Inside Greenspan's Briefcase

Inside Greenspan's Briefcase

Investment Strategies
for Profiting from
Key Reports and Data

Robert Stein

McGraw-Hill

New York   Chicago   San Francisco   Lisbon   London   Madrid
Mexico City   Milan   New Dehli   San Juan   Seoul
Singapore   Sydney   Toronto

McGraw-Hill

A Division of The **McGraw·Hill** Companies

1 2 3 4 5 6 7 8 9 0 AGM/AGM 0 9 8 7 6 5 4 3 2

ISBN 0-07-138913-X

McGraw-Hill books are available at special quantity discounts to use as premiums and sales promotions, or for use in corporate training programs. For more information, please write to the Director of Special Sales, Professional Publishing, McGraw-Hill, Two Penn Plaza, New York, NY 10121-2298. Or contact your local bookstore.

 This book was printed on recycled, acid-free paper containing a minimum of 50% recycled, de-inked fiber.

Contents

Foreword

O ver the last five years, the practice of following the daily fluctuations in American financial markets has gone from the province of money interests on Wall Street to a national phenomenon. Not only do average middle-class Americans now pick up the morning paper to check daily share prices as if they were baseball box scores, but they also will spend hours watching financial networks like CNBC and comb Internet news sites to track the minute-by-minute vicissitudes of the stock market indices.

But many, if not most, average investors enter this arena only minimally equipped to understand the economics driving the markets on a daily, weekly, and monthly basis. Just as even the most basic baseball fan needs to understand how to compute a pitcher's earned-run average or a batter's slugging percentage, today's investor needs to know what the daily economic numbers that come out of Washington's bureaucracy—the Labor Department, the Commerce Department, the Federal Reserve—mean for a retirement plan or a mutual fund investment. Each month there are reams of data—from the unemployment rate to the consumer price index to consumer confidence—that could prove to be a blessing or a curse for every investor's life savings.

There are few people better suited to explaining what these numbers mean than Robert Stein. I first met Rob in New York City almost a decade ago when I started my journalism career covering the ups and downs of the foreign exchange markets at Dow Jones Newswires. At the time, I had only a rudimentary understanding of the inner workings of the currency markets myself. And like any novice investor, I was looking for someone to guide me through the maze of potential market-moving events, including the release of daily economic numbers, nuanced shifts in Federal Reserve policy, and the frequently obtuse declarations emerging from the regular meetings of policymakers from the world's leading industrialized countries, known as the Group of Seven, or G-7.

When I sat down to write my very first weekly foreign exchange column, a colleague of mine suggested I call Rob to get his views on where the dollar was headed in relation to the Japanese yen. At the time, hopes were high that the United States and Japan would reach a trade agreement in the crucial auto sector, a treaty that many believed would mean increased U.S. car exports to Japan. On the expectations of a pro-American deal, the dollar had risen substantially against the yen in the days leading up to the trade meeting.

It was not to be. Not only did talks between the two nations break off abruptly, but instead of announcing a final agreement, the United States ended the weekend talks by saying it was launching a 1-year investigation into the Japanese auto market. It was a huge failure on an international level. I called Rob on a Saturday afternoon to ask him what this disappointing outcome would mean for the markets. In hindsight, the call was relatively easy. Just as the dollar had surged on expectations of a deal, he said, the greenback would plunge when the currency markets opened in Tokyo on Monday morning. But what Rob taught me on that first story was more than a one-time snapshot into how a news event would affect a day's trading. He taught me a lesson I have carried with me ever since: Markets frequently move on expectations rather than on any underlying fundamentals.

Those who followed the esoteric world of global trade policy closely were prepared for the dollar's fall. Those who were asleep at the wheel lost out. While most average investors do not dabble in the volatile currency markets, the lesson behind Rob's call on the dollar applies to understanding the day-to-day economic indicators and using them in investment decisions. The better an investor understands what's happening in the economy, the better she'll do in the long run.

That's not to say that calling a market's direction is always easy. As Rob discusses in his book, there are even times when smart, well-informed people reach completely different conclusions about what investment decision to make in light of a news event. Perhaps the most important example of this is the way investors react to interest-rate decisions by the Federal Reserve, the United State's increasingly powerful central bank chaired by the man frequently known as The Oracle, Alan Greenspan.

In the public consciousness, Greenspan has come to be seen as an economic Svengali, fine tuning the economy behind closed doors while issuing opaque and sometimes incomprehensible policy statements. But in reality, Greenspan's greatest legacy may be his attempt to make the Fed more open about its views of the economy. On the most basic level, Greenspan made it a regular practice to announce publicly the interest-rate decisions of the policymaking Federal Open Market Committee (FOMC). It may seem shocking to those who sit perched in front of their TV sets almost every other month—at about 2:15 p.m. Washington time on a Tuesday—to learn what the FOMC has decided. But when Greenspan took office, there was no public acknowledgment of interest rate moves. Previously, investors would have to make an educated guess about the Fed's policy changes by studying the ebb and flow of the U.S. government securities market.

But not only does the Fed announce its decision to the public, in recent years Greenspan has gone even further. In the late 1990s, Fed officials began releasing statements to accompany their interest-rate moves that both inform the public of the shift and provide an assessment of the risks to the economy.

In theory, this was supposed to take some of the guesswork out of the Fed's moves. After all, with a simple statement on the status of the economy—whether it was shrinking or expanding, facing inflation or stable prices—all who were interested could look into the mind of the central bankers. In practice, however, it caused more confusion. Why? Because different investors had different interpretations of the central bank's policy pronouncements.

When the Fed released a statement after leaving rates unchanged on October 5, 1999, it said it was leaning toward raising rates. Suddenly, the stock market tanked, fearful Greenspan was prepared to choke off economic growth. But an hour later, the market just as suddenly rebounded after confused investors changed their minds, deciding the Fed meant it would raise rates somewhere down the road, but not until after the Y2K barrier was crossed. The result: massive market confusion. If the professional investors couldn't divine the meaning of the Fed's words, how could individual investors even attempt to do so?

In all fairness, the Fed has since revamped its disclosure policy. But there still are those days when even veteran market participants are not sure what the central bank is trying to telegraph. Despite the confusion, investors ignore the Fed's policy statements at their very great peril. After all, an up or down move in the interest rates controlled by the Fed has ripple effects that move billions of dollars in the economy; shaping mortgage rates, business investments, and even the interest the average consumer pays on his or her credit card. And all this has a critical impact on financial markets in the United States and around the world.

So how does one make sense of policy proclamations that are sometimes confusing and can lead to contradictory conclusions? First, a better understanding of the winks and nods that are contained in the statements themselves; hints that are very clear if one knows what to look for. But just as importantly is a firm handle on the tools Greenspan and his colleagues use when they make their decisions: the publicly released economic figures that are at the fingertips of any investor who cares to look at them.

That's not to say that forecasting the economy and the markets is easy. But by having a basic understanding of the economy's indicators—why a spike in unemployment can cause a rally in the stock market, why an increase in durable goods orders can lead the bond market to tank—investors can make better-informed choices about where to put their money.

Inside Greenspan's Briefcase is a great place to start. Even long-time investors will enjoy the book. Unlike the Economics 101 text-book we all dreaded in college, this book gives investors an easy-to-read guide to understanding the economy. It includes color-ful anecdotes from Rob's long career following the markets. And, most importantly, Rob has somehow managed to incorporate humor into his writing—not always an easy task when writing about relative growth rates and average annual price levels.

In the decade I have known and worked with him, Rob has become an invaluable source, not only clarifying what the economic numbers mean in a broader context, but also providing true-to-life examples of how the daily economic releases affect individual com-panies and individual lives. In fact, it would not be an overstatement to say that Rob has taught me which numbers coming out of Wash-ington were important and why. I hope you enjoy learning from him as much as I do.

Laura Cohn
Economics Correspondent
BusinessWeek magazine
January 2002

Acknowledgments

S itting down to write a book is one of those challenges that seems a lot easier in theory than in practice. The support required in all aspects of your life is enormous.

When taking on a project like this, the support falls into two categories. There are those whose help made this project a lot smoother and enjoyable. And there are others without whose help *Inside Greenspan's Briefcase* may not have been accomplished.

My experience at Astor Asset Management and Stockbrokers.com has been invaluable in helping with the ideas and concepts for this book. My partner Jeff Feldman took on more than his fair share of responsibilities during the time I was engulfed in my writings. Thank you, Jeff. Sarah Cusimano's work as my assistant cannot go without notice. Her ability to perform the most challenging tasks, particularly her management of the tedious details of database administration, her organizational skills, and her supervision of my business overall, continues to exceed even my wildest expectations. I appreciate her loyalty to me and to our organization.

The support of my friends must be acknowledged. My childhood friends from Lincolnwood (the "Wooders") redefine the term "best friends." The same goes for the N.Y. guys at 57th.

My parents, whose encouragement and applause during the many sessions of rewriting chapters, deserves mention even though their opinions sometime seemed biased in my favor. But after all, that's what parents are supposed to do, and mine are no exception, and the same goes for my brother, David, and his family.

I want to thank my sister, Jeanne, and all the staff at Glenkirk, who make the lives of special people like Jeanne even more productive. They have taught me that happiness has several definitions, and sometimes explaining things simply and logically makes me understand them better, too.

Special thanks goes to my wife, Eileen, whose support, understanding, and love show that accomplishing goals is all the sweeter when someone shares your glory.

My editor, Kelli Christiansen of McGraw-Hill, believed in this project and kept me motivated and on track to see it through.

Thanks goes to my friend Laura Cohn of *BusinessWeek*, who wrote the foreword. Our conversations have often sparked interesting economic discussions over the years.

Last, but not least, is the person without whom this book would not be possible, Patricia Crisafulli. Her help in writing this book cannot be described in just a few short words. She guided me on chapter outlines and chapter rewrites and encouraged me constantly to keep going. At the start of Chapter 1, when I thought that the task of writing a book was too large to take on, Tricia said, "Rob, it's like eating an elephant. Just take it one bite at a time." Well, Tricia, what's for dessert?

Thanks for the opportunity to write a book for everyone to learn from and enjoy.

Introduction

I was in a deli in Chicago the other day, buying a corned beef on rye, when Harvey squinted at me from behind the counter and asked, "Aren't you a stockbroker?"

As the portfolio manager of Astor Asset Management and the co-founder of a Web site known as Stockbrokers.com (as well as being an economist and a former trader), I figured that "stockbroker" was a close enough description of what I do. "Sure," I nodded, watching Harvey slice up my corned beef, making sure it was lean like I always ordered it.

"Well, can you tell me if the Fed did anything about rates today?"

This was not the question I was anticipating. At best, I thought Harvey might ask me about a "hot stock" he had heard mentioned on television or that some prosperous looking customers were discussing at the counter. But the actions of the Federal Open Market Committee (better known as the FOMC or the "Fed")?

"Tell me," I replied. "Two years ago, did you even know when the Fed was meeting?"

Presumably Harvey was a long-term investor with a portfolio of mutual funds, a few stocks, and maybe a 401(k) plan. But he certainly wasn't an active trader. So why was he watching the Fed's actions so closely?

"Well, I know they're meeting today and they might cut rates," Harvey explained, wrapping up my sandwich to go. "That will be good for the stock market, right?"

Clearly, investor awareness of economic reports is at a heightened state. And if the deli incident didn't convince me of that, a visit with my own Aunt Roberta would confirm it. My aunt is an investor of the long-term variety, with a portfolio of buy-and-hold stocks, mutual funds, and bonds. She's hardly what you'd call a swing trader.

When I went to visit her the other day she asked me, of all things, what I thought was going to happen with the employment report. I answered her question with a question: "Aunt Roberta, when did you start paying attention to the employment report?"

"They were talking about it on the television this morning," she replied quickly, making sure her economist-nephew didn't get all high and mighty on her. "It's going to be a big number."

Of course Aunt Roberta and Harvey, the deli man, were right. The actions of the Federal Reserve and the employment report are important. But they're important to the economy. The economy and the stock market are two entirely different creatures.

What's happened these days is that investors of the short-term and long-term variety—thanks to the proliferation of financial media—have become hyperaware of the latest economic report or "number" to come down the pike. When they hear that the employment number showed a slowing economy, they're looking for the Fed to cut rates and for an uptick in the stock market to swell their portfolios.

Economic news is front-page news these days. What would have merited a one paragraph mention in a market or economic wrap-up in the business section a few years ago now warrants its share of page-one space. It doesn't matter if your portfolio consists mostly of a 401(k) that you won't tap into for another 30 or 40 years. If the Fed's going to do something, the employment report is going to give a glimpse of economic conditions, or something else is going to rock the stock market, you want to know about it now!

But do investors really understand what these numbers mean? Do they know the difference, say, between the consumer confidence, consumer sentiment, and the Consumer Price Index? Do they know how these reports are calculated and analyzed?

There is a need for today's investors—particularly those who are active in the market on a short-term basis—to have a fuller understanding of economic reports, how they're compiled, what they reveal, and how professional market participants (the professional traders at brokerages and banks, for example) view these reports and use the information to trade. Moreover, they need to know how they, as investors, should process this information and possibly include it in their investing strategies.

When it comes to importance, economic reports ebb and flow. I remember when I was a clerk for my cousin, Jimmy (Filo), on the trading floor during summer breaks from college. I received my introduction to how economic reports moved markets—whether money supply or the trade deficit—back then. There was always some number we were on the lookout for.

Today, with the focus on the economy—especially given the recession that the U.S. economy slipped into in March 2001 (as defined by the National Bureau of Economic Research, as I'll explain in Chapter 3) —economic reports such as GDP, unemployment, the ISM Report, and the Consumer Price Index (CPI) are in everyone's sights. Who knows what will wield the biggest influence next year!

As of this writing, the "Big Three" in economic reports and events are

- Actions of the Federal Open Market Committee, better known as the FOMC or the Fed.
- Gross domestic product (GDP). How much (or how little) growth is in the U.S. economy?
- Employment report. What's the state of joblessness in the United States?

In this book, we'll examine each report carefully, looking at how they're calculated, what they reveal, and what the market tends to "read into" them. Moreover, we'll discuss how economic reports can affect investor sentiment, market activity, and most importantly how the Federal Reserve uses economic reports to gauge the state of the economy and plots the course of its monetary policy.

It is important to note when working with statistics and economic data that sometimes they lend themselves to interpretations that can be confusing and at times on the surface misleading. Additionally, quarter-to-quarter comparisons may cloud annual comparisons, which show different results over a longer time period. Further, there can be some confusion over terms like quarter-to-quarter "declines." Sometimes, declines are actually a lower rate of increase. For example, if something rose 10 percent in the first quarter and it rose only 2 percent in the second quarter, that's a decline—meaning the growth rate has slowed dramatically. Nonetheless, it's still growth. The bottom line is, when looking at economic data, you're looking at the relationship between statistics for the same time periods, i.e., quarter-to-quarter or year-to-year. Moreover, there are times when you're looking at percentage rate of change and times when you're looking at other absolute values.

Inside Greenspan's Briefcase is far from a dry textbook listing definitions. The book seeks to enlighten investors by letting them understand what the numbers stand for and how the professionals in the market interpret them. With this new awareness, investors will be better judges as to whether, for example, a market decline after a "disappointing" rate cut by the FOMC is an emotional overreaction or something they should pay attention to in their own investment strategies.

1

The Stock Market
Is Not the Economy

Over the course of this book, I'm going to repeat this mantra many times: "The stock market is not the economy." When it comes to this basic premise, there's no such thing as over-statement.

Many individual investors have the mistaken perception that Wall Street and Main Street are one and the same. This is a relatively new phenomenon stemming from the beginning of the big bull market circa 1981, or at least the great popularity of 401(k) employee retirement programs, profit-sharing, stock options, and matching programs that began life in the early 1980s. These "invest for your future" programs brought the stock market to mainstream America. No longer was the stock market an exclusive club for the wealthy and fiscally privileged. The stock market became the investing ground for Middle America, as Charts 1-1 and 1-2 clearly show the growth in equity investment in the United States.

As individual investor money was pouring into the stock market, a great bull run was being enjoyed on Wall Street. In fact, this great

CHART 1-1　Number of Individual Shareholders (millions), 1989–1998

	1989	1992	1995	1998
Individuals owning stock directly, through mutual funds, retirement savings accounts, or defined contribution pension plans	52.3	61.4	69.3	84.0
Individuals only owning stock directly	27.0	29.2	27.4	33.8

Source: New York Stock Exchange "The Investing Public" report, 2000

CHART 1-2 Percentage of Stock Ownership by U.S. Households

	1989	1992	1995	1998
All Families	31.6	36.7	40.4	48.8
Annual Income				
$25,000 – $49,999	31.5	40.2	45.4	52.7
$50,000 – $99,999	51.5	62.5	65.4	74.3
$100,000 or more	81.8	78.3	81.6	91.0

Source: "The Roots of Broadend Stock Ownership," April 2000 Report to the Joint Economic Committee, U.S. Congress

bull market has taken credit for the robust economic times we've seen in the past 2 decades. That begs the essential question: Did the strong economy create the great bull market, or did the great bull market create the strong economy? While the answer(s) to that question could be argued for some time, it's important to remember that the market and the economy are two separate and distinct entities. While Main Street and even Wall Street may blur the distinction, it's vitally important as an investor to remember that the stock market and the economy are not the same.

Here's a case in point. Consumer spending accounts for 67 percent of gross domestic product (GDP), the broadest measure of economic output (see Chapter 5). Until recently less than 50 percent of the U.S. population owned stocks. Of those who did own stocks, the majority had an average holding of less than $15,000. Therefore, the stock market just did not affect them as much as one might think. Whether they got their paychecks at the end of the week was more important to their spending habits than their investments were, and thus to the overall economy as measured by GDP. Therefore, it becomes clear that unemployment has a bigger correlation to the health of the economy than the stock market!

Keeping that in mind, imagine if you saw this scenario on your favorite financial news television show.

TV anchor: "A bit of bad news in this morning from Wilkes-Barre, Pennsylvania, where Joe Smith lost his job today. That brings the unemployment count to 351,421 nationwide. But wait! This just in! We have received a report that Jill Rose was hired today as a sales associate in San Diego, California! Jill's new job brings the U.S. jobless rate back down to 351,420! Way to go Jill!"

Kidding aside, it's important to note that the actual state of employment (or unemployment, as the case may be) in the United States is far more relevant to the economy—and thus to you, the investor—than the endless stream of so-called financial information that "IBM is up 2 . . . Dell is down 1 . . . GE is up 3 . . ."

I don't want to underestimate or belittle the importance of the stock market or even its vital place in the overall economy. But the reality is, the stock market is a capitalist venue that exists to channel resources (capital) to business, helping to create, strengthen, and enhance our economy. Of course, in a capitalist society such as ours, capital requires a return for the risk that is taken and this return is reflected in either higher stock prices or (not so much lately) greater dividends. Additionally, many companies perform better during good economic times, creating some correlation between a good stock market and a healthy economy.

The basic function of the stock market, however, is to create a marketplace in which investors can buy shares in a corporation in return for the capital they invest. The shares received represent a minority ownership in that company. Stock exchanges were created to provide a single place in which buyers and sellers of shares could meet to exchange shares at an agreed upon price. Thus, share prices fluctuate depending upon supply and demand for shares, and depending largely upon the outlook for that particular company. Admittedly, this is the most basic explanation of why Wall Street exists, although in reality the functions of Wall Street have far greater complexities beyond what I just described. Still, this simplistic picture does illustrate the point. The basic function of Wall Street is that of a marketplace—not as an economic barometer and not as a means to stabilize, enhance, or otherwise help (or hurt) the economy.

Over the past 3 decades, many financial instruments have been created to speculate on the future price of a company's stock or to hedge a portfolio of stocks. These instruments include options on stock, stock-index futures, and warrants. The business of profiting from the fluctuations of the price of these stocks and related financial instruments has become almost as important as the companies themselves. In fact, many academics feel that these products, collectively referred to as derivatives, have been responsible for the increased volatility of the stock market. Some people even blame them for the Crash of 1987. I, on the other hand, suggest that these instruments have actually helped smooth out the volatility in the market, reduce the risk, and make it easier for investment managers to create balanced portfolios. That's all well and good, but the fact remains that Wall Street, the stock market, and the financial markets are marketplaces for investors and speculators to employ their capital in return for what they hope to be a gain. As many investors have learned the hard way in late 2000 and through

2001, an investment in the stock market is no guarantee that your money will grow.

True, long-term data have indicated that over any extended period of time, the return on stock investments has outweighed every other investment, including bonds and other fixed-income instruments (investments that pay a certain interest rate). There are fluctuations, however, that have more to do with perception, relative value, speculative interest, and other investment considerations. That's why it's vitally important that you, the investor, draw a definite distinction between the stock market and the economy. If you confuse the two or consider them to be one and the same, you will make economic decisions based upon stock prices and stock decisions based upon economic conditions. While the latter is not such a big deal, the former could hurt you—potentially a lot.

The purpose of this book is to give you a look at what makes the economy tick, helping you to become more educated on its various facets. Moreover, this understanding will go a long way toward helping you make the best investment decisions. Thus, by knowing your time frame, your goals, your risk tolerance, and so on, you will be able to make educated decisions for yourself. You won't be tempted to make a knee-jerk investment decision in reaction to the latest "economic headline" that flashes across the television screen.

Knowing that the economy is not the stock market will help you to weather the financial storms, both fiscally and emotionally. You'll have the knowledge, and with that the discipline, to know when the economy is in the midst of one cycle or the other. This will prevent you from putting your money in a box under your mattress because the market has "crashed" or, conversely, buying the latest, greatest, hottest stock because some pundit says prices are going to the moon!

Perspective is everything. Consider the Crash of 1987 when things looked, in a word, terrible. A looming trade war with Europe. Concern over the value of the U.S. dollar. The new Fed chairman (one Alan Greenspan) had just *raised* interest rates. Then poof! The market sold off almost 20 percent in one day after having a huge run over the past year or so. The focus on equity prices was as high as it ever had been. Every newspaper headline was about the stock market crash, and stories forecasting a 1929-like depression permeated the financial community.

Everyone was scared, including me, even though I had finished my internship at the Federal Reserve under the chairmanship of Paul Volcker and was a currency trader for a major bank. Then one day after the infamous Black Monday crash, I walked past a Walgreen's drugstore in Chicago. Looking in the store's plate glass window, I saw a line at the checkout counter. People were still buying toothpaste, shampoo, and aspirin! The sky, it seemed, had not fallen.

Later that day, I spoke with my mother who had visited the retailer The Gap for the first time. She told me that while she had expected to find only clothing for my generation, she had been pleasantly surprised to discover a few things at the store that she could mix into her wardrobe.

That night, my father called me from Arizona, where he was on a business trip consulting with a steel company that wanted to raise prices in light of a pickup in demand.

We had the stock market gyrating wickedly that week after Monday's crash, providing a powerful example of fear and greed at its best. The market had to close early during the week to reconcile trades. There were 10 percent daily swings in the market, which looked unsteady at best.

The economy, meanwhile, kept chugging along. I had tickets to a preseason Chicago Bulls' basketball game later that week and found it difficult to get a reservation at a trendy restaurant near the Chicago stadium. Parking lots surrounding the stadium were full, and I remember being boxed in at a remote lot. Clearly, there were plenty of people going out to dinner and a basketball game. So even though the stock market had just taken a severe nosedive, economically things couldn't be all that bad. Supermarkets, drugstores, shoe stores, movies, and restaurants all remained open, busy, and profitable.

Today, some 15 years later, it's important to keep this perspective, despite the "tech wreck" and the "Nasdaq crash" that have consumed the business-page and front-page headlines. Yes, the Nasdaq has seen a steep correction. Yes, in 2001 and in early 2002, there is some question about the health of the economy and when it might pull out of a recession. But the two situations must be viewed as distinct occurrences. In fact, given the events of 2000 and 2001—with the big drop in equity prices, a 6-week-plus standoff during the presidential election in the United States, and some unexpected rough weather in many parts of the country—it was probably quite a surprise that unemployment had remained so low. Housing starts and home sales remained near record levels through mid-2001 and consumer spending remained healthy. What would it take, one wondered at the time, to slow this economy down?

Low inflation, low unemployment, and robust consumer spending don't exactly make for a dismal economic scenario. In fact, if you looked at just those three elements, things would have appeared quite rosy. But the stock market was sure having troubles by the end of 2000 and into 2001, and it did not look like it would be getting better any time soon. Yet, if you looked only at the economy *at that time*, you would have thought that the stock market was likely to keep rising. For a more complete understanding of why the economy may appear strong even as the stock market declines, let's take a look at the function of the stock market.

This is particularly important as more and more individuals invest in the stock market. You must never lose sight of your own goals and your time horizon. Yes, it is true that the average return on the stock market's broad averages over a 60-year period is about 9.5 percent. And the best way to reap that gain is with a buy-and-hold strategy using dollar-cost averaging. (With dollar-cost averaging, you purchase securities, often mutual funds, with fixed dollar amounts at regular intervals, say $100 a month in stock or fund XYZ. The theory is that by investing the same dollar amount, you can, in effect, smooth out the volatility and buy at a range of prices that, over time, will average out.)

But a whole book dedicated to the buy-and-hold strategy would not only be boring, it would be misleading. In fact, in some cases, one would have had to buy and hold for 50 years to achieve the so-called long-term averages. If one started investing in the late 1920s, his/her average annual return would not have approached 9 percent until the late 1980s. That's why many economists and market strategists that frequent the financial news shows become a bit like weathermen during a drought, continuing to predict, "Rain is coming!"

Meanwhile, you get hotter and thirstier, while you begin to doubt the weathermen and their predictions. But in the long run, it will rain again. After all, one of the main objectives of a capitalist democracy is to achieve economic growth and expansion.

With today's markets being easier to access, thanks to electronic trading, and with more participants who have different goals and shorter time horizons, it would be nice to know, in economic terms, if we should stock up on water and ice for the next drought. Also, just how much water and ice will we need?

My goal in writing this book is to try to prepare you for the droughts, floods, sunny days, and rainy days that, as sure as the weather and the seasons change, occur in metaphoric terms in the market. Using the weather analogy again, I want you to be able to tell *for yourself* when you need an umbrella and when it's time for sunscreen. A little rain never hurt anyone, but it's nice to have protection when it starts to pour. Additionally, this will enable you to be proactive, giving you more control over your financial future.

In keeping with the theme of this chapter—that the economy is not the stock market, and vice versa—we'll take a look at how to sort through the smattering of economic data that is released continuously. As you'll learn, some data about the strength or weakness of the economy are more important than other data. Some data are more important at certain times of the economic cycle than other data are. And some data are just downright useless. The information is too volatile to give an accurate picture or it's meaningless because it reflects past conditions. It's like saying let's focus on the high and the low temperature of the day (or the day before). Most of us want to know what tomorrow's weather is going to be and what the weekend forecast looks like.

As an economist, I produce a report called "Logical Economics," in which I explain various economic data in plain English. I try to give a look at what's in Greenspan's briefcase (meaning the economic data that the Fed, which is charged with managing the U.S. economy, is also looking at). As an investor, you need this information in "English" with the knowledge of how can you profit from it.

You need to know which news and data reflect what's really going on and how you should react. Of the data that are released

regularly, I have seen short-term market reactions in both directions
to the same news. Let's say retail sales are released (see Chapter 7)
and the number is stronger than expected. The market rallies, as
investors assume the economy is stronger than expected and that
retailers will make bigger profits, which will in turn push up stock
prices for retailing firms. But do you know what happens sometimes? The market can go down on good news. The rationale is
sometimes that this good news can't last; therefore next month's
numbers are going to be weak, and stocks should go lower. Or the
thinking is that the economy is overheating, and the Fed will have
to raise rates, which is historically bad for stocks.

If that's not confusing enough, sometimes the market goes up on
bad news on the thinking that the economy is weak, and the Fed will
have to lower rates, which is historically good for stocks. Or else it's
a case of the old adage, "it can't get worse than this," which entices
the buyers and bargain hunters to venture into the market.

I wish I could give you a rational explanation about when to look
at the economic glass as half full or half empty, but, unfortunately, I
can't. What I can do, though, is give you an understanding of the data
and of the different interpretations of the data. That will allow you to
make rational decisions based on facts and statistics, not on market
hysterics.

A HISTORY LESSON . . .

As we examine why the stock market is not the economy, let's take a
look at some events from recent economic history. Indeed, the last 15
years or so have been punctuated with notable economic events, from
crashes to bubbles. The important lesson to derive from these
sketches of economic history is to look at what the economy was
doing and what the market was doing. Very often, the two entities
displayed their unique natures and their separateness by reacting in
opposite directions. This distinction is even more important given the
large growth of investor participation in the stock market, as evidenced by the overall growth in volume traded on the New York
Stock Exchange (see Chart 1-3).

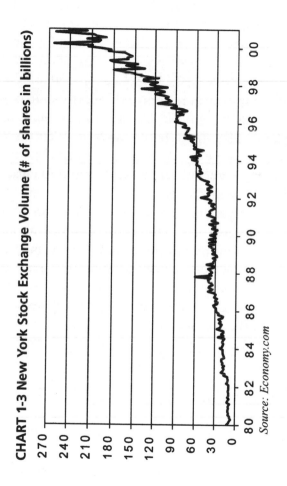

CHART 1-3 New York Stock Exchange Volume (# of shares in billions)

Source: Economy.com

THE CRASH OF 1987

First, the facts: On Black Monday, October 19, 1987, the stock market took its biggest drop ever, with the Dow Jones Industrial Average falling 508.32 points for a loss of 22.6 percent of its total value. That far exceeded the 1-day loss of 12.9 percent experienced in the great stock market crash of 1929, which preceded the Great Depression. Up to Black Monday, the market had enjoyed a 5-year bull run, with the Dow rising from 776.92 points in August 1982 to a high of 2722.42 in August 1987. Black Monday is indelibly etched in the memories of many Wall Streeters and investors alike. (For the later baby boomers who are too young to remember the Kennedy assassination, Black Monday might be the historic event we can ruminate about.) More than a few scared traders wondered about the solvency of the market in general. When markets closed to clear trades, some wondered if they would reopen.

How many people recall how quick the rebound was after the crash? How many people are aware that the market posted a 1-day gain of 102.27 *the day after the crash* and 186.64 points *2 days later*! Or that the market actually closed positive that year. By September 1989, the Dow had regained all the value it had lost in the crash.

Looking at a single event in time, however, you could easily fixate on the crash. But that was the stock market; what about the economy? As I stated earlier in the chapter, shoppers were still shopping, diners were still dining, and moviegoers were still filling the seats in the theaters—even on the day of the crash. The economy hadn't crashed; the stock market "corrected" 500-plus points.

What caused the crash? Some point to "program trading," which involves computer models that generated massive "sell orders." Once the market started to decline, it made the sell off even more precipitous. However, that's too simple an answer. Many economic factors contributed to the crash, including (and notably) the value of the U.S. dollar and its steep decline. In the mid-1980s, the dollar was so overvalued that U.S. exports were uncompetitive in foreign markets. That, in turn, severely increased the trade deficit. Then the value of the dollar began to fall, at first to the approval of the central bankers, but later to their concern. The dollar declined—and yet the U.S. trade deficit situation continued to deteriorate. This was not a healthy economic picture. In February 1987, finance ministers met in Paris to discuss how to support the price of the dollar. If the dollar became "too low," it would hurt foreign exports in the U.S. market as well as adversely affect capital flows into the United States, which help fund the budget deficits.

What was needed was either an improvement in the U.S. trade picture (which didn't materialize) or an increase in interest rates, which would attract investment back into the United States. Thus, the Fed raised interest rates to help the dollar. While the Fed will not admit to changing interest rates to support the dollar, it is clear that Mr. Greenspan was very impressed with how the Bundesbank (the German equivalent of our Federal Reserve) was operating. The deutsche mark was strong, growth was positive, and inflation was low. In short, the freshman Fed chairman was suffering from Bundesbank envy. But as we know, an increase in rates typically hurts the market. The proverbial other shoe was about to drop. The stock market continued to rise, increasing the price-to-earnings ratio (P/E) that we associated with a climbing market. (P/E, which is one measure of a stock's value, reflects the ratio of the price of a stock compared with its earnings. Typically, if a stock price is inflated, it has a high P/E, which means the price of the stock is disproportionately high compared with the earnings of the company.) At the same time, bond rates were also rising. The long-term government bond rate, which had been at about 7 percent in early 1987, was above 9 percent in September. On the morning of October 19, 1987, the long-term bond yield had reached 10.47 percent.

In mid-1987, Alan Greenspan became the new Fed chairman and a long-term and sometimes difficult chairmanship was just beginning. His predecessor, Paul Volcker, was still being applauded for killing inflation, albeit at the expense of growth. The conventional wisdom was that controlling inflation would lay the foundation for stable growth ahead.

In learning a lesson from the past, it's important for investors today to remember that inflation was the biggest economic concern of the 1980s. (During the Ford administration, the catch phrase was Whip Inflation Now, and "WIN" buttons and slogans proliferated.) Everyone feared inflation: the markets, corporations, investors, and consumers. History taught us that inflation contributed to World War I and had brought down some of Europe's strongest countries. In the 1970s, OPEC and the Arab oil embargo had contributed to "stagflation," or inflation without growth, which was the worst of all scenarios. In the 1980s, inflation was wreaking havoc on Latin American countries whose currencies devaluated overnight to the point that it took a proverbial wheelbarrow full of currency to buy a loaf of bread. Thus the Volcker Fed had wanted to avoid hyperinflation at all costs. With a weakening dollar creating a trade deficit and the United States having to spend more dollars to buy the same goods, there were potential inflationary implications.

This all had to be on the mind of the new Fed chairman, Alan Greenspan, when he announced that interest rates were being raised. While the stock market initially ignored the rate hike, in hindsight we can see that this was a contributing factor to the October 1987 crash. Add to that the fact that retail investors were active in the stock market, and these uninitiated participants were likely to panic when they saw (or thought they saw) the bottom drop out of everything.

That's when Fed Chairman Greenspan stepped in to take decisive action to ease the panic on Wall Street, which not only could have impacted the U.S. banking system (brokerage houses faced billions in margin calls, but didn't have the funds to pay them), but also the psychology of the nation. The Fed immediately reduced interest rates and pledged to "serve as a source of liquidity to support the economic and financial system."

The Fed's immediate response saved the day and prevented further panic. Greenspan already knew that the economy was okay. GDP was positive (showing growth) and unemployment was around 5 percent. His top priority in the days after the crash was to make sure that the financial system also was okay.

What's the lesson from the crash? Once again, the economy and the market were and are two separate entities. The number one priority of the Fed back then was the control of inflation. While that contributed to the Crash of 1987, the correction was a comparatively brief one. One could say that Greenspan's Fed made the right decision in raising rates, and that the stock market overreacted. Later, Greenspan continued the tightening cycle, raising rates again in 1988.

Inflation post crash was still under control, albeit with a threat to rise, and unemployment was low—establishing all the makings of a healthy economy. Although interest rates appeared to be on the rise again, the housing market was stable. In fact, housing shortages existed on both coasts, as retirees migrated to warmer climates. Meanwhile, there was a large influx of educated workers in the work-force, as the last of the baby boomers graduated from college. It was the largest pool of educated people to enter the workforce in the history of the United States. When it came to the job search, they were not about to take *no* for an answer. This was a workforce that was going to be employed—even if the economy had to grow to accommodate it! Entrepreneurs started small companies. Consultants went to work for themselves.

According to the Small Business Administration, employers with fewer than 500 employees increased from 4,941,821 in 1988 to 5,261,967 in 1994. With the rise of small companies, self-directed individual retirement accounts (IRA) and Keogh plans also increased. The major shift toward the entrepreneur spurred capital spending and investment in the market. We were entering a new phase of the market and the economy as the bull kept running.

THE S&L CRISIS AND BAILOUT

First, the bailout: In February 1989, President George Bush unveiled a plan to bail out the savings and loans (S&Ls) that had gone bankrupt due, in large part, to fiscal mismanagement. Later that year, S&L regulation was switched to the newly created Office of Thrift Supervision, and the Resolution Trust Corporation was created to deal with the insolvent S&Ls. In short, the federal government bailed out the S&Ls, averting a crisis that could have spread through the U.S. financial system.

Now, consider the cause. According to the FDIC's chronology on the S&L crisis, one of the problems for these financial institutions was their inability through the 1970s to keep up with interest-rate increases. Every time interest rates rose, consumers withdrew substantial amounts of money from their S&L accounts to deposit them with large institutions where they received a higher rate of return. To compete, S&Ls, which had been allowed only to accept deposits and grant home mortgages, were given more liberal authority to invest. For example, in 1982, the Reagan administration gave expanded powers to federally chartered S&Ls and enabled them to "diversify their activities with the view toward increasing profits, according to the FDIC. States responded in kind. For example, California, Texas, and Florida allowed S&Ls to invest 100 percent of deposits in any kind of venture.

Insolvency, and in some cases criminal activity, was later uncovered at some S&Ls, with Charles Keating's Lincoln Savings and Loan the most infamous. The subsequent failure of Lincoln alone was estimated by the FDIC to have cost taxpayers more than $2 billion. While it cost the government—and therefore the taxpayers— billions of dollars to bail out the S&Ls, the cost of *not* doing so would have been even higher, including a loss of savings, stifled economic growth, and higher taxes.

In light of the economic dangers, the solution was a brilliant one. The Fed and government regulators would work together to monitor the type of appropriate investments that institutions could make. By limiting the types of risky investments made by banks, they could keep some control over the problem for the time being. As a result, the Fed would keep long-term interest rates artificially high for a period of time. This would allow financial institutions to borrow short-term funds at low rates, say 4 percent, and lend out money or buy 30-year U.S. Treasuries at say, 8.5 percent. That would lock in a return of 4.5 percent. Banks and other financial institutions could employ this strategy with very little money down, increasing the magnitude of the effect.

In a few short years, the banks became solvent again. However, the impact of this solution would take its toll on the economy. The banks and lending institutions tightened up on credit restrictions, which made it very difficult for consumers and businesses to borrow money. The result was a very serious liquidity crunch, which set the stage for a big downturn in the real estate market in the early 1990s and a light recession in 1990-91.

In the broader picture, this economic result was a small price to pay to avoid what could have been an even bigger problem. The potential direct cash outlay to solve this problem would have been in

the hundreds of billions of dollars, which could have been a significant blow to GDP at that time. Instead, the brilliant solution was to
allow banks to profit from the interest-rate spread, thus helping them
to bulk up their balance sheets. The way that the U.S. government
bailed out the S&Ls—with a minimum of impact on the average cit-
izen—averted what could have been one of the greatest financial
catastrophes faced by this country. This also set the stage for the
deflationary times ahead. Today we see a parallel between the liquidity crunch, resulting in a turndown in the real estate market, and the
decline in 2000 of IPOs (initial public offerings), which all but terminated a source of liquidity for technology companies, causing
them—and other Nasdaq issues—to turn down as well. Money is the
blood of the economy, and its availability and cost (interest rates) are
important in understanding the economy. That is one lesson of the
S&L crisis and bailout.

THE 1990-91 RECESSION

A recession began in July 1990, ending what was then the longest,
peacetime expansion in U.S. history. The recession ended, officially,
8 months later, in March 1991. But the impact on the labor market
was felt for some time to come. As an article by Jennifer M. Gardner,
an economist in the Division of Labor Force Statistics, Bureau of
Labor Statistics, stated in the June 1994 issue of *Monthly Labor
Review*: "Employment declines were more widespread across the
major occupational and industry groups in the 1990-91 recession
than in past contractions. White-collar workers in general, and workers in the finance, insurance, and real estate industry in particular,
were at greater risk of losing their jobs in the early 1990s than at any
time in the past. Also, the rate of employment decrease in both
wholesale and retail trade was nearly twice that of the averages of
prior contractions."

Looking at employment as a major indicator of economic health,
the 1990-91 recession would be considered a serious one. But what
about the stock market at this time? Historic statistics from the New
York Stock Exchange reveal that the market, overall, was not in "as
bad" a shape as the economy. In fact, the cutbacks, layoffs, and overall downsizing that increased the unemployment rate may have actually made companies (and therefore their stock prices) healthier in

the eyes of Wall Street. Consider that the average share price of New York Stock Exchange (NYSE) stocks in 1989 was $36.51. This declined in 1990 to $31.08. But in 1991, a year that included 3 months of official recession, the average price of NYSE stocks rose to $37.27—more than what it had been in 1989!

This was typical of the behavior of the stock market, which declines during good times as we head into a recession, bottoms while we are in a recession, and often rallies before the economy turns around.

Meanwhile Greenspan's Fed was noticing some inner changes in the U.S. economy. Small companies and start-up companies were hiring at a frenzied pace (as we discussed earlier in this chapter). Curiously, many of these companies "outsourced" work using contractors and third-party providers for various services. This rise in outsourcing did not show up in the employment figures. But at the same time, elsewhere in the technology sector, there was an unusual number of orders for telecommunication equipment and computers. If the big companies weren't creating this demand, then who was ordering so many telephones and computers—and why?

This was the first sign of what was to become the greatest technology revolution, leading to a bull market and economic growth. Newly unemployed white-collar workers began to use their skills and entrepreneurial spirit to start new companies. Many two-income families could survive on one paycheck while the other wage earner started up a new company. These professionals knew how to jump from one employer to another, taking many benefits with them. This was the fertile breeding ground of being able to "go it alone." During the recovery of the early 1990s, investment from small businesses and employment by small businesses became the engine behind a growing economy. Greenspan saw this phenomena and wanted to monitor it, as it would give signals about the economy.

INVASION OF KUWAIT

On August 2, 1990, Iraq staged an "unprovoked" invasion of Kuwait. While the United Nations imposed sanctions against Iraq, which impacted the Iraqi economy, it did not end the occupation of Kuwait. Thus, in January 1991, the Bush administration issued

"National Security Directive 54," which authorized "military actions designed to bring about Iraq's withdrawal from Kuwait." And so the Gulf War began.

A few months later, the United States proclaimed victory in the Gulf War even though Saddam Hussein was still in power in Iraq. (Of course, getting rid of Saddam altogether was not listed as one of the U.S. goals in the Gulf War; getting Iraq out of Kuwait was.) What ensued after the Gulf War victory was a stock market rally.

The U.S. economy, meanwhile, appeared to be teetering on the brink of recession. White-collar workers faced the greatest risk of being laid off. The real estate market, particularly in New York and Los Angeles, was in recession. Against this backdrop there was uncertainty as to what impact a war would have on the economy. (For one thing, it had been a while since the United States was involved in a war, and war was different now.) Many investment managers and investors alike exited the stock market for what appeared to be safer ground in dollar-denominated assets, U.S. fixed-income instruments, and gold. This brings up another important lesson from the economy vs. the market school of thought: From an investment point of view, gold does not glitter.

In fact, gold no longer was a store of value fixed to currencies. Truly, it doesn't represent anything. Supply and demand is hard to monitor because gold is not consumed or used in any practical purpose as other metals are. In fact, one might say that the only value gold has is an intrinsic one because of the jewelry made from it.

During times of economic uncertainty, inflation, and war, anything is better than gold. A tanker of oil . . . A bushel of wheat . . . A side of beef . . . All are better than gold! Now, granted for gift-giving occasions, gold is a far better choice than, say, a pork belly. But if you're hungry and times are hard, then that pork belly is looking mighty tempting!

Once speculators and investors had finished pushing up the price of gold prior to the invasion of Kuwait, (by the way, even with all the buying going on, gold still did not take out its highs for the year) the price retreated to levels that were *even lower* than before the war.

The dollar, which had been suffering amid an economic slowdown and interest-rate differentials that favored foreign currencies, increased in value prior to the invasion. Once the invasion was announced, the dollar started to slide as the economic fundamentals regained control.

I remember the night of the invasion well. As a currency trader, I had watched the dollar rise significantly against the Japanese yen for the previous month or so. Then came the announcement over the news wires that the United States had begun its offensive against Iraq with an air attack. It was evening in the States, but the morning trade was about to begin in Asia. The dollar was poised to open higher. I saw the first price quoted, with the dollar up over 2 yen. My decision: I sold dollars and bought yen. This was directly opposite what many other traders, including my colleagues, were doing. They were feverishly buying dollars. When I saw this buying frenzy I wondered why the dollar wasn't even higher. Then came the bigger question in my mind: What was everyone going to do with these dollars, as well as with all the dollars they had been buying all month long?

The economics had not changed in the currency equation, which is what led me to sell dollars and buy yen, figuring that the relationship between these two currencies was going back in line. By the opening of the market in the United States the next day, the dollar was down considerably.

What's the investment moral of this story? The economy is not the market (in this case the currency market). While a frenzy may sway things, you have to remember that fundamentals will regain control eventually. Rudyard Kipling defined bravery and valor as "keeping your head while those around you are losing theirs." Frankly, that's good advice—especially in these times for investment.

MEXICAN PESO CRISIS

On December 20, 1994, the Mexican government devalued the peso. The impact of that action was felt around the world. In a nutshell, it began with a strain on the Mexican financial system, including overzealous monetary and fiscal expansion in 1994. As a Council on Foreign Relations report, "Lessons of the Mexican Peso Crisis: Report of an Independent Task Force," noted: "Recent studies indicate that Mexican investors grasped the fragility of the situation much more aptly and sooner than did foreign investors and observers. Thus

Mexican, not foreign, investors triggered the initial outflow of capital in November and earlier December 1994."

The action taken to address this fiscal and monetary crisis was to allow the Mexican peso to float against the U.S. dollar. In effect, this devaluated the peso by 15 percent. "In the ensuing months, the peso plummeted to an exchange rate of seven and a half to one U.S. dollar, its lowest level in 2 decades, dropping below levels reached in the depths of the 1982 debt crisis."

Additionally, overnight rates on pesos exceeded 70 percent in some cases, and 3-month rates were over 50 percent. This was more proof that higher rates don't support a nearly worthless currency if the fundamentals are not in place.

In the aftermath, markets in Argentina, Thailand, Spain, Hong Kong, Sweden, Italy, Canada, and Russia experienced a "varying degree of turbulence," the report noted. "Already in 1994, gradual declines in equity and bond prices in emerging markets had signaled a market correction that was not considered out of the ordinary."

The Fed, meanwhile, was between a rock and the proverbial hard place. Mexico was (and is) one of the largest trading partners with the United States. Thus, the Mexican economy is very important to the United States in many subtle ways. Therefore, the Fed needed to help Mexico, but concerns ran high about possible inflation in the United States, and we were still not completely over the S&L crises.

The lesson: one economic event can have a major impact on another and another (i.e., the Mexican peso crisis, the need for stability in the United States, and the continuing bailout of the S&Ls.) Nothing in the economic picture is ever 100 percent clear or 100 percent cloudy.

THE LTCM CRISIS

First, take a bunch of really smart guys—Nobel laureate types—and add some very sophisticated economic models. Mix in a financial crisis in Russia, which defaulted on its domestic debt and devalued its currency, the ruble. Put that in an economic blender known as an unstable world economic picture and what do you get? You get the Long-Term Capital Management (LTCM) debacle.

Long-Term Capital was a hedge fund that used models designed by Robert Merton and Myron Scholes, who won the Nobel Prize in economics. These models, Long-Term Capital believed, would allow it to do *safely* what hedge funds do: that is, leverage capital (borrowing 25 to 1 and then borrowing some more) to invest and (hopefully) make big returns. Based upon these Merton/Scholes models, Long-Term Capital believed that it was safeguarded against a market turndown.

But what the smart guys at Long-Term Capital didn't take into consideration was a variable such as the Russian government defaulting on its domestic debt. Long-Term Capital held Russian domestic paper, and, as things got dicey, it sold off safer things like U.S. Treasuries, hoping that the Russian stuff would recover. Well in the end, Long-Term lost just about everything, and the Fed had to orchestrate its bailout.

What does that have to do with you, the investor? The Russian debt debacle was a global problem that rippled through a world economy that was already shaky, especially in Asia and certain countries of Latin America. Secondly, there was Long-Term Capital, and a few other hedge funds as well, that were caught with near worthless paper and other investment problems in the wake of Russia's debt default. The market hiccupped but kept on chugging in spite of it all.

Long-Term Capital seized financial headlines for a while. But your 401(k) was (at least in 1998) probably safe and secure and gearing up for the 1999 blast off of the Nasdaq. What does Long-Term Capital have to do with you? Nothing. And that is the point. A bunch of very smart guys did some very dumb things that made news but that didn't affect the economy one iota, although some may argue that without the carefully planned bail-out by the Fed, some large banks and brokerages would have gone under, creating a bigger problem (although I don't doubt that).

BUBBLES AND BURSTS
In recent years we have seen some dramatic ups and downs in the equity markets, including the skyrocketing Nasdaq of 1999, followed by the bursting of the proverbial bubble in 2000 and 2001. Let's take a look at a few of these recent market events.

- **October 1997**. The Dow Jones Industrial Average (DJIA) dropped a record 554 points, or 7.2 percent. (While this was a larger point drop than the infamous Crash of 1987, it was smaller on a percentage basis.) A few days later, it staged a 337-point rebound, and then finished the week at 7442, down only 4 percent. As a November 1997 *U.S. News and World Reports* article, "The Market's Bumpy Ride," noted: "Whether the market heads up or down this week, investors are bracing for more violent mood swings."

- **December 1999**: The Nasdaq Composite (an index of all Nasdaq stocks) rose nearly 86 percent by year-end. Dot-com fever had struck this market, propelling tech stocks to lofty P/E levels.

- **December 2000**: The Nasdaq Composite was off 39 percent by year-end.

- **First quarter 2001**: The Nasdaq Composite declined 25 percent from the fourth quarter of 2000 and was 60 percent lower then the first quarter of 2000.

Enter the age of the tech wreck. Throughout 2001, equity markets continued to trade lower with no end in sight to the bear market. Investors were not only nervous about their stock holdings, they were also downright scared about their retirement savings—401(k) plans that included stock holdings and other investments that promised a brighter future.

The market is front and center in everyone's attention. The daily gyrations up and down (and these days down some more) consume much of the news media's focus as well. "The market" is part of the vernacular, and not just on Wall Street.

This brings us full circle to our point of entry on the topic: What does Wall Street have to do with Main Street, and vice versa? There is no doubt that the speculative bubble on Wall Street, particularly when it comes to the Nasdaq, has burst. But what does that say about the U.S. economy? Does it say anything relevant at all?

Investors making decisions today about tomorrow must sift through the news and nuances. Just as you're in charge of making your "asset allocations" in your 401(k), so are you in control of your economic future. Yes, you are at the mercy of the whims of the market as much as anyone (unless, perhaps, if you have as much money as, say, Bill Gates). But then again, you can decide how and when you're going to invest based on your criteria, not the nonsensical ramblings of an economist and/or talking head.

So what's inside Greenspan's briefcase? Of course only he and his closest advisers know for sure. But somewhere in there, among confidential reports and letters from central bankers is quite a bit of data that looks at what you, the investor, is doing right now with your money.

It's the economy. It's all about you.

THE LESSON

As investors, both long term and short term, we've all had the bejeepers scared out of us. Equity prices, particularly Nasdaq issues, have declined. The value of pensions and 401(k) plans has evaporated. Many people, literally, had less money at the end of 2001 than they did 2 years ago. At the same time, the summer of 2001 brought headlines of rising unemployment as layoffs continued. Mortgage rates in 2001, meanwhile, were below 7 percent. The fed funds rate was at 3.5 percent, and headed lower. Unemployment was at 4.5 percent (but would soon head higher). Inflation stood around 2 percent. In August 2001—well before the National Bureau of Economic Research (NBER) proclaimed that the United States had entered a recession in March 2001—the gross domestic product (GDP) showed the economy was growing at a rate of 0.2 percent. That wasn't full steam ahead, but it was in positive territory.

The stock market, meanwhile, was down. The tech sector continued to suffer, with the Nasdaq Composite some two-thirds lower than its heights of over 5000 in March 2000. However, the Dow was down a comparatively smaller 6 percent or so. The values of our homes, in general, were at all-time highs. Housing starts and new home sales had been strong. It probably wasn't the time to bet the farm with a large investment in stocks, based on the stock market activity in the first and second quarters of 2001. The mixed economic signals, with a slowing GDP yet low unemployment, would have raised a red flag for you, the investor, that something was changing. In other words, while some things looked good—the value of our homes and the low level of unemployment—the slowing of GDP should have signaled that the economy was cooling off. And a slower economy for an investor typically means lower equity prices.

2

The Fed: What It Does...
What It Doesn't Do

Picture a small house somewhere and inside a family huddled around the dining room table. Upon a closer look, you see there is a newspaper open on the table. A man and his son (imagine Bob Cratchet and Tiny Tim) are scanning the stock tables in the newspaper by the dwindling light of the setting sun. A woman sifts through brokerage account statements. Her brow is furrowed with worry. The daughter, no more than 12 or 13 years old, is also at the table writing a letter.

Dear Mr. Greenspan:

Mom and Dad are so worried these days. Even my brother wonders if he'll be able to keep up with the traveling soccer team. Uniforms are so expensive. As for me, I've all but given up trips to the mall. Won't you please help us?

The stock market has fallen so low. Our mutual funds are down 20, 30, or even 50 percent. Father thinks it's the end of Tech as we know it, and Mother thinks that even Blue Chips aren't a safe haven anymore.

Please, Mr. Greenspan. Can't you make the stock market go up? I know you've tried with rate cuts. But if you pardon me for saying so, it doesn't seem like you've done enough.

We want to go on vacation this year. But Mother says we won't be able to afford to go if the market keeps going down. Father thinks we're headed for a depression and that everyone will lose his or her job.

Please Mr. Greenspan. We've been such a good little family. Can't you do this for us?

Sincerely,
Virginia (Who *believes* in the Fed)

Sorry, Virginia. The Fed is no Santa Claus.

Before we discuss the role of the Fed, it's important to note what the Fed *doesn't* do. It doesn't regulate the stock market. It's not the Fed's job to support the price of Microsoft, GE, or GM. It's not the Fed's job to ensure a bull market. It's not the Fed's job to make sure your 401(k) shows a positive annual return.

But wait, you say. Didn't the Fed rescue Wall Street after the Crash of 1987 by offering sufficient liquidity to the banks and brokerages? Didn't the Fed help bail out Long-Term Capital Management—and that was a bunch of investors—after the Russian debt default? Why won't the Fed help me?

Sorry. That's not what the Fed does, or is supposed to do. In fact, I'll go a step further: The Fed is far more concerned with mundane, bureaucratic responsibilities—like making sure that checks clear—than people realize. In fact, the image of the Fed as some kind of financial "swat team," armed with the latest in the tools of economic good and right, is a disservice to the Fed and to you, the consumer and investor. The Fed is an important, if difficult to define, quasi-government, pseudo-private, bank oversight body. And when things are economically difficult—as they were in mid- to late 2001, the time of the writing of this book—everyone gloms onto the Fed like the last shred of hope. That view distorts the power and therefore the responsibility of the Fed. Alan Greenspan isn't Santa Claus or Daddy Warbucks, folks who are going to make sure you have bus fare and spending money in your pocket. If you want to know who has the real power in this economy. . . . If you haven't figured it out so far you might as well read the rest of this chapter.

At this point, I've probably raised a few hackles in the "I ♥ Greenspan" circle. Personally, I have nothing negative to say about

Mr. Greenspan, or his predecessor, Paul Volcker, the inflation-fighter who ran the Fed when I was a lowly intern there. But if investors are going to make wise decisions about their own futures, they have to understand what the economic forces do—and don't do. Understanding the Fed is a very important step.

Now hold on, the monetarists say. The Fed controls money supply and that controls the economy. Monetarists believe that money supply is everything. Increasingly it pumps up the economy, but too much causes inflation. Controlling inflation is achieved by controlling money supply. Fair enough. Money supply is an important factor in the economy, helping to control inflation or stave off recession. Although if you look at what the Fed did in 2001 and the condition of the economy in September 2001, horrific events of September 11 notwithstanding, I'd argue that ratcheting down the discount rate and freeing up more money was not the proverbial silver bullet.

Wait one moment, the Keynesians cry. Keynesians believe that the economy needs the intervention of the government to manage demand. Thus, the economic levers are in the hands of politicians (heaven help us) through taxation, fiscal stimulus packages, and so forth. Once again, I point to current events. The tax-break package passed in 2001 by the Bush administration did bring a little windfall into many taxpayers' lives, but it didn't erase mounting unemployment figures.

I'm in the camp of the free market advocates. I don't believe that there is any one body or any one person who is synonymous with our economy. I believe that our economy is simply our economy. It's made up of a variety of factors that do include the Fed's money supply activity and government policies that put or don't put a strain on business. But at the core of our economy is the consumer/investor, who either buys that big screen TV/washer-dryer combo/living-room set/mini-van/ultra-deluxe coffeemaker cappuccino machine . . . or not. Who controls the economy? You. (When businesses expand, that is obviously an important element of the economy, but often it is a result of increased consumer demand.)

The Fed is a mechanism that helps to grease the wheels of the economy when the economy is shaky and tightens things up when it's going too fast. Here's an entirely different metaphor. Think of the Fed (in the persona of Alan Greenspan) as a kind of economic personal trainer. The Fed shows up at the door of the economy in sweats and cross-trainer sneakers and tries to get the economy in shape with various exercises. If the economy has been working too hard and risks an injury (inflation) due to too much exertion, the Fed trainer will say, hey, it's time to take a break. But the Fed is only the trainer. The economy has to do the work.

You may be feeling a little economically abandoned right now. In this time of your economic distress, with your 401(k) a mere shadow of its former self, you believed that Alan Greenspan could push some magic button and make everything okay. Now some spoilsport has told you that the Fed is not Santa Claus. Welcome to the harsh but far better world of economic reality.

The perception of American investors that the Fed will bail them out has parted ways with economic reality. In order for investors to make sound investment decisions, particularly for the long term, they must understand the role of the Fed. The goals and objectives of the Fed are to create an environment of optimal growth, productivity, and employment without high inflation, labor shortages, and currency fluctuations—all the while preserving an orderly and efficient banking system.

Granted, as the monetarists would have us believe, the number one tool of the Fed is monetary policy. That involves increasing or decreasing the money supply using open market operations (buying and selling U.S. Treasury securities) and lowering or raising the federal funds rate, as well as setting bank-reserve requirements. That's the first thing that investors must understand, a subtle point though it may be. The Fed doesn't set interest rates or mortgage rates per se, although the Fed's actions will affect the rate at which you, the consumer/investor, can borrow money. It also can influence the rate that an interest-bearing account, say a money market account or fund, will pay you. What the Fed does is set the rate that banks must pay each other for short-term (as in overnight) loans.

Banks and other financial institutions are required to hold reserve balances at the Federal Reserve. When one institution is below the desired reserve position, it can borrow from other banks and institutions that are above their positions. The financial institution that lends the money charges a short-term interest rate, which is known as the *federal funds rate*. Meanwhile, the Fed's policy of easing the supply of money or tightening it up has an immediate effect on the supply or demand for reserves and the federal funds rate.

When the Fed wants to take an action that will have direct impact on the money supply (and therefore the U.S. economy), it has three options.

- **Reserve requirements**. The Fed's Board of Governors sets reserve requirements for depository institutions (banks and financial institutions that hold deposits for businesses and consumers).

- **Discount rate**. The discount rate is set by directors of the Reserve banks, subject to review by the Board of Governors. This is the interest rate at which the Federal Reserve lends money to member banks, and it also directly impacts the rate at which banks and financial institutions lend each other money.

- **Open market operations**. The Federal Reserve buys and sells securities, which, in effect, changes the volume of reserves in the depository system. When the Fed buys securities, that action adds to the reserves, while a sale reduces them. Here's how the Fed itself explains it.

> When the Federal Reserve buys securities, it pays, in effect, by issuing a check from itself. When the seller of those securities deposits the check in its bank account, the bank presents the check to the Federal Reserve for payment. The Federal Reserve then honors that check by increasing the reserve account of the seller's bank at the Federal Reserve. When the Federal Reserve sells securities, the opposite occurs. Payment for securities by the banks reduces the reserves that they have on deposit with the Fed. "This characteristic—the dollar-for-dollar change in the reserves of the depository system with the purchase or sale of securities by the Federal Reserve—makes open market operations the most powerful, flexible, and precise tool of monetary policy," the Fed explains on its Web site.

Clearly, this monitoring of the bank reserves and setting the levels of the reserves makes the Fed far more of a fiscal post office than most people realize. And, I'm not knocking the Fed for that. We need the Postal Service. The Fed does provide a vital function when it comes to monitoring the money supply and controlling the liquidity that is, quite frankly, the lifeblood of the banking system. Each of us needs our checks cashed and the money moved from account to account. That's important. If it didn't happen, we'd be in trouble. If the Fed didn't undertake these functions, the inflation spikes in an overheated economy and the valleys of recession when the economy cycles downward would probably be more pronounced. The Fed does help to smooth out those bumps in the road. But the Fed cannot and should not try to make the road completely flat. The economy runs in cycles. Certain events impact those cycles, from the state of the world economy to consumer fears and confidence. But the economy will do what it will do.

The role of the Fed is to watch what the economy is doing at the moment and try to influence things a bit. The Volcker-led Fed was credited with defeating inflation, which was accomplished not by high interest rates alone. The Greenspan Fed has kept a watch on the economy's growth, on alert for signs of inflation while trying to keep a recession from turning into something really bad. One of the things that the Fed can do is increase (or decrease) money supply. Once that action is taken, the economy (meaning you, the consumer) must let things run their course.

Governing money supply is the most important thing that the Fed does (although I believe it is *not* the single most important thing that happens in the economy.) In the 1980s, money supply was a really big deal. Traders and speculators watched money supply figures to see if they rose or fell, which would presage Fed action in the Treasury market. So when I was an intern at the Federal Reserve Bank in Chicago, I knew that if there was any power and influence to be had in this place, it was in the realm of money supply.

Now I was a 20-year-old manually inputting data for money supply statistics. Most of this was automated, but there were still a few figures that had to be punched in by hand. Those hands included mine. I was, in reality, a data entry clerk. I was not pontificating about economic theory or hypothesizing about the role of the Federal Reserve. I was typing in "Federal Reserve Bank System 3 . . . $38 billion. . . ."

Then one day a senior vice president of a very large bank stopped by the Fed for a meeting. I was very impressed by who this man was and nervous about being introduced to him. When I was, he asked me, "So, what do you do here?"

What could I tell him? My job was, basically, entering data into a computer. The only requirements were 10 functional fingers and hand-eye coordination. My interest in the markets, the economy, and all things fiscal was really immaterial. So I got creative in my reply.

"I'm helping to make decisions on money supply," I replied, straight-faced. There was the tiniest grain of truth in that. I was inputting money supply figures that did get crunched with all the other numbers to monitor the overall money supply, which was used by the Fed as part of its decision-making process. So if I didn't type in those numbers, the money supply figures wouldn't be totally accurate. So the more accurate I was in my punching and typing, the better the decision the Fed could make.

"Hmm," the senior vice president said, nodding, and probably suppressing the urge to laugh in my not-so-innocent face.

After a few moments of conversation, the senior vice president looked back at me, amused, and then turned to his associate. "He's helping to make decisions on money supply . . . Do you think Mr. Volcker knows that he's doing that?"

The point of this story (other than my confession of youthful self-aggrandizement) is that the most important things the Fed did then, and does now, are impact money supply and set short-term rates. Period. Money is like grease for the wheels churning in the economy. But it's not the wheels themselves.

Truth be told, I have oversimplified the Fed's role, which goes far beyond bureaucratic functions or raising and lowering rates. Its larger economic-policy role includes a weblike influence that is not only broad but also hard to define. For the purpose of talking about the Fed's direct impact to the economy, I intentionally understate things a bit.

THE FED: PUBLIC OR PRIVATE?

Any discussion of the role and importance of the Fed wouldn't be complete without the perfunctory history lesson and a look at that essential question: Is the Fed public or private? First the history. The Fed was established by the Federal Reserve Act of 1913 under then President Woodrow Wilson and presented to Congress by Virginia Senator Carter Glass. The unique relationship and powers of the Federal Reserve have been debated through the decades. Many think that the Fed is above the laws of other government agencies with regard to reporting and secrecy. Others think that because the Fed is actually owned by the member banks, which are private, nongovernment institutions, the Fed is not a government agency and, therefore, should not have some of the privileges of government agencies. Still others contend that since the Fed governors are appointed by the president and confirmed by Congress, it should be equated to a government agency. In reality, the Fed is a little bit public, a little bit private.

This public and private world that the Fed occupies is reflected in the fact that the presidents of the regional Federal Reserve Banks are voted on by the board of directors of the banks, who take turns serving on the Federal Open Market Committee (FOMC). At the center of the Federal Reserve System is the Federal Reserve Board of Governors, which has seven members. Each governor is appointed by the president and confirmed by the Senate. In an effort to ensure the Federal Reserve's independence, each governor serves a 14-year term, with one governor's term expiring every other January.

The Chairman of the Board of Governors, currently Alan Greenspan, is chosen from among the seven governors and serves a 4-year term. Typically, the chairman of the board will retire once his or her term is up, regardless of how many years remain in his or her term as a governor. (Greenspan has been Fed Chairman since 1987.) The Board of Governors is the top echelon of the Federal Reserve System, with the power to control monetary policy in all parts of the Fed. Further, the seven Fed governors are among the 12 members of the FOMC, which gives them collectively the majority of the votes and thus control of open market operations.

An important part of the Fed is the group of outside governors. These individuals have already enjoyed success somewhere else and they bring with them experience and expertise. So if you're an outside governor and now you're in the service of the Fed, you're there (we hope) on your merits in the financial world. You're not just some bureaucrat whose longevity has pushed you up the ladder until you're sitting at the Fed conference table asking Alan Greenspan to pass the pitcher of ice water.

Consider Greenspan himself. In 1987, when Volcker's second term was about to expire, the name "Alan Greenspan" surfaced as the logical candidate. At that time, he was a 61-year-old New York economist who had served as chairman of the Council of Economic Advisors in the Ford administration. He took the job, apparently overcoming his reservations of decades before. According to Bob Woodward's biography, *Maestro: Greenspan's Fed and the American Boom* (Simon & Schuster, 2000), Greenspan frequently used to visit his mentor, Arthur F. Burns, who was Fed chairman from 1970 to 1978. "As Greenspan learned about the job of Fed chairman, he concluded that it was amorphous, not something he would enjoy doing," Woodward writes. "It seemed to be an arcane exercise, and there were large elements he frankly didn't get. Greenspan liked the mechanical, analytical work of basic business economics—inventories, arithmetic, physical reality. Monetary policy and the setting of interest rates were far more complex. It entailed trying to figure out what business conditions and inflation were going to be in the future. Interest rates had their impact months or a year or more down the road. Seeing the future was about the most impossible task imaginable . . ."

Greenspan is probably the best statistician ever born, and his analysis of the steel industry and the resulting increase and decrease in demand during the 1950s, 1960s, and 1970s is nothing short of brilliant. His thirst for statistics and information that lead to clues about the future direction of the U.S. economy is like fortune-telling.

Although Greenspan himself, as well as many of his admirers, says he is an awful predictor of the future of the economy, I believe that this is inaccurate. Perhaps he responds a little late in the cycles, as many claimed in 2000. For example, in December 2000 he went from a tightening stance, concerned about inflation, to an easing, accommodating stance, concerned about economic weakness. When he made that shift, totally skipping "neutral," the economy really slowed down. The Fed tried to head off the slowdown with 11 unprecedented rate cuts, including three surprise cuts—all because the slowdown was foreseen by his analysis of economic data. However, the Fed could only soften the blow of the economic downturn, not prevent it, as the decline in the economy was exacerbated by the September 2001 terrorist attack on America.

Whatever reservations Mr. Greenspan had about the job of Fed chairman before he took it on, he must have gotten over them. He's expected to stay in this post until at least 2004. As Fed chairman, in addition to sitting at eight yearly meetings of the FOMC, he's an active adviser to the president. He frequently testifies before Congress in addition to keeping an active speaking schedule, addressing various business and economic groups. His comments are combed for hints, indication, nuance, or sentiment that might give the market some inkling of whether the Fed is likely to cut rates, raise rates, or leave them alone. Throughout 2001, the expectations had been for the Fed to make substantial rate cuts with the hope that this would bolster a lagging economy and, in turn, stem the losses in the equity market. In 2001, the Fed made 11 rate cuts, reducing the federal funds rate from 6.5 to 1.75 percent.

While the Fed's statements may be insightful as another view of the economy, they are not the potion that will make the economy healthy or ill. I mean, if you wanted to know about the game of football, wouldn't you listen to a Jerry Rice or a Payton Manning? They are not the game of football, but they sure do play a lot of it. So if you wanted to know about the economy, wouldn't you listen to the Fed?

The FOMC's eight meetings a year means it convenes about every 6 weeks. Most are 1-day sessions, although the first and fifth meetings of the year are extended to 2 days. In addition to the seven Fed governors, the FOMC's 12 voting members include five Federal Reserve Bank presidents. The president of the New York Federal Reserve Bank is always a voting member due to the large share of member banks in its district. Although they do not have the ability to vote, the other seven Federal Reserve Bank presidents attend the meetings and participate in the discussions.

Just how do the Federal Reserve and the FOMC make their decisions? Here's what the Federal Reserve itself says: "In making monetary policy plans, the Federal Reserve and the FOMC are involved in a complex, dynamic process in which monetary policy is only one of many forces affecting employment, output, and prices. The government's budgetary policies influence the economy through changes in tax and spending programs. Shifts in business and consumer confidence and a variety of other market forces also affect saving and spending plans of businesses and households. Changes in expectations about economic prospects and policies, through their effects on interest rates and financial conditions, can have significant influence on the outcomes for jobs, outputs, and prices . . ."

In other words, the Fed monitors the current state of the economy, projects its likely course over the short and long term, and takes action. Because of the direct impact of the Fed's decision on the market, these actions—or hints of possible actions—are closely watched by traders, economists, speculators, and the financial media at large. Continuing the theme of "the economy is not the stock market," it's important to realize that the Fed's role is to watch over the economy, trying to do its part to stimulate sustainable growth while staving off inflation. That's the number one job. What happens to the market is, truly, secondary.

Thus you have the Fed with its collective finger on the economic pulse of the country and often acting in concert with other central banks of the world. It's clear that the powers of the Fed certainly play a part in the health of the economy. But this importance is greatly overestimated. True, the Fed controls the money supply, as well as the rates that banks charge each other for overnight loans. But these powers have less importance these days than they did in the past. That may sound like economic blasphemy, but I think it's a good dose of reality. The Fed is powerful and influential. But it isn't the first or last word about the economy. As I'll discuss later in this chapter, relying on the government or a pseudo-government agency like the Fed to control your investments and your economic future is a faulty notion at best. Ours is not a centrally planned economy by any means. Ours is a free market, which means values rise on supply and demand, with varying degrees of fear, greed, and euphoria thrown in depending upon the prevailing sentiment.

I don't want to discount the Fed. But I also do not want to raise it to a level of an economic demigod. Consumers who feel confident spend more, and the economy chugs ahead. Consumers and investors who are fearful rein in their purchases of anything from refrigerators and cars to stocks and mutual funds. Panicky investors who are eager to sell and too nervous to buy are what send the market lower.

The Fed's influence extends to the economy by making more or less money available. When money is freely available, businesses and consumers can borrow at advantageous rates, thus sparking purchases, investments in homes and other big-ticket items, and capital expenditures by companies. When the money is tight, rates are high, and investment by businesses and consumers is limited. Tax policy has much to do with this as well. When corporations are given tax incentives for research and development, they spend more on research and development, and thus become more efficient. That, in the long run, makes them more profitable. As a result of all this, you, the consumer, get to enjoy lower costs on goods (because companies that are more efficient can price their products more competitively) and you get to enjoy cool stuff because of all the new product development. For example, when the Reagan administration announced a reduction in the capital gains tax in the early 1980s, this was about as good for the market as a surprise rate cut every quarter. Controlling the demand for investments and savings has a great impact on the stock market. But, again, it is still limited in terms of overall impact.

The tools of the Fed in its task of controlling the money supply are its open market operations. Money supply is defined as M1, M2, and M3 (see Chart 2-1). M1 is the narrow definition of money supply, meaning the money that's on hand to be spent or invested. M1 consists of currency in the hands of the public, traveler's checks, demand deposits, and deposits against which checks can be written. M2 includes everything in M1, plus savings accounts, time deposits of less than $100,000, and balances in retail money market mutual funds. M3 includes M2 (which of course includes M1), plus time deposits of $100,000 or more, balances in institutional money funds, repurchase agreements issued by depository institutions, and Eurodollars held by U.S. residents at foreign branches of U.S. banks, and all banks in the United Kingdom and Canada.

As you'll recall from earlier in this chapter, the Fed controls money supply by buying and selling Treasury securities. In financial lingo, when the Fed notifies the primary dealers that it will purchase

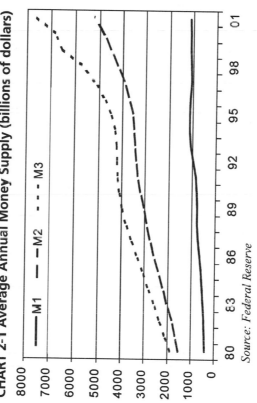

CHART 2-1 Average Annual Money Supply (billions of dollars)

Source: Federal Reserve

securities with the intention to resell them at a later date, that's a "repo"—short for repurchase agreement. When the Fed notifies primary dealers that it intends to resell those securities, that's a "reverse repo." Thus, when the Fed buys securities (repo), it pumps more money into the economy. When the Fed sells securities (reverse repo), the money supply in the hands of banks tightens. Money is not really changing hands in all this; accounts at the Federal Reserve are being debited and credited accordingly.

Before Greenspan took over as Fed chairman, this repo and reverse repo activity was done daily at about 10:30 a.m. Central Time. Traders and economists called it "Fed Time," which was closely watched as an indication of what the Fed's monetary policy was. In other words, how the Fed monitored and controlled money supply could presage changes in rates. Back in the 1980s, we watched M1, M2, and M3 statistics for any hint of a loosening or tightening in money supply. As a young trader, it was possible to get so caught up in watching a number that you forgot just how important, or unimportant, the number was.

I remember a particular day when the money supply numbers were coming out. Based on those numbers, we'd either buy or sell U.S. Treasuries. When the money supply figures were released, there was a decline across the board with M1 at, say, $1.078 billion, M2 at $4.284 billion, and M3 at $5.824 billion.

M1 . . . M2 . . . M3 . . . The figures were rolling around in my head. M1 was money in the hands of retail people. M2 was money in the hands of retail people and larger institutions. M3 was . . . was . . . "Hey," I shouted across the trading room. "What's M3?"

"$5.824 billion!" was the immediate reply.

"No, what *is* M3?"

"I said $5.824 billion."

"Yes, I know. But what *is* M3?" I felt like I was playing the financial version of "Who's on first?" "What" is on second, and "I don't know" is on third.

Maybe in a clearer moment, my fellow traders could have recited the textbook definition of M3, and probably I'd recall what it was too. But in that moment it didn't matter to anyone in that trading room what M3 was. It could have been the value of all the diamonds at Harry Winston's or the dollar value of the angels who could dance on the head of a pin. What mattered to us knee-jerk traders was that M3 was down from the previous month, which meant that the money supply was tightening and that interest rates might go up.

Now, nobody pays a nickel's worth of attention to money supply figures. We traders watch signs of economic growth, or lack thereof, to try to anticipate if the Fed will make further rate cuts and the likely magnitude of those cuts. Why? Because there still is a reaction—sometimes only momentary—to what the Fed says and does. And if you're a trader (especially a short-term, day-trading type), you want to catch that wave of Fed-action reaction.

But you don't have to be caught up in the cycle of Fed watch. Be aware of what is happening, but don't lose your focus on the broader picture—particularly if you have an investment horizon of 5 to 10 years. When it comes to Fed announcements, your most valuable investment insight may come from the Fed's own assessment of the economy. Then like the traders and speculators who hang on every word communicated by Greenspan and the Fed, you can extrapolate what the Fed is likely to do and your own investment response (or not) to it.

Today's Fed is far more transparent than in the past, communicating clearly about its economic views. Take, for example, the statement made by the FOMC on August 21, 2001, after it decided to lower its target for the federal funds rate by 25 basis points to 3½ percent and the Board of Governors approved a 25 basis point reduction in the discount rate to 3 percent. Here's what the Fed had to say:

> Household demand has been sustained, but business profits and capital spending continue to weaken and growth abroad is slowing, weighing on the U.S. economy. The associated easing of pressures on labor and product markets is expected to keep inflation contained. Although long-term prospects for productivity growth and the economy remain favorable, the Committee continues to believe that against the background of its long-run goals of price stability and sustainable economic growth and of the information currently available, the risks are weighted mainly toward conditions that may generate economic weakness in the foreseeable future . . .

It doesn't take an economist to see what the Fed was driving at. As of August 21, it saw inflation under control but still viewed economic weakness in the foreseeable future. That's an environment in which the Fed would be likely to cut rates further (which, of course, it did). The Fed makes announcements not only on its actions but also on what the meanings of those actions are and what its stance is on rates and future "bias."

Whatever the Fed action, the consensus of the market is that rate hikes are bad for the stock market (investor money is attracted instead to fixed-income instruments, and companies have to borrow at higher rates for expansion). Subsequently, rate cuts are good for the stock market (as investors go to the stock market for higher returns than they could get on bonds, and companies can borrow more cheaply to finance expansion).

There can be any number of permutations on those basic views, including that a rate cut may prompt a selloff on Wall Street when the rate reduction "isn't enough" to spark economic growth, or because it indicates a period of prolonged economic slowdown.

In 1989, the Fed had been pretty quiet in terms of rate action. There was some indication of inflation in the picture, and the dollar had been weaker all year long. Concern about the value of the dollar had started to permeate the markets. It was a quiet day and I was on the phone with a counterpart on the West Coast. We had been speculating on how much lower the dollar could go without sparking inflation and a run on U.S. assets because foreigners would flee our markets due to a deteriorating currency. We went so far as to suggest what it would take to turn the dollar around. We never thought of a Fed rate hike.

Ding . . . Ding . . . Ding. The alert on the news wire! The Fed had raised the discount rate by 50 basis points.

My colleague and I stayed on the phone for a minute, asking each other what we should do. We made up our minds simultaneously.

"Buy!" I shouted to the trading desk in Chicago.

"Sell!" He shouted to the trading desk in Los Angeles.

Same scenario. Same set of events. Different conclusions.

My West Coast colleague's rationale was that higher rates would be bad for bond and stock prices, prompting sales of these assets by foreigners who would sell dollars to repatriate the currency. I thought that higher rates would mean lower inflation ahead and higher yields for U.S.-denominated currencies.

I hit the button on my computer terminal to buy U.S. securities, and my counterpart in L.A. was selling.

What this anecdote shows is that the market (or more specifically traders, speculators, and investors in the market) reacts when the Fed takes action. Clearly the powers at the disposal of the Fed make it and its functions important to the economy and, by extension, to the market. After all, the Fed controls the supply of money, which is the lifeblood of the economy. The price we pay for this "blood" impacts the cost of everything. Additionally, the availability of money is vital to businesses, enabling them (or preventing them) from making purchases or capital improvements.

The Fed acts on the premise that it can control the economy by controlling the supply and price of money. This was a good theory when the Fed was the only game in town. But now, financial markets are so mature and sophisticated that there are many other ways to borrow money and finance projects. Even banks have created new, innovative sources of funding. Therefore, the actual fed funds rate and discount rate are less important now than they were in the past. In fact many times after a Fed action, interest-rate sensitive instruments move in the *opposite* direction. It's like the prime rate. This used to be the rate that banks charged their prime clients for money. Hardly anymore borrows at prime anymore.

Yes, the Fed does adjust the reserve requirements of banks, in effect making more or less money available for lending (and costly or less costly in the process). But banks aren't the only sources of capital in the same way that the Fed is not the only cog in the economic wheel. Today, companies can raise capital in any number of ways that exclude banks. They can issue bonds, float stock, sell off a subsidiary or part of the company, or even get funding or an investment from other companies. How willing a company, a financial institution, or the investing public is to buy the securities or notes that a company is selling reflects the economic reality of supply and demand. Do they like what this company is selling, whether it's a bond issue or a manufacturing operation or not? That's as basic as it gets when it comes to the economy.

I believe that the market actually does a lot of work for the Fed. Frequently the lenders of money have a better gauge on interest rates and the cost of money than the Fed does. Frequently, these money market rates are telling more about the economy than the Fed's actions tell. If you're trying to raise money by selling bonds or notes and you can't get takers, you need to raise the rate that you're offering. This free market mechanism truly gives a clearer picture of demand for funds in the short run than the Fed.

In fact, we could argue that the Fed is constantly behind what the markets are already saying. Take, for example, 2000 when the Fed was still raising rates as late as May of that year. Interest rates on the 10-year note and the 30-year bond, however, stopped rising in late January.

In 2001, even with the aggressive easing by the Fed that we saw throughout the year, long-term rates actually made a new high in mid-April, after 100 basis points worth of rate cuts by the Fed. Even the stock market, which was clearly not ready to turn around in January, rallied for a week or two after a rare intrameeting surprise cut in January 2001, only to fall even lower in February and March. To bring the point home, the market is the final judge of when—and if—it's ready to make a turn, regardless of the immediate actions of the Fed.

Of course, there are times when the Fed does step in with swift, decisive action, such as after the Crash of 1987 when Greenspan acted quickly to lower rates and calm the markets. Another time was in September 2001, after the tragic terrorist attacks in New York and Washington, which resulted in the complete destruction of the World Trade Center. After the attack, the Fed cut rates by 50 basis points, cutting its target for the federal funds rate to 3 percent and the discount rate to 2½ percent. In a statement dated September 17, 2001, the Fed said it would "continue to supply unusually large volumes of liquidity to the financial markets, as needed, until more normal market functioning is restored.

"Even before the tragic events of last week, employment, production, and business spending remained weak, and last week's events have the potential to damp spending further," the Fed stated. It continued, "Nonetheless, the long-term prospects for productivity growth and the economy remain favorable and should become evident once the unusual forces restraining demand abate."

No tea leaves needed here. The Fed stepped in with the promise of liquidity and ample money supply in the wake of the tragic terrorist attack on New York and Washington. Chart 2-2 shows a steep decline in the target fed funds rate, while Mr. Greenspan & Co. pursued an aggressive economic stimulus program. Longer term, however, the Fed sees "favorable" prospects for growth. But how well the economy will do in the short and long run will depend on what you, the consumer, do. If you run for cover out of fear for your job and your investments, then the economy will decline further and take longer to recover. If you loosen your purse strings a little and buy that appliance, car, stock, or mutual fund as you had been planning all along, then it won't.

That's why the two biggest assets of Mr. Greenspan and the Fed are (1) being able to listen to what the markets and the economy are saying and (2) acting accordingly to ensure order and creating the perception that everything is under control. But this is more illusion than reality. When it comes to control, the power rests in the hands of the market—the collective consciousness, if you will, of retail and institutional investors. Yes, the Fed can take action that will sway sentiment. But the Fed is reacting to what it sees. In other words, the decisions and actions of the Fed are the effect, not the cause.

In that, Mr. Greenspan is reminiscent of the "man behind the curtain" in that great movie *The Wizard of Oz*. The smoky, ethereal face of the "wizard" looked menacing, but as Dorothy and her companions were soon to discover, it was all just special effects from the "man behind the curtain." And as Dorothy quickly learned, the real power for her own destiny was in her own hands, or in her case, her ruby slippers.

So investor, don't look to the Fed to make all your worries disappear. You have the power to control your fate and, by extension, the economy. Don't forget that consumer spending makes up more than 67 percent of our GDP. When it comes to the economy and the market, we control our own fates.

So just click your heels together and repeat, "There's no place like home. There's no place like home."

Then, while the mortgage rates are favorable, go out and buy one, or at least refinance one.

CHART 2-2 Federal Funds Rate

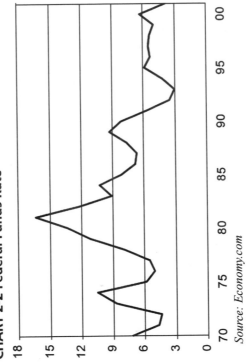

Source: Economy.com

3

What's Economics Got to Do with It?

conomic News Bulletin. . . . Recession *not* a dirty word, economist says. . . . What goes up must come down. . . . Always darkest before the dawn. . . . Without sadness we cannot value joy. . . . Now you know the theme of this chapter.

Seriously, many investors are so afraid of the "R" word that they won't contemplate it, let alone think about its place in the economic cycle. True, nobody really *likes* a recession. We don't look at a shrinking economy and rising unemployment and say, "Oh goodie! We're gonna have some fun now!" But at the same time, you can't be so afraid of the "R" word that you make poor—or even disastrous—economic and investment choices for yourself. The reasons that recession isn't, figuratively, a four-letter word are basically twofold.

First, there is the kind of reason your grandmother would give you: "Remember, if there were no cloudy days, we wouldn't appreciate the sun." If the economy didn't contract once in a while, you wouldn't know the value of it when it expands. That's not only a philosophic point of view meant to raise your spirits when things are less than sunny (personally, financially, economically, or otherwise), it also holds the truth that things move in cycles—and more on that in a minute.

Then there is the kind of reason that an economist like me would give you: "A recession is like the economy going on a diet. Excess is eliminated, and leaner companies are more efficient and poised for sustainable growth." In other words, the economy moves in cycles, and a recession is part of those cycles.

It is the relative performance of the economy rather than the actual economy that is most watched. In other words, we look at whether the economy is doing better or worse than last year. We want to know if the economy is going to keep doing better or if it is going to soften. These are valid questions because we have all learned that these cycles continue to repeat themselves. The problem for us is that these different cycles affect our quality of life. Learning to understand and accept the cycles will go a long way toward helping you both as an investor and personally.

The standard joke goes that if your neighbor loses his job, that's a recession. But if you lose your job, it's a depression. Well to the extent that the latter (you losing your job) has an even greater impact on your quality of life than the former (him losing his job) does, it sure is depressing. But truth be told, we need contractions in the economy in order to continue having the recurring cycles that, in the long run, are good because they yield more innovative products, technological advancements, and efficiency, which in turn increase the wealth of each person.

From a purely economic standpoint, it is actually better for your neighbor to lose his job rather than for you to lose yours. The point is that when there is a recession, companies can lay off some workers (your neighbor, for example), but others (hopefully you) keep their jobs and can still buy things. Companies will get leaner and more efficient, increase productivity and profits, ramp up new spending, expand, and hire workers. Then comes the economic equivalent of Nirvana, when all seems bright and beautiful. That is, of course, the expansion stage, which is the first of four phases of the economy (sometimes referred to as the business cycle). Put together, these four phases are expansion, peak, contraction, and trough. I am a big believer in the business/economic cycle, and I use economic data to determine what stage we're currently in. Then based on the evidence of the particular cycle, I make my investment decisions. My premise in this book is that you will be able to interpret economic data to determine what business cycle we're in and make your own investment decisions.

The *expansion stage* of the economic cycle usually lasts the longest and produces the greatest amount of wealth. Unemployment is low, as companies hire aggressively, trying to keep up with the increased demand. With demand strong, the marginal cost of hiring a new worker is offset by the increase in output and revenue generated. Stock prices usually rally during the expansion, as corporate profits increase and revenue grows substantially. Interest rates and inflation remain low. Consumer spending is growing during this stage of the cycle, and real estate appreciates because of increased demand as well as because of low interest rates and inflation. In short, this is the "life is good" phase of the economy.

The *peak stage* of the cycle is characteristic of euphoria. Stock prices appreciate radically, while consumer spending surges. Rampant consumption on big-ticket items is evident. Stock price-to-earnings (P/E) ratios increase. Companies start to overbuild, overbuy, and overhire, as they feel the increased demand will never end. In short, this is the "eat, drink, and be merry," phase of the economy. Lately this stage has lasted longer than in the past due to just-in-time inventories, greater technology advancements that allow business to manage their inventories, and a more sophisticated consumer.

The *contraction stage* is the most painful and unpleasant stage, but it is a very necessary one. During this stage, the economy might slip into recession (or at least into a slowdown). Unemployment ticks up, and stock prices generally depreciate. Overall growth and investment slows. Wealth deteriorates, as capital cannot be employed efficiently enough to produce a return. Labor costs increase at first, as companies are producing less, so worker productivity shrinks. Consumer spending generally slows, as does investment. Eventually we see large layoffs, declining stock markets, and a tightening of credit extended to borrowers. In short, this is the "repentant" phase.

Eventually, this leads to the fourth stage—the *trough stage*. During the trough stage a lot goes on, some of it unnoticed. On the noticeable side of things, companies lay off employees in large numbers. Stocks decline at a rapid pace. High unemployment leads to a drop off in consumer spending, and GPD is clearly negative. At this point the Fed continues to lower rates and stimulate the economy with monetary policy tools. As part of fiscal stimulus, tax breaks and incentives for companies to invest and for consumers to spend are put into place. With both monetary and fiscal stimuli in place, something happens in the middle of the trough cycle that may not be noticeable at first. Leaner and hungrier companies eventually start to make money, or, in some cases, more of it. With the labor force trimmed so lean, interest rates so low, and the government providing either tax breaks or incentives, companies have a good environment to make a profit. Additionally, labor costs are low, and worker productivity per worker is extremely high. In short, this is the "12-step program is working" phase, and the economy is getting healthy again.

From the trough onward, the stock market begins to recover, and the tracks are being laid for the recovery and expansion stage of the cycle. When companies start to show profits and then eventually spend those profits on R&D, new plants and facilities, and more efficient production processes, guess what happens next? They begin hiring new employees, who spend their paychecks and voila—stock prices increase. This new wealth in stocks and salaries creates a wealth effect. Consumer spending increases, and the whole cycle starts over again.

These cycles are very important because without them we would not have the long-term growth and productivity of the economy. We need to contract to cut the fat from the economy in order to produce a long-term change in our standard of living. Out of every contraction or recession have come great innovations. Maybe some seemed ridiculous or at least unnecessary at the time, but eventually they became staples for our standard of living. From the 1990-91 slowdown came the beginning of the Internet, telecommunication growth, and advancement in cellular wireless communication. Before that, the 1980-82 slowdown yielded advancements in the PC (personal computer). Why? Slowdowns allow companies to focus on creating innovative products, services, and advancements that eventually increase the wealth of the economy not only on a monetary basis, but also in terms of standard of living and quality of life. The advancements and innovations also play a role in pulling the economy out of recession, as demand for the new, more efficient, and otherwise desirable products help to fuel the all-important consumer spending.

The cyclical nature of the economy—up and down, down and up—is important to keep in mind when things don't look so good at the moment. It's also important to keep in mind as an investor that the economy will again improve, and the companies that survive and thrive will be stronger as a result.

This was especially important for investors, for example, at the start of the fourth quarter of 2001 with recession at the top of everyone's mind. The economy had been in the midst of a classic slowdown or contraction period caused by a speculative bubble and a buildup in inventory. (Later, in November 2001, the National Bureau of Economic Research [NBER] issued its opinion that the U.S. economy had slipped into a recession in March.) The economic slowdown or contraction was caused by overbuilding during the late 1990s, excessive spending on technology and communication channels, and concerns over Y2K. Remember, Y2K? We thought the dreaded double-zero date would shut down everything from nuclear reactors to ATMs to elevators. Companies spent billions on Y2K prevention programs, which sidelined a lot of other spending and product research in the process.

Back in the good ol' late 1990s, it was hard to find quality employees in a tight labor market. Money was cheap, and overall demand appeared strong. So, U.S. businesses built—a lot! And while the economy is not the stock market (nor vice versa), the effect of all this expansion in inventories was reflected in stock prices. The high stock prices, in other words, reflected not the actual economy but rather the anticipation of demand. As a result, equity valuations far exceeded rational economic logic.

But reality and logic catch up to things eventually. In terms of stock prices, that catching up began in late September 2000.

According to my models, that is when the bear market in stocks began—even though I continued to see strength in the economy at that time. After all, unemployment was relatively low, interest rates were low, and inflation was low.

Much has happened in the time since September 2000. The horrific events of September 11, 2001, with the terrorist attacks in New York and Washington, have given this generation its own "day that will live in infamy" (to quote FDR and his famous Pearl Harbor speech). The impact on the economy, and most visibly consumer spending and consumer confidence, solidified the belief that the slowdown and increased unemployment would result in a recession. Now most investors would not greet this as particularly "good news," nor am I portraying it as such. But at the same time, a recession does carry a few long-term benefits that cannot be denied.

First, let's discuss what happens after a recession compared to what happens after a slowdown. In a slowdown, we never reach a point at which enough of the "fat" is cut off to allow corporations to make the kind of profits needed to increase spending. Or, to use our dieting metaphor, a slowdown is like cutting out a second helping of dessert but not making any real change in diet and exercise. The consumer keeps spending in a slowdown, as long as he or she has a job and a paycheck. What is needed, therefore, is a boost of corporate spending—not only to help the economy, but also to help companies become more innovative and efficient.

In a recession, however, companies are able to cut enough excess to become very efficient and more profitable. Plus, as the economy heads toward recession, you can count on the Fed as well as on Washington to provide support in the form of lower interest rates and tax benefits that spur capital spending. During a recession, unemployment increases as production is cut back. In fact, companies will continue to cut costs and lay off workers until they either become more profitable or go bankrupt. However, while unemployment is increasing, some good things happen: Worker productivity also increases. For example, let's say a company has 100 workers and produces 100 boxes. A downturn in the economy decreases demand, and the company reduces its workforce, let's say to 80 workers. Then things begin to improve, and demand returns to previous levels, but the company does not call back those laid-off workers. Thus, 80 workers are producing 100 boxes. This means that the output per worker has increased. This allows the company to improve its profitability. Then, with sustained profitability and an outlook for improving demand, the company can increase its spending and rehire workers. You know what happens then? Stock prices go up, reflecting the improvement in companies' profitability and the outlook for increased demand.

Thus, while a recession may look bleak, especially as the number of those laid off or without jobs rises, it's important to remember that the economy won't always stay that way. If you lose your job during a recession, it's especially important to keep that in mind. There will be jobs created eventually, and you will be rehired. If you doubt that, then you will fight two battles, one economic and one psychological. Or as your grandmother would have said, "Even in the darkest time of night, you know the sun will come up tomorrow."

WHAT IS A RECESSION?

Now you know that a recession is part of the economic cycle, and that it usually ends up being good for the economy in the long run. But what is it, exactly, that determines a recession? In other words, when is it really a recession and not just a slowdown from the peak into the contraction?

A recession usually is defined as the slowing of economic activity. But wait! How do you know if it's just a slowdown kind of slow, or if it's a recession kind of slow? The short answer is that it depends on whom you ask.

The NBER defines a recession as a "significant decline in activity spread across the economy, lasting more than a few months, visible in industrial production, employment, real income, and wholesale-retail trade."

According to the NBER, "A recession begins just after the economy reaches a peak of output and employment and ends as the economy reaches the trough. Between trough and peak, the economy is in an expansion. Expansion is the normal state of the economy; most recessions are brief, and they have been rare in recent decades."

A recession, like much in life, is best viewed in the rearview mirror. When the economy has obviously declined and may be starting to improve, that's when most of the economists will come out and make their appearances on the financial television networks saying, "Yup, it's a recession." That's like telling your best friend after his or her marriage or significant relationship breaks up that "well, this one has some trouble."

But that is the nature of pure economics. It's more about measuring than it is about forecasting. Unfortunately many economists think it is more important to try to forecast, which gets them into trouble. The need for forecasting, especially beyond a few quarters, is irrelevant. It's like asking for the weather forecast for the July 4th weekend on New Year's Day. The forecast that far ahead does not matter or even affect your plans, and it's certainly subject to change. The real ability, which is far more important than one may think, is defining where the economy is now and identifying what stage it is in.

A case in point is the 1990-91 recession, the length of which was debated even while it was going on. It was only after it finally ended that the time frame of the recession was actually determined. In its report, "Recession Dating Procedure," the NBER stated: "The Bureau announced in April 1991 its determination that July 1990 was a peak, and in December 1992 announced its determination that March 1991 was a trough. This particularly long lag for the trough date resulted from the slow pace of growth in 1991 and 1992. Had the economy reversed course and declined below its March 1991 level during that period, the period would have been counted as a single longer recession. The Bureau could not set a date for the trough until, in late 1992, the economy had regained its July 1990 peak, and a subsequent contraction would have been considered a separate recession."

If you read that carefully, you can see that economists have less in common with weather forecasters than they do with baseball umpires. It's a hard enough job to determine what's happening now as opposed to what's going to happen tomorrow. And unlike baseball umpires who have basically one chance to determine "out" or "safe," the economist gets seemingly endless replays. If you're not sure if the economy is really in a trough, you can wait until more data comes in, or you can change your mind at a later date.

To illustrate what goes on when the economy is in a recession (or should I say appears likely to be heading or to have headed toward a recession), let's take a look at some real-time reports, which include the 1990-91 timeframe (see Chart 3-1). First, here's what we know now with the benefit of a decade of hindsight. Real GDP grew at an average annual rate of 2.3 percent for the four quarters prior to the 1990-91 contraction and posted an average decline of 2.0 percent during the 1990-91 recession, according to the "Key Economic Indicators Update" report, (which tracks economic data in the United States as a whole and in the state of Michigan) published in May/June 2001 by the House Fiscal Agency.

But what was going on in real time during the recession of 1990-91? Here are excerpts from the Federal Reserve's "Summary of Commentary on Current Economic Conditions," which is commonly known as the "Beige Book."

- **October 31, 1990**: "Economic activity appears to have grown slowly in most Federal Reserve districts since early August, but seems to have declined somewhat in others. Many districts reported a weakening in business and consumer confidence. Retail sales, including new car sales, were sluggish or down in most of the country. Indicators of manufacturing activity were mixed to weaker ... Manufacturers in several districts were concerned about their business prospects in the coming months. Some planned further reductions in employment and were cautious about their capital spending plans. . . . "
- **December 5, 1990**: "Business conditions are somewhat mixed in different parts of the country but on balance display a weaker pattern. In many of the Federal Reserve districts, economic activity appears to have declined recently while it has remained sluggish or grown slowly in the rest. Several districts report a decline in consumer and business confidence and many refer to expectations of continued diminution in economic activity. ... Most districts report that retailers were pessimistic about sales prospects for the Christmas season as well as for 1991. . . . "
- **January 23, 1991**: "The level of economic activity appears to be declining in most districts. The Persian Gulf situation is frequently cited as a key determinant of both current and future economic activity. Nominal retail sales during the holiday season differed little from a year earlier. Inventories are near their desired levels. . . . Nearly all districts report weak or declining manufacturing activity. . . . "
- **March 13, 1991**: "Economic activity remained soft in much of the nation but there were some indications that the decline may be slowing. The pattern of retail sales varied among districts with the majority reporting either sluggishness or results below planned levels. . . .

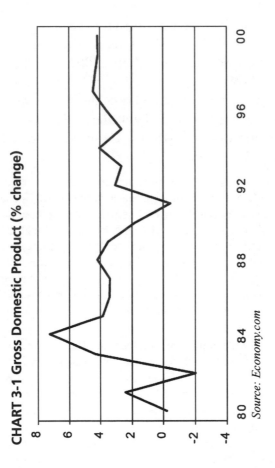

CHART 3-1 Gross Domestic Product (% change)

Source: Economy.com

Manufacturing activity was sluggish in most of the nation, though
several districts noted either a slight improvement or an easing of the
downward trend. . . . "

The point is that we know now that the economy peaked in July
1990, contracted through third and fourth quarters of 1990, and hit a
trough in March 1991, at which point it began to slowly swing
upward. But when you read the economic reports for that time frame,
you see that things weren't so clear. Things were softer in places, but
not as bad in others. Sometimes business conditions are "mixed."

Now that you understand that, you can see that economics is not
an exact science (or is it an art?). That's why you need to consider a
variety of data to form your own consensus. You also understand that
certain stages of the economy, such as contractions or expansions,
can last for long periods of time. Thus, if you know what cycle the
economy is in (or is likely in, or is headed toward), you can make
your investment decisions accordingly. This, once again, is one of the
goals of this book: to help you define what stage of the cycle the
economy is in and to invest regardless of what the market is doing at
the time (or at least with little emphasis on what the market is doing).

For example, the main measure of the growth of the economy (or
lack thereof) is GDP (gross domestic product), which we'll get into
later in this book. But GDP is measured only quarterly and is contin-
ually revised, sometimes years later. I like to think of GDP as akin to
what the Dow Jones Industrial Average is to stocks. While some
stocks can go up or down irrespective of the DJIA, so can other economic data fluctuate irrespective of the stage of the cycle. But just as
the benchmark for the market is the Dow, the benchmark for the
economy is GDP, with employment running a close second.

According to the NBER, in 2001 the United States was in the
midst of a recession, ending a 10-year economic expansion—a very
long time, indeed. So that right there should tell you, the investor,
something. When the economy was chugging along in the early
1990s and really burning up in the late 1990s, a bell should have
gone off in your head: Why is this happening? How long can this
last? Is this is the end of the expansion cycle? Once again, that
rearview mirror sure looks clearer than the windshield we're looking
through as we drive ahead.

This time we're going to approach the whole economy/ market/investing thing with the benefit of hindsight and a lot more experience and wisdom. To that end, the business headlines were filled with the "R" word post-September 11 even though the NBER had not made its official recession proclamation. But even as recession was creeping into our view of reality, there was talk about the other "R"— recovery. For example, Reuters News Agency ran an article "Economists Look Ahead to Rebound in 2002" (by Caren Bohan, Reuters, September 29, 2001), which appeared very timely since it came before it was confirmed that we were in a recession. The article stated:

> Even though most economists say a U.S. recession is inevitable in the wake of the September 11 terror attacks, many have become increasingly optimistic that when a recovery finally arrives, it will be a strong one.
> There is widespread agreement that over the next 6 months the economy—which was weak well before the deadly attacks in Washington and New York—will sink into an even deeper slump as nervous consumers shy away from vacations, trips to the shopping mall and even house-hunting. But recessions, as painful as they are, are often followed by periods of strong growth. After months of hunkering down and bolstering their balance sheets, businesses and consumers can spend more freely and often do because of "pent-up" demand.

There was no denying even before the September 11, 2001, tragedy that the economy was slowing. "From the third quarter of 1999 through the second quarter of 2000, real GDP advanced at a very robust average annual rate of 6.1 percent," the "Key Economic Indicators Update" for May/June 2001 stated. "However, the three most recent quarters (third and fourth quarter 2000 and first quarter 2001) indicate that the pace of economic activity has slowed significantly to 1.5 percent—a decline of 4.6 percent from the 6.1 percent rate."

Regardless of what the economic pundits declare the mid- to late-2001 time frame to be (recession, contraction, near recession), it's obvious by all accounts that the economy was slowing. Now the question becomes how you, the investor, should be viewing things.

AND THE MARKET
The first thing you know is that things may look economically dismal for a while and sadly, but inevitably, some people will lose their jobs. But eventually things will get better, and the economy will grow once

more. After all, the point of our capitalist economy and democratic political system is to create an environment to foster growth, expansion, and prosperity. As an investor, it's important to acknowledge the phase the economy is in and to realize that cycles last longer than just a few days. That way, you don't let one economic number or one big day in the market—up or down—sway you from your long-term investment game. Further, understand that these cycles last long enough to make well thought out investment decisions. That way you won't worry if you didn't catch today's or this week's big turn in the market. With a longer term perspective and an acknowledgment of which cycle the economy is in currently, you can make your decisions regarding allocations to individual retirement accounts (IRAs) and 401(k) plans, along with your decision to borrow money to buy a new home or to refinance your existing one. In other words, you know when it might be better to buy bonds and when money market instruments aren't just for safety but rather are actually good investment ideas.

Once again, I beat the drum and chant my mantra: "The stock market is not the economy. The economy is not the stock market," (along with my other mantra, "Remember to identify the business cycle"). And yet I can't turn a deaf ear to the investors nor to my fellow traders and their stories of participation in this stock market over the past few years. They bought this stock at $2 and the next day (or so it seemed) it was at more than $300. Or shucks, they say with self deprecation, wouldn't you know they sold the stock *the day before* the software company announced a new product that would change life and revolutionize business, or they sold their shares in the biotech company the day before it discovered the Fountain of Youth. They watched stocks go from $10 to $100, and bought it at $95— only to watch it go back to $10 before selling it.

I myself am not immune to having a few of these stories. I remember a time when I was lucky enough to get some shares in a hot IPO. It opened $20 higher than its IPO price. So, acting quickly, I sold the stock and pocketed a good profit. Then the very next day the stock rose another $20 points, and in a few short weeks the stock had gone from its IPO price of $15 to nearly $100 a share. "I made a profit, but I missed the proverbial boat," I said, kicking myself.

When the stock started to sell off a bit, I decided to look for my opportunity to get back in. I was mad, after all, that I had missed this huge opportunity. (Yes, I had made $20 a share, but I could have made $85 a share!!!) This is the first warning bell I should have heeded. You see, when an IPO comes out, it's supposed to be priced fairly. So someone out there in investment brokerage land thought it was a $20 stock. Okay, so lots of IPOs were exploding in their early days. But a stock that basically goes up five or sixfold within a couple of weeks should have raised a red flag. Ever watch fireworks on the Fourth of July? Sure, they zoom up like the little rockets they are. Then they reach a peak, explode, and fizzle.

When the stock came down to $85 a share, I bought twice as many shares as I had originally bought in the IPO. My reason? I was basically PO'd that I had missed the opportunity and wanted to get even. Even with whom, you might ask. Myself . . . the market . . . *them* (you know, the other, nameless, faceless folks who didn't sell as quickly as I did.)

I bought at $85 a share, and the stock never traded at that price again. In fact, the stock price declined all the way back down to where I sold the original IPO shares on that first day of trading. And if you want to do the math, it was about a $50 a share decline.

Not being able to stand the pain any longer, I sold those shares I had purchased at $85. My loss was many magnitudes greater than what I had made on the IPO. To rub a little salt into my wounds, after I sent the sell order to my broker, I checked the price of the stock. I saw on my screen that the stock was halted. When I called my broker to find out what was going on, he informed me that he had managed to sell the shares before stock trading was halted. I wasn't sure at that moment if I should be happy (maybe the stock would reopen even lower) or nervous (like, maybe it was going to blast off higher again).

(Un)lucky me. The reason the stock was halted was that a large telecommunications firm announced the purchase of this company for a price of more than *two times* where it was currently trading. And of course my broker had managed to sell just before the stock was halted.

Then I remembered a little something that dramatically increased the amount of salt in the wound that was getting larger by the hour. I had broken up with a woman I had been dating. She worked for the company that was buying out my stock deal. She was now a stockholder. Okay, so it is irrational to think that this whole deal was her way of getting back at me, but do you think . . . ?

The point of this anecdote, other than letting you laugh at my misfortune, is to show that there are a plenty of stories out there of investment mishaps. Why? Because the markets are volatile, and valuations often have nothing to do with reality. Stock prices go up or down based upon perception. The stock market changes every day, to a greater or lesser extent. Do you really think that the economy is moving that fast? It's a recession! No, it's an expansion! We're in a peak. No, it's a trough. Get real.

As you, an investor with your own tales of woe and triumph to tell, look at the market, keep in mind that you want to steer away from the emotion. If I had done so, I would have pocketed my nice little $20 a share profit on the IPO and kept myself out of trouble. Maybe I would have watched the stock decline back near the IPO level and decide to reinvest then and not at the peak. And then I would have benefited from the buy-out bonanza. But once again, that ol' rearview mirror shows things clearly.

When we think about the stock market, the images that come to mind are the pictures we see on the television: People in trading jackets and business attire running around inside a hive of activity. Or we think of the façade of the New York Stock Exchange, an ornate and serious-looking building. Or maybe we think of trading floors with people shouting out orders amid a sea of computer screens.

But what does GDP look like? If you passed the consumer price index (CPI) and its components on the street would you recognize them? Maybe you saw a graph in an Economics 101 textbook. The economy today seems like a screen shot of a graph that's flashed on the screen while a market commentator talks about jobless claims, or factory orders, or some such thing.

What does the economy look like? Take a look around you. The economy is everywhere and it runs 24/7. The stock market opens with the ringing of a bell at 9:30 a.m. Eastern Time and closes at 4:00 p.m. It's like an elementary school in Hackensack, N.J., (after-hours trading notwithstanding).

The economy, which is *far* more important than the stock market, is every job, every paycheck, every business, every factory, every retail store, and every dollar saved, spent, earned, or unearned. Everything you do, including paying taxes and dying, has some impact on the economy. As I mentioned earlier, the broadest measure of our economy is the GDP (gross domestic product), which is the measure of all goods and services produced in this country (see Chart 3-2). I think the unemployment rate and inflation rate are also very instrumental in measuring the economy. The workers make the stuff that becomes the output measured by GDP. Additionally, these workers are consumers of some of the output, a very important and interesting relationship. We will discuss each of these components in upcoming chapters—and I promise you these chapters will not be as boring as you might think.

So sit back, relax, and read as we take a peek at what (I think) is in Greenspan's briefcase.

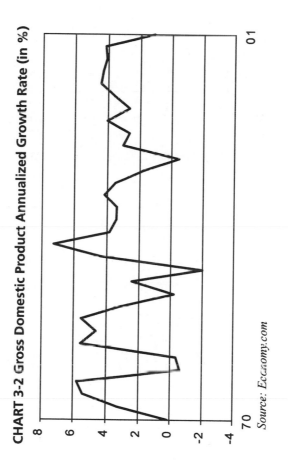

CHART 3-2 Gross Domestic Product Annualized Growth Rate (in %)

Source: Economy.com

4

Making Sense of Dollars

The currency market is the most liquid and least regulated of all markets and has the most diverse participants. Currency trading, or foreign exchange as it's called, represents capitalism and the laws of economics at their best, with supply and demand and free market theory all rolled up into one. The value of the U.S. dollar is part and parcel to almost any financial transaction—from you buying a car to a large multinational firm investing in raw materials on another continent. Yet, the value of the dollar receives very little media attention and even less public attention.

Foreign exchange is a subject that holds a special appeal to me since I cut my teeth in this market as a currency dealer in the early 1980s following my internship at the Federal Reserve. What I saw firsthand then, I continue to preach today. It is vital for investors to understand the nature of the currency markets, which offer a window into the relative economic strength or malaise of any number of countries. Moreover, the currency market is one arena in which the Fed takes direct action, increasing or decreasing the supply of dollars to fight inflation or to create economic stimulus. While the Fed denies any intent to dollar-fixing, it seems to intervene when the price of the dollar hits undesirable levels.

In the currency markets, there are few (if any) barriers to entry, little or no regulation, and very low transaction costs. The price of a currency is truly determined based upon supply and demand, with the market price reflecting the highest bid and the lowest offer. The currency market is open 24 hours a day, but there is no one "exchange" to complete transactions. The result is a perfect instrument to represent free markets, and a barometer of a country's relative strength (economically speaking) compared to its trading partners.

The bulk of currency transactions—more than $1 trillion a day— takes place in the interbank market, where large money-center banks in the United States and abroad buy and sell currencies on behalf of their customers and the banks' proprietary accounts. There are, of course, some regulations imposed upon the participants in the interbank market. Very little "exchange trading" takes place in the streets. But all the basic market principals still apply.

Currency trading is the oldest form of exchange and trading, with roots dating back centuries before stock exchanges were even dreamed of. Looking at more recent history, there were periods of fixed exchange rates, such as prior to 1973 and the Breton Woods Agreement, when the U.S. dollar was on the gold standard, and the price of gold was fixed at about $32 per ounce. The dollar was only allowed to fluctuate in a narrow band of about 3 percent. When the foreign exchange price of the dollar would get near the top or the bottom of the band, central banks were forced to intervene in the market by buying or selling dollars in exchange for foreign currency.

When intervention did not work at extreme times of pressure, the central banks would increase short-term interest rates to try and support their currencies. When all else failed they would just change the bands. It was believed that we could regulate the currency market or fix exchange rates by targeting inflation and interest rates. This would create a pricing parity model that would allow efficient transfer of capital between trading partners. This was an important ingredient to central bank policy.

In the early 1970s, inflation was starting to heat up. The increase in government spending due to the Vietnam War and the corresponding huge military build up, along with low interest rates and low unemployment of the 1960s, created an inflationary spiral. Then came higher oil prices with shrinking supply due to the Arab oil embargo and greater demand. Inflation was out of control. Gold had already started to trade above its fixed level on the foreign markets, while the U.S. dollar was trading below its "band" of allowable value. The supply of gold was no longer able to back the dollar because of the tremendous amount of dollars that the U.S. government had to print. At this point, the U.S. government had no other choice but to abandon the gold standard and once again allow the dollar to float freely on international markets.

What Kryptonite is to Superman, inflation is to currencies. Once the dollar was allowed to trade freely, it was demolished. Even as interest rates neared double digits because of double-digit inflation, the dollar could not find support.

I started out as a currency trader because, quite frankly, that's where I was hired. But ending up in currencies, or "forex" as we called it, was a wonderful opportunity for me. In the 1980s, currencies to me were the center of the financial universe. The flow of capital starts and ends with currency transactions, and the magnitude of the deals that I saw in my early days was staggering.

I remember a debt offering of Eurodollars, which are the interest rates on U.S. dollars on deposit overseas. The size of the offering was about $10 billion. That's an amount that boggles the mind and the imagination. It was bigger than anything I had seen before. Far larger than the $1 billion currency order we once received from a U.S.-based multinational firm that was buying deutsche marks to fund an investment in Germany.

I remember vividly that day when, as a young currency trader, our bank was given an order early in the morning to buy $1 billion worth of deutsche marks (DM), which at the exchange rate at that time was worth some 1.7 billion DM. Luckily, it was the middle of the week, so we had a 24-hour global window in the Asian and European markets. Thus, when our markets are winding down in the United States, it would be Thursday morning in Japan. Our instructions from the U.S.-based multinational firm were to complete the order by the end of the day.

For a currency trader, this kind of deal is a dream come true. You have major size to move ($1 billion) and with that kind of volume you are the market. By 2 p.m., I had bought the entire 1.7 billion DM order, and the currency market seemed quite stable. I would have thought that a currency order of that magnitude would have skewed the dollar-DM relationship somewhat, but that had not occurred.

So I went to my manager with a suggestion that we put some of the bank's money on the line as well, buying DM and selling dollars. Clearly our customer knew something we didn't know, and the signs were pointing to the DM moving up sharply in value against the dollar.

The manager heard me out and then gave me the green light to take on a small position based on my convictions.

All I can say is thank goodness I had to wait for the elevator. By the time I went from the eighth floor down to the trading room, the DM had depreciated in value by nearly 2 percent. Had I been faster on the trigger, I would have been handed an instant loss in the DM-dollar position. Later, I found out that an opposite order—buying dollars and selling DM of equal or greater size—had been done by an investment banking firm that needed to sell DM and buy dollars for a huge bond offering. What's the moral of this story? In the vast currency market, the need for capital flows dominates. And no one—not even a U.S. multinational firm that's buying $1 billion in currency—is bigger than the market.

THE "VALUE" OF CURRENCY

For you, the investor/consumer, currency exchange rates have a far greater meaning than what you might think. Obviously, a strong U.S. dollar makes foreign goods less expensive and a trip to Italy or France even more tantalizing when you can by that Prada bag at half what you pay in a chic boutique on Chicago's Oak Street.

A strong dollar also attracts investment in the United States, with more foreign individuals and institutions buying U.S. bonds (our government debt) to help us finance even more growth and build even more infrastructure. Further, a strong dollar attracts money into our stock market, helping companies expand and make capital expenditures. Lastly, a strong dollar helps keep inflation down by "exporting" our inflation. A strong dollar increases the ability to purchase like goods at lower actual prices because the dollar buys more. For example, let's say a like good is priced at $10 in the United States and at 10 euros (the pan-European currency) in Europe. In addition, let's assume that you can exchange 10 euros for $10 (and vice versa). Then, effectively, the price is the same in each currency. Now let's say that the price of the good goes up 10 percent to $11 in the United States and to 11 euros in Europe. However, if the U.S. dollar also strengthens by 10 percent so that $10 is equivalent to 11 euros, then the price in U.S. dollars is essentially unchanged because of a favorable currency move. That helps keep price pressure or inflation under control. Thus, because of their correlation to inflation, large exchange rate changes have a similar impact as the raising and lowering of interest rates.

Overall, a strong dollar reflects a healthy economy—at least on the surface (see Chart 4-1). A report from the Federal Reserve Bank in New York, "To What Extent Does Productivity Drive the Dollar?" (August 2001), looked at the relationship between the U.S. dollar and U.S. labor productivity. As the report noted, "Between 1995 and 1999, the dollar appreciated 4.8 percent against the yen and 5.8 percent against the euro on an average annual basis. For some observers, the productivity boom and the dollar's rise were twin manifestations of U.S. economic strength. Indeed, the parallel timing of these trends suggested that productivity gains were driving the appreciation of the dollar.

If the dollar gets too strong, it can cause problems with our trading partners, our own manufacturers, and even laborers in the United States. While it is nice as a consumer to buy imported goods for a cheaper price, the question becomes what happens to our "stuff" when it's sold over there? If the U.S. dollar is too strong, then our exports are overpriced in local currency terms in foreign markets. That results in weaker demand for our exports, and the effect will be felt at the U.S. company level in the form of lower sales and weaker profits. Further, a strong U.S. dollar means imports enter our markets more cheaply, further decreasing demand for equivalent quality U.S.-made goods in our market.

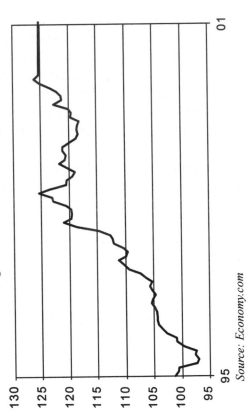

CHART 4-1 Trade Weighted Value of the Dollar (index 1995 = 100)

Source: Economy.com

As an example, the U.S. auto industry suffered the consequence of a strong dollar in the early 1980s and early 1990s when the price of a Toyota was less than the price of an equal-quality Chrysler. The Japanese gained huge market share, and as a result U.S. autoworkers lost jobs. Eventually, U.S. automakers set up shops abroad to make cars overseas where it was cheaper to produce. The bottom line was that the U.S. trade deficit with its partners widened as American consumers bought more goods made abroad and U.S. manufacturers exported less.

The strong dollar scenario also is not good news for the U.S. labor market if rising imports cut demand for domestic products. If unemployment goes up, then there is less money to buy all those cars (U.S. or foreign made) or those Prada bags and Armani suits even if they are cheaper. When left unchecked, a "too strong" dollar can be hazardous to American business, employment, and the economy.

During the Reagan administration, the dollar started to gain momentum again after the economically dismal Carter years. But the momentum went too far, and the dollar became too strong. Among those complaining about the strength of the dollar were the auto companies that couldn't compete effectively against cheaper imports—with Chrysler's Lee Iacocca heading the complaint department. Everywhere, businesses were screaming that the United States had to do something to stem the rise in the U.S dollar, which was creating a huge imbalance in the trade deficit. Things were clearly out of balance.

What I didn't fully appreciate at the time was how weak the dollar had been in the 1970s and the early 1980s, and now how concerned the Treasury was with the strength of the dollar. But when I saw a headline flash across my Reuters news terminal that said President Reagan wanted to see the dollar-to-yen exchange rate lower, I thought this was the opportunity I had been waiting for to get short dollars, buy yen, and make the proverbial killing. After all, this was the president of the United States of America talking.

So I went to my manager and asked just how much of a position I could take to get short dollars and long yen. Clearly this was the opportune time for such a strategy given the strength in the dollar. And now the president, himself, was advocating a weaker dollar.

"Rob, the administration has been saying this for 3 years," he told me, and the dollar had been appreciating in spite of the jawboning.

Little did I know that this time the president would be correct (and by extension so would I). When the central banks and finance ministers of the G7 got together one weekend later that summer, the result was the Plaza Accord under which exchange rates would shift to a more acceptable level. The president got his wish; the dollar weakened against the yen. It took several years of jawboning, many compromises with business leaders, and the coordination of seven finance ministers; but they got the desired results. As for my strategy, I had participated in this move in only a very minimal way.

Currency trading aside, you can see that for political and economic reasons, the United States has pursued a strong-dollar policy with the caveat that the strength of the dollar not get out of hand. The impact of a strong dollar or a weak dollar is certainly well known to the Fed, as well as in Treasury and central bank circles. The Fed cannot set levels in the stock market or even set mortgage rates. But what it can do is intervene in the currency markets to support or to halt the rise in the U.S. dollar. This is akin to the "rabbit out of a hat trick," which the Fed uses to help achieve certain monetary goals. For example, a recent Federal Reserve report shows how the Fed monitors the relative value of the U.S. dollar and the actions it takes or directs to intervene.

In the third quarter of 2000, the U.S. dollar appreciated 8.2 percent against the euro currency and 2.0 percent against the yen. "On a trade-weighted basis, the dollar ended the quarter 4.1 percent stronger against the currencies of the United States' major trading partners," noted the report entitled "Treasury and Federal Reserve Foreign Exchange Operations."

On September 22, 2000, the U.S. monetary authorities "intervened" in the foreign exchange markets, purchasing 1.5 billion euros against the dollar. (Buying euros and selling dollars would have the effect of strengthening the euro by decreasing supply and weakening the dollar by increasing supply.) "The operation, which was divided evenly between the U.S. Treasury Department's Exchange Stabilization Fund and the Federal Reserve System, was coordinated with the European Central Bank (ECB) and the monetary authorities of Japan, Canada and the United Kingdom," the report added.

While the Fed will intervene (as it did in the example above) when the dollar becomes too strong, we know that a relatively strong dollar is better than a weak one in terms of inflation. Thus, pursuing a strong dollar policy as a way to help keep inflation in check is prudent as long as the strength doesn't hinder growth and employment.

The health of an economy can be measured by the strength of the home currency, since basic economic conditions show up in the value of the currency. Inflation, which decreases the real rate of return, will cause a currency to depreciate, and decreasing GDP will weaken a currency. Political instability, which makes foreign investors shy away from committing their capital to a foreign country, an oversupply of debt, and a decline in equity markets all are reflected in the value of a currency. Likewise, low inflation, a healthy stock market, stable bond prices, and other attractive investment conditions help to support the currency.

Further, employment (cost of labor), as well as shifts in manufacturing costs and production, influences the value of a currency. The relative relationship among currencies allows resources to be deployed around the globe, favoring places where efficiencies reside. (Read: The cheaper the labor or the raw materials, the more likely we will use them.) This kind of environment can be encouraged with exchange rates.

Additionally, the risk and reward of investing globally shows up in the exchange rate of the currency. If the reward for buying U.S. dollars and investing in a company or stock in the United States is offset by the loss on the currency rate, then the flow of capital will be less. That means that in order to attract capital we need to pay higher rates, which in turn can increase borrowing costs for companies. That further reduces their corporate earnings, which will be reflected in lower stock prices. The chain reaction will continue into our investment portfolios and individual retirement accounts (IRAs), which will decline in value as equity prices soften. That ends up extending the time we need to work in order to save enough for retirement. And if that weren't enough, having to work more or longer could increase our exposure to health risks, raise our stress levels, trim our life expectancies, and increase our medical bills. If you haven't gotten the message thus far, let's say it in plainer English:

The value of the U.S. dollar has a direct impact on your life, your wealth, and your well-being.

THE BIG MAC THEORY

No wonder then that the Fed watches the relationship between the U.S. dollar and foreign currencies. In the Federal Reserve Bank of New York report, "To What Extent Does Productivity Drive the Dollar?" Fed economists explain how the value of a currency is measured. "The best gauge of this value is a currency's real exchange rate against a foreign currency," it notes. "The real exchange rate—defined as the nominal exchange rate adjusted for the ratio of foreign prices to domestic prices—allows us to compare the purchasing power of different currencies."

Enter the "Big Mac" theory used to measure the purchasing power parity of currency. Under this theory, one would compare the price of a Big Mac hamburger in the local currency of several different countries and then convert that price back to dollars. The country in which the Big Mac was the most expensive (in U.S. dollar terms) was considered to have an overvalued currency compared to the U.S. dollar. Conversely, the country in which the Big Mac was the cheapest (in U.S. dollars) was considered to have an undervalued currency compared to the U.S. dollar. After all, the price of a Big Mac is supposed to be relatively consistent.

While this theory is just an example of what we would like to achieve with currency rates, the reality is that many factors other than purchasing power parity are relevant. These factors include the cost of labor, the actual demand for a product (which may differ vastly from country to country), the available resources that could be more or less expensive, and interest rates that may be higher or lower depending upon prevailing economic conditions. By allowing exchange rates to fluctuate, a value for a currency can be established that will efficiently factor in all these variables and allow investors and the flow of capital to be employed efficiently.

The "Big Mac" theory and the purchasing power parity all point to the impact of currency values on the trade deficit. More explicitly, we know that there is a direct link between the value of the U.S. dollar and how much our trade deficit is shrinking or growing. Today, the trade deficit is no longer studied as the next best thing in economic reports. To say that no one cares about the trade deficit would be putting it too strongly, but certainly less attention is focused on it today as opposed to a couple of decades ago.

In the 1980s, the trade deficit number was so significant that it became the "report *du jour*" to watch. It took a front seat to even GDP and unemployment, which are the stars in the economic sky these days. Back in the 1980s, the fear was that if the trade deficit grew to unmanageable levels, the U.S. economy would crumble. Foreign investors were snapping up undervalued U.S. real estate, from Rockefeller Center to the Pebble Beach golf course.

All things economic, including trade deficits, move in cycles. Today, there is little concern about the trade deficit, or that the United States will somehow be shut out of the market at home or abroad because a strong dollar will keep it from competing with manufacturers in countries with comparatively weaker currencies. Rather, U.S. multinationals have become more global, setting up operations in countries with favorable currencies (when it comes to importing goods and components back into the United States) as well as available resources and cheaper labor.

Still, it behooves us to take a look at the trade deficit as it stood in late 2001, with the understanding that what was once important, and then became less so, may someday take center stage again.

TRADE BALANCE

According to one recent report, the U.S. trade deficit continues to correct, with the September 2001 trade balance (see Chart 4-2) coming in at −$19.4 billion compared with −$28.4 billion in August. Exports contracted by $7 billion, but imports fell by an even larger $15 billion. The decrease in imports represents insurance claims by U.S. institutions on foreign reinsurance companies associated with the September 11 terrorist attacks.

While these statistics show trends on the surface, they sometimes mask other issues. For example, a shrinking deficit might be due to a slowing economy in the United States (and thus consumers are not buying as much) rather than to increased exports. Likewise, an increasing deficit may actually be due to higher prices for products

CHART 4-2 Trade Balance (in billions of dollars)

	Nov-01	Oct-01	Sep-01	Aug-01	Jul-01	Jun-01	May-01	Apr-01
Balance	−28.5	−29.6	−19.4	−28.4	−30.7	−29.8	−28.9	−31.8
Goods	−34.3	−35.1	−35.6	−34.1	−35.9	−35.6	−34.4	−37.7
Services	5.8	5.5	16.2	5.7	5.2	5.7	5.6	5.8

Source: Economy.com

we import, like oil. When the price of oil increased in early 2001, the trade deficit measured in dollars was expanding even though we imported roughly the same amount of oil. However, the price of each barrel was more than 50 percent higher than the previous year, artificially increasing the deficit. Furthermore, (as we will discuss in Chapter 5) imports are subtracted from GDP. Thus, if imports are constant but the amount we paid for them goes up, it may cause GDP to look weaker than it actually is.

Looking at the value of currencies from the "real world" view of trade statistics makes the relative strength of the dollar more tangible to you, the consumer, as well as to the Fed. It also goes a long way to explaining why and how the Fed uses currency market intervention as one of its "secret weapons" to manipulate exchange rates. While the jury is still out on the longer-term impact of intervention, I am one of the jurors who is not convinced that intervention alone will support a currency. In the short term, it is a good technique that identifies a problem and the concerns of an unstable currency and that can be used as a bargaining chip when coordinating with foreign central bankers and policy makers. Thus, exchange-rate policies can be used to entice them to alter prices, taxes, trade restrictions, interest rates, and so forth, which will affect the U.S. trade position and have a direct impact on the value of the currency and, by extension, the U.S. economy.

I do not believe that exchange rates alone make this happen. Rather, the currency market sounds the alarm so that the real economic rescue efforts can begin.

The value of the dollar to the retail investor is clear. Just as diversification is the key to a sound investment portfolio for U.S. investors as well as international investors, the impact of your return is directly tied to the value of the currency. For example, an investment in a Japanese equity fund will be greatly impacted by changes in the yen exchange rate. Furthermore, large currency fluctuations provide the warning signs of economic problems that can impact your investments as well as the overall economy. It is one of the warning signs to be on the lookout for. Many of the economic problems of the mid-1990s started out with weak currency values, resulting in major devaluations across Europe and South America. These problems eventually made their way to our markets, causing great volatility in the value of U.S assets and even shouldering part of the blame for the debacle of the hedge fund Long-Term Capital Management, whose demise at one point, some say, may have threatened our financial system.

So the next time you see a report on the value of the dollar or hear about exchange rates, take note. A weaker dollar can signal potential problems and higher interest rates. A stronger dollar may mean a healthy economy in the short run, but could result in a shift to more manufacturing abroad, which would not be a good situation for U.S. workers. While a strong dollar appears to be more desirable, the reality is that a stable dollar is the best scenario for long-term economic stability.

5

Gee, No GDP!

First, the facts: Gross domestic product (GDP) is released by the Bureau of Economic Analysis, U.S. Department of Commerce (*www.bea.doc.gov*). The report is released on the third or fourth week of the month for the prior quarter. It is typically revised twice in the second and third months of the quarter. The first is the "advance report," which is based upon data that are incomplete or subject to further revision. Then comes the "preliminary" report, which has more complete data, and finally the "latest" estimates, which include both annual and comprehensive revisions.

Now the spin: GDP—the indicator formerly known as gross national product—is one of the most important measures of the economic condition of the United States. In fact, I'll go as far as to say that it's one of the most important economic indicators in the world. Over the years, other economic indicators—whether money supply or trade figures—have been more "in fashion." But when it comes to the day in and day out health of the economy, there is no better measure than GDP. The reason is that GDP is the broadest measure of economic activity in the country. Now there are some inherent draw-backs and inaccuracies in GDP, especially since the economy has changed a bit since 1950, but we'll discuss this later in the chapter (see the GDP Chat with Delos Smith, Senior Business Analyst at The Conference Board). But when it comes to economic reports today, the most potent is GDP because of the breadth of activity that it mea-sures—or attempts to measure.

It is true that GDP, as I mentioned in Chapter 3, is a lagging indicator that is subject to several revisions, which means it lags even further by the time the final report is issued. However, that does not diminish its importance to measuring the economy, espe-cially the manufacturing of durable and nondurable goods. In fact, as I've stated, GDP is as important a measure for the economy as the Dow Jones Industrial Average is for the stock market. The Dow's past performance is yesterday's news. However, it is impor-tant to tomorrow's investment as well as spending and savings deci-sions, which in turn makes it important to tomorrow's performance of the Dow.

Of course, the Dow only represents a small sample of stocks, 30 to be exact, that from time to time do not reflect the overall market's performance. But over time it has proven to be a good barometer of the stock market. Likewise, the GDP number may not represent the growth rate of every sector. More recently, its structure does under-state service and technology and has not fully accounted for the open and global economic system we now enjoy. You could even find some sectors that are inversely related to GDP and the business cycles, such as attorneys who file bankruptcy papers and who repre-sent landlords in eviction hearings.

Over time, however, GDP has proven to be a good indicator of not only the health of the economy, but also what business cycle we are in. One might ask, "What good is old or used news? Who cares how much the economy expanded or contracted *last* quarter? I want to know what is going to happen in this quarter." The simple answer is that the U.S. economy, all $10 trillion of it, is like a Formula One race car at the Indy 500. After the flag is dropped, it's a pretty good bet that the car will go around the track a few miles (500 of them, in fact). So if I told you that 278 miles were just completed (which is the old news), it is probably assured that at least one more mile (and probably 222 more) around the track would be forthcoming.

The U.S. economy is so big and multidimensional that the direction in which it is now moving (its current lap around the track) is generally sustainable for multiple quarters. With this kind of "momentum" behind it, it's easy to see why it takes so much to result in even a tenth- or a quarter-percentage point of change in the growth rate. Thus, even a small incremental change in GDP is very significant.

That being said, a few factories adjusting output isn't going to make for one iota of difference in GDP. Massive ramp up or reduction of production by many, many factories could make for a significant shift. That's why if GDP comes out with a significant shift in economic output—upward or downward—you know that the force behind that change had to be a big one.

Think of the economy as measured by GDP as a rocket bound for Mars. The engines propel the rocket out of the Earth's atmosphere, but once it breaks through, no auxiliary power is needed. With its course set, the rocket will continue toward its destination. The only time the engines are fired is when the rocket, for some reason, strays off course and a quick boost is needed to get it back on track or to slow it down so that it doesn't crash into Mars. Similarly, the economy is propelled along by its own forces and only when it strays significantly off course (growing too fast or slowing down toward recession) should the Fed (in the role of the booster engine) take action.

The Fed doesn't and shouldn't micromanage the economy, because the economy experiences much slower changes in direction and in magnitude of growth than, say, the Dow Jones Industrial Average. On a given day, the Dow could go from being down 50 points to being up 50 or more points. Intraday on any given day, the direction that the Dow takes is irrelevant compared with the overall trend.

The GDP, on the other hand, does not fluctuate as much. It is not going to jump one-tenth of 1 percent just because you bought a new pair of shoes, or even if 100 people go out and buy new pairs of shoes. There probably won't even be a blip on the GDP radar screen if a shoe manufacturer has to step up production because he sees demand for four more truckloads of shoes per day. With a base of $10 trillion in this economy, it takes a lot more than that to move the GDP needle. But when it does move, you can rest assured that something is going on. Conversely, the economy cannot expand without it showing up in the GDP report.

When a GDP report is released, the most attention tends to be focused on the quarter-to-quarter change in the growth rate. In other words, the question is, "how is the economy doing compared with last quarter?" Is it accelerating or decelerating? Is the economy revving up, slowing down, or skidding backward? For example, the GDP report for the third quarter of 2001 showed a decline of 1.3 percent, the first negative GDP number since the first quarter of 1993. That compared with a positive annual growth rate of 0.3 percent in the second quarter of 2001. If you didn't know anything but those two numbers, you could surmise quite accurately that the output of U.S. businesses and factories had dropped, signaling a weaker economy. By the fourth quarter of 2001, however, GDP had returned to positive territory with a reading of +1.7 percent, largely due to strength in the auto sector, which was bolstered by consumer incentives. Additionally, some of the slowdown that occurred in the third quarter of 2001 actually showed up as deferred activity in the fourth quarter of 2001. The long and short of it, the third quarter probably wasn't as weak it looked, but at the same time the fourth quarter was not as strong as the numbers suggested.

Looking at Chart 5-1, you can see the ebb and flow of the economy, steaming well into positive territory in mid- to late-1999 and early 2000 (remember the Nasdaq stock bubble during the same time frame). That was followed by a slow decline in mid-to late-2000 and into 2001, until GDP slipped into negative territory in the third quarter.

What exactly does a negative GDP reading mean? Obviously, we can't produce negative amounts of goods. The factories aren't "unmaking" products. Rather, the rate at which we produce has declined from the previous period, so that on an annualized basis, our output is measurably less. For example, if second quarter real GDP is +0.3 percent, and in the third quarter the reading slips to −1.3 percent, that's a negative, or contracting, economy. This differs from a declining economy, in which the real GDP reading is still positive— meaning it is greater than the previous quarter—but the rate of that growth has slowed. For example, if the first quarter had a real GDP

CHART 5-1 Gross Domestic Product (billions of chained dollars, SAAR)

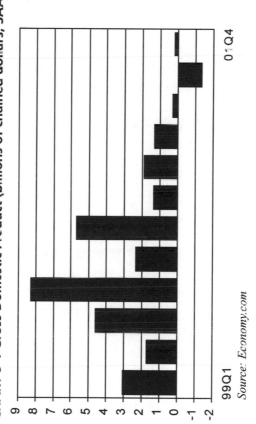

Source: *Economy.com*

rate of +1.3 percent, and the second quarter has a rate of +0.3 percent, that's a declining economy.

In the GDP report, there are some curiosities about the number that make it unique. First, GDP includes two sets of statistics: "real" and "nominal." "Real" estimates are based on 1996 dollars. (The benchmark year is updated frequently.) This gives the proverbial "apples to apples" comparison for economic output without inflation putting its thumb on the scale. Nominal GDP is the same output, only using current dollar values. The deflator, which is an inflation indicator that is closely watched by the Fed, gives us a value by which to discount the nominal GDP to take us back to 1996 dollar values. Here is a purposely oversimplified example to show how this works. Let's say that the total output of the economy in 1996 was two Chevy Cavaliers. Each cost $12,000, making the total GDP for that year $24,000 (not counting parts, labor, taxes, shipping, advertising, gasoline, and so forth). Now, let's say that in 2001 the price of a Chevy Cavalier was $15,000. But the output of the economy was still only those two Cavaliers, which were produced and sold. In "nominal" (today's dollar) terms, that would make GDP equal to $30,000—two Chevy Cavaliers worth $15,000 each. That looks like a whopping 25 percent increase in the economy from 1996.

But if we use a deflator number (in this case 1.25) for the 2001 GDP to put it into 1996 dollars, then you'd see that the output of two Chevy Cavaliers would be $24,000 (two cars valued in 1996 at $12,000 each). Thus, the economy in this example shows 2001 as flat compared with 1996 (a 0 percent change) compared with an increase of 25 percent in nominal terms.

The U.S. economy, needless to say, is far more complex than two Chevy Cavaliers. But the concept is the same. If we bring everything back to a value standard (1996 dollars), then we get a better view of actual output.

Further, while the reports are issued quarterly, the figures reflect annualized output, on a chained basis (meaning over four sequential quarters). In other words, if the current report is for the third quarter of 2001, the annualized rate of growth reported is based on the third quarter of 2001 along with the second quarter and the first quarter of 2001 and the fourth quarter of 2000. In some businesses, it is misleading to compare, for example, the second quarter with the first quarter. Consider the case of a snow-removal equipment manufacturer.

But just what is that output showing? We recall from our old "Econ Days" the formula for GDP is: $GDP = C + I + G + X - M$. In other words, GDP equals consumption, investment, government spending, and exports minus imports. Of these individual components, the largest by far is consumption, which accounts for some two-thirds of the total. The formula does not include inventories, which are discussed in the report even though they don't factor into the GDP number per se. The reason is that what is held as inventory today was counted previously as output, even though it ended up in a warehouse somewhere. There are some insights and conclusions that can be drawn from inventory numbers that aren't part of the GDP formula. We'll discuss that later in the chapter.

To understand what GDP is all about, let's take a look at each of the components. This is far more than just defining a formula. The economy is a complex machine, with many components that are in turn complex. So while you may be lulled into a certain belief or assumption about the economy—thanks to the headline GDP rate that just flashed across the screen—there's a lot more going on behind the scenes than you might otherwise realize.

- **Consumption.** As I have stated repeatedly, the consumer makes up more than 67 percent of the GDP, in both spending and investing. The theory is that for every dollar that you earn, you either spend it, invest it, or save it. You can't measure every little piece of gum you bought to calculate consumption. Instead, it is based on something far easier to track—income. Say someone makes $2,000 in a month. Of that amount, he or she manages to put $500 in the bank. That shows up as investment or savings. The person pays $500 in taxes, which shows up in the money supply figures, and the person puts $500 in the stock market, which is also easily tracked. That leaves $500. And the assumption is that it was spent on "something," whether it was shoes, CDs, or fees paid to an accountant (who can't figure out how the person managed to save 25 percent of what he or she made).

- **Investment.** Money supply and securities accounts are fodder for the investment category. Curiously, this also includes investments and improvements in real assets, i.e., your home. Now there is some overlap between investment and consumption, which is one of the reasons why the GDP report is revised so often.

- **Government spending.** Government spending is difficult to get a read on. The government sets its own spending patterns and prices, with little rhyme or reason to economic events. It's not like the government decides, "This would be a good time to build a highway." With government spending such a big part of GDP, it has to be viewed at face value in order to get a handle on it. Increases or decreases in government spending have a huge impact on GDP, which some may argue is a problem for a capitalist society such as ours. But like it or not, government spending still is a big piece of the economy, so we can't ignore it. One thing to remember: Even though government spending is big and has a major impact, it is far less than what the consumer will contribute.

- **Exports.** Given that GDP measures all goods and services made in the United States, it obviously includes exports. (Imports are subtracted from GDP.) The rationale is that GDP measures all goods and services produced in the United States, even though exports are made here and used "over there."

- **Imports.** Goods that are made "over there" and used here are subtracted from GDP. The rationale is that imports used in the economy would lessen demand for U.S.-made goods. Therefore, imports are subtracted from the GDP number. This is where the double-negative positive comes in. If imports decline, this would show up as a positive. (Subtracting a negative is a positive.) In reality, however, when imports are down—assuming that the decline is not related to politics, trade wars, or currency fluctuations—it generally means that the economy is contracting. Further, in our global economy, more and more companies are manufacturing overseas, where costs may be lower, and then selling back into the United States. Thus imports are not always a replacement for U.S-made goods, but also products that are made by American companies overseas as part of their global operating strategies.

Dissecting a GDP report isn't something that only an economist can do. While the focus is on the "headline number," the GDP reports (which are readily available at the Bureau of Economic Analysis web site (*www.bea.doc.gov*) give a good breakdown of what increased and what decreased during the quarter.

Taking a look at the report for the third quarter of 2001, as stated earlier, real GDP declined 1.3 percent. This was a downward revision in GDP from the advance report, which had shown only a 0.4 percent decline. According to the Bureau of Economic Analysis, the major contributors to the decrease in GDP included exports, equipment and software, nonresidential structures, and private inventory investment. These negative factors were offset somewhat by positive contributions from personal consumption expenditures (PCE) and federal government spending. Imports, which are a subtraction in the calculation of GDP, decreased sharply.

That was a prime example of the import double negative. GDP wasn't as bad as it could have been, due to the double-negative positive effect of imports. Imports in the third quarter of 2001 declined, which ended up being a positive. Without this impact, real GDP would have shown an even greater decline.

This brings us to the topic of inventories. You made it before (when it was part of the "output" figures of a previous GDP report) and you'll sell it (hopefully) in the future. Right now, it's in a kind of GDP-limbo known as inventories. Still, it's important to look at inventories for insights into current demand and the outlook for future production. Let's say that GDP decreases, but inventories also decline. You could argue that the reduction in the "headline number" was really because companies did not need to produce, since they could sell from inventories. (Why make 4,000 cartons of widgets when you have 6,000 cartons on the shelf?) This would lead some economists to conclude that production will have to pick up again in the months ahead so that diminishing inventory levels could be replenished. This reduction was nothing more than a statistical blip.

I would go so far as to argue that the economic slowdown we saw in 2000 and through mid-2001 was really an inventory correction. Things were so good in 1999 and 1998 that producers overproduced, thinking that demand in the future would stay as strong as it was then. (They were wrong, of course). Plus in 1999 we had Y2K fears. Y2K increased demand and consumption for everything technology related. Why buy it twice? Companies didn't want to invest in a short-term fix and then replace the system in a few years. Just invest in a new system now. The end result was that we overbuilt in the United States and created huge inventories. When the Y2K spending stopped, demand for more technology softened, and the economy got caught holding the proverbial bag—a bag that was chock full of stuff at a time when demand was weakening. There were 10 buyers for every 50 computers and cell phones.

The economy, after all, works on a cycle, and the time had come in 2000 and into 2001 to begin the inventory work-off cycle. Production was cutback so that inventories could be depleted. That inventory depletion did put a damper on the economy, which slowed dramatically into the first and second quarters of 2001 to growth rates of 1.3 percent and 0.3 percent, respectively.

When inventories reach a low enough level, companies will begin to ramp up production. And when that occurs, GDP generally increases. Therefore, while not a part of the GDP figure per se, I track inventories as a signal of when GDP (and the economy) may turn around. (One caveat, of course, is that many companies need to build up inventories because of the cyclical or seasonal nature of their businesses. Or if production cycles are long, a company may see some times as more opportune for production than others.)

Inventories, of course, are a basic function of supply and demand. When demand goes down and supplies go up, inventories build. When demand goes up and supplies go down (or at least, if there is demand and supplies don't increase) then inventories are depleted. While supply and demand are the basics of economics, they can be more complicated—or at least trickier—than they appear. The following anecdote illustrates this point.

A group of entrepreneurs founded a company called Dollar Bill, Inc., which sold a one-dollar bill for 90 cents. Yes, it took a 10-cent loss on each bill sold, but demand was incredibly high for this product. Demand was so high, in fact, that it raised the price of a dollar bill to 95 cents, and sales didn't slack off one bit. With this kind of revenue stream, it went public. At the same time, it raised the price of a dollar bill to 98 cents, and demand was even stronger because there was a concern among consumers that it might raise the price of a dollar bill to $1.00! Some smart analysts projected that at this rate of revenue growth and the ability to raise prices, Dollar Bill, Inc. would be profitable in the third quarter of the following year. Looking at the current rate of revenue growth and the shrinking of the net loss, this was one hot company!

Dollar Bill, Inc. then raised the price of a dollar bill again, this time to $1.01. Sales dropped dramatically. The stock price got hammered. Dollar Bill, Inc. eventually filed for Chapter 11 bankruptcy.

This anecdote clearly shows that you can't take supply and demand figures on face value. Sure you could sell a dollar bill for 95 cents. But you can't sell it for more than it's worth. When it comes to projections of demand and supply, you have to use a good dose of reality.

Clearly, one of the biggest factors in an increase in GDP is the building up of inventories. But that is a reflection of the perception of demand, not actual demand. Consumers aren't suddenly going to demand 10 percent more of some product overnight. Tomorrow morning, you're not going to need eight new pairs of running shoes even if you do decide to take up jogging. True, GDP can rise as companies build inventories in anticipation of demand, but that apparent demand and its impact on GDP must be studied carefully. And there remains the fact that some inventories will never be sold. If a product is obsolete, there won't be demand for it at any price. Corporations have to find a way to write these inventories down or write them off as they continue down the road to becoming more profitable and making better and more innovative and useful products to sell.

There are other things that can impact inventories that have nothing to do with the health of the economy. By the end of 2001, inventories declined by more than $120 billion. At first, that would appear to be a good sign for turning GDP around. But the fact remains that the terrorist attacks on September 11, 2001, disrupted the U.S. manufacturing supply chain. Many companies had no choice but to draw down their inventories.

Given the importance of inventories on GDP, one of the most significant changes of the past several years has been the push toward "just-in-time" inventory management at companies. Simply put, just-in-time allows companies to keep a very low supply of inventory of parts and components, sometimes only enough for a day's production or even a few hours of production. Then new parts arrive "just in time" from suppliers. This efficiency has reduced costs in the manufacturing supply chain and has kept inventory levels low.

The impact of this inventory efficiency is that it has made GDP a more reliable indicator of the current state of the manufacturing economy. Since companies eschew high inventory levels, inventory building isn't a part of the supply chain. (Thus, when inventories do build, it is because supply is out of whack with demand.) Additionally, this efficiency carries productivity benefits that enable companies to manage inventories better and to keep costs down. This in turn prevents situations in which companies have to discount products to reduce their inventories. Thus, they have better prices and higher margins. Also, the consumer benefits by enjoying lower costs, shorter waiting times for products, and newer, more innovative products. Manufacturers can introduce up-to-date products more quickly because they don't have to wait for old models to sell out.

INDEX OF GROWTH

Inventory anomalies notwithstanding, GDP remains important in determining the current state of the economy—not as an absolute measure, but as a kind of index or gauge of relative growth. For the investor, this then presents an opportunity to use the economy to dictate an investment strategy. In fact, this is the backbone of the model I use at my firm, Astor Asset Management LLC. Astor Asset uses economic data, such as GDP, to determine the current economic cycle and, thus, whether the portfolio should have a long or short bias. GDP is one of the important barometers that determines whether we are in an expansion stage or contraction stage. Therefore, when I talk about the importance of knowing what the economy is doing as opposed to what the stock market is doing at the moment, I am literally putting my money where my mouth is.

Using GDP to measure the relative strength or weakness of the economy can be seen in the Nasdaq bubble of 1999-2000 and the burst that followed. Granted, it may seem easy to look back upon the bubble and comment upon it. And the fact remains that the economy in 1999-2000—as evidenced by the strong growth of the Nasdaq during this time, with an 85 percent gain for 1999 alone looked like a bubble many times before it actually burst, and yet kept going. So how do you know whether the bubble is about to pop or if it will keep expanding for a few more months or even years?

The answer is you don't. Market valuations often get ahead of economic reality, and sometimes economic reality catches up with market valuations. And that is actually what traps us in the bubble in the first place! In the case of the U.S. economy in 1999-2000, we all thought that the Internet and the related technology revolution would eventually increase productivity and output as well as create many efficiencies that we couldn't even quantify. This kind of thinking supported the rationale for higher stock prices, again particularly in the technology-dominated Nasdaq.

This reminds me of a meeting I attended in the mid-1980s about a new company that made disk drives for personal computers and was about to go public. An analyst at the meeting explained so convincingly that every computer eventually would have at least one disk drive in it, and some would have two. It seems like forever ago when not all computers had disk drives built in. But that was the niche that this company had, and the potential on the surface seemed enormous. As the analyst told us, every desk in every office would have a computer on it before the end of the 1980s. Every home and every college dorm room would have a computer in it, and every computer would have a disk drive.

When the company went public, the stock increased tenfold from its initial price of $10 a share to $100 a share over a very short time. The disk drive market was being valued in terms of hundreds of billions of dollars. (At one time the disk drive business was being valued greater than the PC business.) Indeed, the analyst was right. Every desk in every office had a computer. The explosion was phenomenal. The prediction of the near-term growth of the market was on target. But over time the stock price declined, almost to the original price of $10 a share. The reason was simple. At $100 a share, the price had already factored in the future growth. Thus, valuations for the stock had far outpaced reality, even though the analysis about the sector was correct.

This is analogous to what happened in the Nasdaq during 1998, 1999, and early 2000. Valuations were based upon projections of explosive growth but were not supported by actual economic activity. It was so hard to quantify that even very smart investors were caught in the technology euphoria. In the third quarter of 2000, however, economic reality caught up with perception, as GDP slipped from 5.7 percent in the second quarter of 2000 to 1.3 percent in the third quarter of 2000.

It would be difficult in hindsight to imagine equity valuations continuing higher, since the economy had already started to show signs of slowing growth. Even the stock market was starting to doubt these unrealistic valuations by the third quarter of 2000. The Nasdaq was down almost 19 percent from the end of the second quarter, and then down on the year as well. My own "Logical Economics" model noticed the divergence between economic growth and equity valuations during 2000. At the end of the third quarter of 2000, when both equity prices and economic activity turned down, it signaled to me it was time to exit the equity markets.

Since GDP tends to be a comparative statistic—the rate of growth or contraction of the economy in the most recent quarter compared with the one before that—it's good to take a longer-term perspective. In Chart 5-2 you can see quarterly changes in real GDP from 1990 through 2001.

As you can see in Chart 5-2, quarterly changes in real GDP at annual rates have been in positive territory since mid-1991. Since that time, there have been some impressive peaks, including a quarterly rise to above 8.0 percent in late 1999, a time when the Federal Reserve used increases in interest rates to slow the economy and

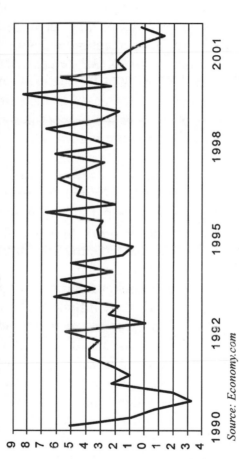

CHART 5-2 Quarterly Changes in Real GDP at Annual Rates 1990–2001 (in percent)

Source: Economy.com

combat any potential rise in inflation. Real GDP then had a precipitous decline in 2000 and into 2001. Not surprisingly, the Fed responded with increasingly lower interest rates to help jump-start a slowing economy.

For an even longer-term perspective, Chart 5-3 shows annual percentage changes in real GDP from 1970 through 2000.

The rate of increase in real GDP has been higher in the last several years than in the first part of the 1990s and much of the 1970s and 1980s. Economic growth, as measured by average annual changes in real GDP, was 4.4 percent in the 1960s. Average rates of growth decreased during the 1970s (3.3 percent), the 1980s (3.0 percent), and the first half of the 1990s (2.2 percent). In the last 5 years of the 1990s, the rate of growth in real GDP increased to 3.9 percent, with the last 3 years being over 4.3 percent per year. A 5 percent increase from 1999 to 2000 is the highest level of yearly increase since 1984.

This then begs the question: What's a "good" growth rate for GDP? Like much in life and economics, the answer is, "well, that depends." The Federal Reserve, that watchdog of the economy, wants to see steady growth, not runaway growth that could spark inflation, and not stagnation because the economy is contracting. The actual number, however, is something of a debate.

Some economists used to believe that if GDP got much beyond 4.5 percent growth, it would spark inflation. The fear was that the economy, at a positive 4.5 percent rate, would grow too quickly and too strongly and, therefore, would be unsustainable. However, advancements in technology and worker productivity have changed that percentage. Now it is thought that a GDP growth rate of 4 to 4.5 percent could be sustained without sparking an inflationary cycle.

IMPERFECT INDICATOR

As good an indicator as GDP is, it's far from perfect. In fact, it is antiquated when it comes to evaluating a global economy. Thus, while GDP is a great yardstick by which to measure the economy, it has its limitations. Cycles in certain sectors that are longer than a quarter or a few quarters can have material impact on GDP, leaving the GDP number itself open to interpretation in the short run. However, as a

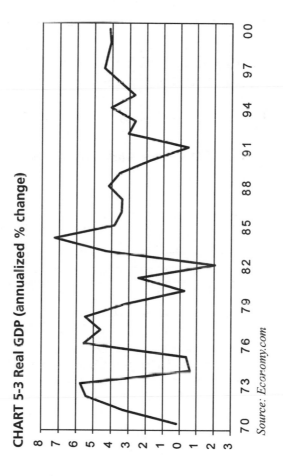

CHART 5-3 Real GDP (annualized % change)

Source: Ecoromy.com

long-term investor, the value of the GDP is clear. The economic trends measured by GDP tend to be long term, and thus quarter-to-quarter "blips" in certain sectors have very little impact on a long-term scale.

The GDP Chat with Delos Smith, The Conference Board

Economists like to talk to each other. Maybe it's because we speak the same language or because we find things like inflation deflators to be fascinating. Truthfully, I think it's because we like to bat around ideas about the economy, indicators, and the newfound investor fascination with numbers.

I chatted with Delos Smith, senior business analyst at The Conference Board, just as we do every week for WebFN, an Internet-based financial news program. Delos has a long history in economics, most of it at The Conference Board where, for a brief time in the 1950s, he worked with Alan Greenspan. Delos is also the founder of The Conference Board's "Help-Wanted Advertising Index," which surveys 51 major newspapers across the country each month to gauge changes in the local, regional, and national supply of jobs. But on one Monday in November, Delos and I discussed the GDP, in particular its value as an index and its shortcomings.

> ROB: When it comes to numbers, shortcomings not withstanding, I think that GDP is one of the most important measures of the economy.
>
> DELOS: Without question, it is the heart of our nation's income system, which makes it a major number of importance. When the national income was introduced in the 1930s, it was a revolutionary system because it looked at the U.S. economy as if it were a company with a balance sheet of assets and liabilities.
>
> ROB: But that was the drawback, right? It assumed that the United States was a closed economy. And at that time, it was. We have a different story now.
>
> DELOS: That is where the problem lies today. We don't have a closed economic system. So when you look at GDP, the personal consumption and expenditure (PCE) part is fine. And the fixed investment portion is fine. But there is a real weakness in the international sector. Today, companies are truly worldwide. Given the current GDP system, we cannot account for all American companies and what they do.
>
> ROB: Exactly, companies regularly make components or parts in one country to take advantage of labor costs or to be closer to a source of raw

materials. Then they import those parts and components into the United States, produce finished goods, and then re-export a portion of those goods. It's all one U.S. company, but it is able to improve its costs by having a global infrastructure. And you cannot deny the fact that Company X in the United States is able to support R&D to generate new products and have strong performance in its sales and marketing departments because it enjoys good margins from manufacturing at least part of its products overseas. The jobs in the United States—the income they generate and the personal spending they support—are directly correlated with the overseas manufacturing operation.

DELOS: And take the example of a Boeing aircraft. Some 60 nations participate in the making of that aircraft, with 25 percent of production of components belonging to Japan. But when Boeing sells a finished aircraft to an airline, 100 percent of that sale is accounted as U.S. GDP.

ROB: So to be more reflective of the global economy and the reality of how many of our products are manufactured today, GDP figures eventually will have to be able to account for companies that make or purchase components and parts overseas.

DELOS: There are some efforts to do just that. GDP was perfect for measuring the 1950s U.S. economy, but not for the global economy.

ROB: Plus, while the United States has evolved from a manufacturing economy to technology to a service economy, GDP has not kept up with those changes. As a result, it cannot completely capture services that are a vital part of our domestic output. While it constantly miscalculates the service and technology sector, I can still use these numbers in my analysis as long as I'm aware that GDP is inaccurately capturing some 30 percent of our economy—but it does so consistently.

DELOS: Exactly. When the national income accounting system was launched, the focus was on durables and nondurables. The service side of the economy was tiny in those days. Now, it's the other way. The durables and nondurables are comparatively small and it's the services that dominate.

ROB: And there is the whole problem with inventories in the GDP. When companies ramp up production in anticipation of strong demand, then GDP looks great. But if those inventories just sit there, then GDP has given a false signal. Still, even with those shortcomings I think GDP is one of the best indicators we have to gauge the relative strength or weakness of the economy. I say *relative* strength or weakness because we know that as an absolute gauge of how much the United States produced in terms of goods and services, it has some flaws. But those flaws are consistent from quarter to quarter. Therefore, I think GDP is helpful to look at as if it were an index, with a 1950s base. Knowing that exports and imports skew the picture, but consistently, you can extrapolate from the GDP numbers a pretty good indication of how the U.S. economy as a whole is performing.

DELOS: I agree. That's why I believe you can't just look at "one number," but rather a family of numbers that give you a broad picture of the economy. You can't just look at one number and decide that's what the economy is doing.

ROB: You can't do that any more than you can glance at the television and see if the Dow is up 50 points or down 100 points and decide your investment strategy based on that one snapshot.

DELOS: You know Rob, back when I started as an economist, these reports were really a "private number for a private club." The expectation was that once these reports were released, they would be analyzed at a place like The Conference Board where there are economists on staff. We never dreamed that they would be broadcast instantly and then analyzed in 2 minutes by a bunch of amateurs.

ROB: Times, they are a changing. Information is instantaneous, and most investors are looking moment-to-moment at the market and the economy and trying to make long-term decisions. Delos, what you and I are trying to do with our weekly financial news show and what you do in your regular appearances on CNBC and CNN is help investors to interpret the numbers as we do; not only as economists but as logical thinkers of the data and then try to apply this information in investment portfolios.

There are many inherent shortcomings with the current GDP data as an accurate measure for the entire U.S. economy. Those include underestimating sectors of the economy, such as service and technology; not fully accounting for imports accurately; assuming that the United States has a closed economy; and not taking full account of foreign participation in our country's output, such as when a U.S.-based company operates a production plant offshore to take advantage of economies of scale or other benefits.

Just as the Dow is a measure of the overall stock market, GDP can be viewed the same way. Granted, it has its shortcomings, but it is an excellent and consistent barometer of economic output. Even if it doesn't measure everything accurately, it does measure everything consistently, which is more important. When making investment decisions it is less important to know the actual output number and more important to acknowledge the relative change in output.

6

Working for a Living

First, the facts: The "Employment Situation Report" is a monthly report released by the Bureau of Labor Statistics. The report covers the total payroll employment and the unemployment rate.

Now, the spin: If GDP is a gauge of the "physical health" of the economy, how much and how well it's producing, then the employment situation is its "psychological health." Employment statistics really hit home in a way that other reports cannot because of their very topics: who has a job, who doesn't, and who is still looking. Think about the impact of employment on your own life. There is no greater *financial* worry than losing a job, and no greater *financial* relief than getting a job or getting a better one. Employment is a measure of the labor force and the mood of the economy.

For that reason, the employment situation is the "two" in the one-two punch of economic data, with the first being GDP. Many other reports and economic measures, such as consumer confidence, consumer spending, and even inflation, have direct ties and correlation to employment. Clearly, it is one of the key conditions monitored by the Fed, and one of the reports that has the biggest impact on investor sentiment. Very often recessions, expansions, and economic peaks are defined in terms of stock market values, but they don't really hit home until we view them in terms of the employment situation.

For example, the Great Depression of the 1930s had many indicators that defined it. But the one you hear about the most—after the 1929 stock market crash—is the 15 to 20 percent unemployment rate that followed. As a result of the war years and post-World War II, the United States witnessed some of the greatest economic expansion in its history as defined by low unemployment, which is still used as a benchmark today.

Employment's psychological aspect shows that it's more than just an economic statistic. It gives people a sense of worth and a sense of security (or lack thereof). You can tell the average person that consumer sentiment fell to an 8-year low, and he or she might happily anticipate more sales at the mall with thoughts of, "hey, that's good for me who has stuff to buy and money to buy it with!" People can even lose money in the stock market and be able to shake it off with thoughts of, "I'm a long-term investor, it will come back." Then you can tell the average person that the unemployment rate rose, and it's a different matter. That strikes the "home, health, and security" chord in many of us. If the unemployment rate rose, it's because of layoffs or business failures à la the dot-com world. Put in the most basic human terms, that means somebody out there lost his or her job (poor them), and maybe I might, too (poor me!). And if I do lose my job (oh, no!), I might have a really hard time finding another one (e-gads!).

The employment situation has the power to stop spending, slow savings, and even deplete nest eggs. Employment trends change people's lives. I've never heard of people moving from Chicago to Tulsa because the stock of a Tulsa-based company they bought went up 30 percent. But you hear that people relocate for a job or even a better job opportunity. From the Joad family in Steinbeck's *Grapes of Wrath,* who went to California in search of work in the midst of the depression, to the Wall Street-wannabes who head to New York, to Generation X'ers, who surfed to Silicon Valley in hopes of catching the Internet gold rush, we as a society regularly uproot ourselves for a new job and a better life. Therefore, it's understandable that the employment situation—regardless of whether you're personally affected—packs a wallop on consumer spending and investing (see Chart 6-1).

A strong correlation exists between the employment situation and consumer and investor confidence (which we will address in Chapter 7). While many individuals curtail spending and investing as the employment situation deteriorates, fearing a downturn in the economy and with it stock prices, it is important to remember the importance of the business cycle. At the end of a contraction or a recession, unemployment can still be on the rise while corporations become more productive and profitable—which in turn usually leads to stock price appreciation.

As layoffs take place, the labor-cost component of making a product declines, and although output may decline as well, worker productivity eventually increases. In fact, layoffs typically continue to occur until worker productivity increases and companies improve their profitability. If not, the company will likely go bankrupt (unless it is Chrysler in the 1980s and the government will loan it money). During this trough in the business cycle, as labor productivity increases, often stock prices advance to the surprise of some investors who wonder how stocks can go up in light of a high unemployment rate and low consumer confidence.

Because employment is a kind of economic linchpin, it is of great importance to the Fed and its policies. Fed policy isn't supposed to target stock market prices, boost up stock valuations, or even target GDP levels. What the Fed does is manage an environment that creates jobs. In the Fed's own words, the FOMC is "responsible for formulation of a policy designed to promote economic growth, full employment, stable prices, and a sustainable pattern of international trade and payments." Looking at it another way, that means the employment situation (or more accurately the *un*employment situation) can alter Fed policy.

Clearly, the unemployment rate is very important both financially and emotionally. But how do you analyze this report? What is considered to be high unemployment? What is a low level? What are the consequences of both situations?

The general belief is that low unemployment is basically good for the economy. Indeed, the U.S. economy has enjoyed, on average, low

CHART 6-1 Unemployment vs. S&P 500

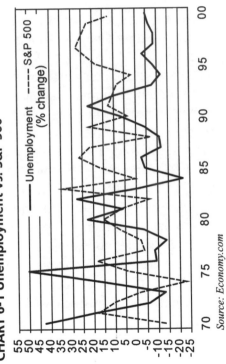

Source: *Economy.com*

unemployment. Chart 6-2 shows the month-by-month unemployment rate from 1991 through 2001. As the chart depicts, unemployment climbed steadily through 1991 and peaked at 7.7 percent in July 1992, as the 1991 recession gave way to recovery. The rate then declined steadily, dropping below 5 percent in mid-1991 and then declining further to a low of 3.9 percent in September and October 2000. The rate began rising in late 2000 and into 2001, reflecting the bursting of the Nasdaq bubble and the cooling of the dot-com and technology-related sectors. In the wake of the terrorist attacks of September 11, 2001, the unemployment rate rose over 5 percent (to 5.4 percent, then to 6.0 percent) for the first time in more than 3 years.

Taking a longer-term perspective, you can see that the United States has enjoyed a relatively low unemployment rate (see Chart 6-3).

While much attention is focused on the unemployment rate, it shouldn't be viewed as an absolute number. By that I mean, it's more important to see if the percentage is going up or down—meaning more or less people are unemployed—than to take the number as absolute gospel. Just because the average annual unemployment rate for 2000 is 4.0 percent, you shouldn't assume that 4.0 percent of the people in the work force were looking for jobs. The fact is there is a lot of ambiguity in the unemployment number.

I don't want to undermine the value of the unemployment statistics as they relate to the economy. In fact, as I've stated previously, the state of employment in the United States is one of the most vital components of economic analysis. But just as GDP—while important—has its share of flaws, so does employment. For that reason, I believe the most important use of the unemployment statistic is to look at the relative change versus prior months. That way, regardless of how the actual "counting" is done—and who is or isn't included in that tally—the employment report retains its value as a relative measure. In other words, I treat the unemployment statistic as if it were an "index."

The Department of Labor determines the employment situation based upon a series of broad surveys. The "Current Population Survey" is a sample of 60,000 households, which collects data by personal and telephone interview. As the Bureau of Labor Statistics (BLS) explains, basic labor force data are gathered monthly and data

CHART 6-2 Monthly Unemployment Rate 1991–2001

Year	Jan	Feb	Mar	Apr	May	Jun	Jul	Aug	Sept	Oct	Nov	Dec
1991	6.4	6.6	6.8	6.7	6.9	6.9	6.8	6.9	6.9	7.0	7.0	7.3
1992	7.3	7.4	7.4	7.4	7.6	7.8	7.7	7.6	7.6	7.3	7.4	7.4
1993	7.3	7.1	7.0	7.1	7.1	7.0	6.9	6.8	6.7	6.8	6.6	6.5
1994	6.6	6.6	6.5	6.4	6.1	6.1	6.1	6.0	5.9	5.8	5.6	5.5
1995	5.6	5.4	5.4	5.8	5.6	5.6	5.7	5.7	5.6	5.5	5.6	5.6
1996	5.6	5.5	5.5	5.6	5.6	5.3	5.5	5.1	5.2	5.2	5.4	5.4
1997	5.3	5.3	5.2	5.1	4.9	5.0	4.9	4.8	4.9	4.7	4.6	4.7
1998	4.7	4.6	4.7	4.4	4.4	4.5	4.5	4.5	4.5	4.5	4.4	4.4
1999	4.3	4.4	4.2	4.4	4.2	4.3	4.3	4.2	4.2	4.1	4.1	4.1
2000	4.0	4.1	4.0	4.0	4.1	4.0	4.0	4.1	3.9	3.9	4.0	4.0
2001	4.2	4.2	4.3	4.5	4.4	4.6	4.6	4.9	5.0	5.4	5.6	5.8

Source: Economy.com

CHART 6-3 Average Annual Unemployment Rate 1950–2000

Year	Avg.	Year	Avg.	Year	Avg.	Year	Avg.	Year	Avg.
1950	5.3	1960	5.5	1970	4.9	1980	7.1	1990	5.6
1951	3.3	1961	6.7	1971	5.9	1981	7.6	1991	6.8
1952	3.0	1962	5.5	1972	5.6	1982	9.7	1992	7.5
1953	2.9	1963	5.7	1973	4.9	1983	9.6	1993	6.9
1954	5.5	1964	5.2	1974	5.6	1984	7.5	1994	6.1
1955	4.4	1965	4.5	1975	8.5	1985	7.2	1995	5.6
1956	4.1	1966	3.8	1976	7.7	1986	7.0	1996	5.4
1957	4.3	1967	3.8	1977	7.1	1987	6.2	1997	4.9
1958	6.8	1968	3.6	1978	6.1	1988	5.5	1998	4.5
1959	5.5	1969	3.5	1979	5.8	1989	5.3	1999	4.2
								2000	4.0

Source: Bureau of Labor Statistics

on special topics are gathered in periodic supplements. The systematic gathering of data to determine the state of employment is a concept that dates back to the 1930s, when the United States was still in the midst of the Great Depression.

The BLS (*www.bls.gov*) states the following in its "Handbook of Methods":

> Before the 1930s, aside from attempts in some of the decennial census, no direct measurements were made of the number of jobless persons. Mass unemployment in the early 1930s increased the need for statistics, and widely conflicting estimates based on a variety of indirect techniques began to appear. Dissatisfied with these methods, many research groups, as well as state and municipal governments, began experimenting with direct surveys or samples of the population. In these surveys, an attempt was made to classify the population as employed, unemployed, or out of the labor force by a means of a series of questions addressed to each individual.

The survey produced some basic classifications: Those who were employed were defined as "persons with occupations" or "gainful workers." The unemployed were defined as those who were not working but were otherwise "willing and able to work." But that didn't seem precise enough to really capture the state of employment at the time. Thus, more precise categories followed in the late 1930s that classified people according to their actual activity for a specific period of time. In other words, was someone working, looking for work, or engaged in other activities (such as retirement)?

These three basic criteria are the basis of today's measurements as well. In monthly interviews of sample households for the statistical survey, household members 16 years of age or older are asked questions to classify, in the words of the BLS, "the sample population into three basic economic groups: the employed, the unemployed, and those not in the labor force." This seems logical and encompassing, right? Not exactly. There is a lot of gray area in employment that may not be captured by household surveys. Here's a scenario seen often in the late 1990s when the unemployment rate dropped so low (measured at 4.2 percent in 1999) that the U.S. economy was assumed to have at least theoretic "full employment." Retired workers—from executives to machine shop employees—were enticed to come back to work. Now, prior to this, they were in the "engaged in other activities" category. They had not been among the "unemployed," because they were retired. But based upon the demand, they were lured into joining the ranks of consultants, part-time laborers, and even temporary help.

Then the economy began to slow, and by late 2001 unemployment statistics were rising. Many of these formerly retired workers were now among those who were laid off or otherwise terminated When they lost their jobs as employees, they were counted as unemployed. But in fact, they had returned to the status of "engaged in other activities." This kind of calculation inflates the unemployment rate, since a portion of those who lost their jobs were not really part of the "looking for work" group to begin with.

Further, there are many "gainful workers" who operate under the radar, so to speak, of the employment surveys. This includes a host of contractors, freelancers, and consultants who are self-employed but who provide services to companies. In addition, as we saw during the economic recovery of the 1990s, the gathering of statistics can miss groups of people that, taken together, make up a large population. What occurred in the 1990s was that new, small companies springing up were creating jobs. They were hiring 4, 8, 10, or 20 people, who were not counted in the employment statistics. Now while one Internet service company with six employees would not cause a blip on employment statistics, that scenario repeated thousands of times would. Clearly, what was happening was the formation of new companies in the technology sector.

What this anecdote from the 1990s shows is that the actual counting of the employed, unemployed, and "otherwise engaged" is far from perfect. But what remains important is the relative increase or decrease. Let's take a look at an announcement from the Bureau of Labor Statistics of the U.S. Department of Labor from more recent history—November 2001.

"Employment fell sharply in October, and the unemployment rate jumped to 5.4 (percent). ... Nonfarm payroll employment dropped by 415,000 over the month, by far the largest of three consecutive monthly declines." The first number that jumps out, of course, is the 5.4 percent unemployment rate. Once again, rather than using it as an absolute number, this rate is important when compared with the previous month. In other words, does this measure show that more or less people are out of work? What this report shows is a 0.5 percentage point rise in the unemployment rate (which the BLS will tell you in the next paragraph is the highest unemployment rate since December 1996).

Then, we come to the nonfarm payroll. The "nonfarm" terminology dates back to the days when the mass hiring of seasonal workers on the farm skewed employment statistics. But, of course, the United States has gone from being an agrarian economy to a manufacturing one—and from manufacturing to a service economy. Nonetheless, the term "nonfarm" persists. What the payroll employment number shows is the rise or fall in the number of people working, in this case a drop of 415,000 people from total payrolls. The BLS then goes on to give a little insight into what happened during the month. "The job losses in October were spread across most industry groups, with especially large declines in manufacturing and services."

Reading this, a bell should go off in your head. The unemployment rate rose, with a significant jump in those out of work compared with previous months. The number of people on the payroll dropped and the declines were shown across-the-board, especially in manufacturing and services. Just with those facts alone, you could piece together a pretty troubling economic picture—especially in combination with GDP, which you know from the previous chapter had been showing a declining economy. Now the employment situation, which is a barometer of the mood or psychology of the economy, is gloomier than before. As an economically savvy investor, this would be your tip-off that the economy is certainly contracting.

Reading further into the report, BLS states that its household survey found that the number of unemployed persons increased from roughly 7.0 million in September to just under 7.7 million in October. Further insight can be gained from the "number of newly unemployed persons," whom the BLS defines as those who are unemployed for less than 5 weeks. That number, according to the report, rose by 401,000 to 3.2 million. In addition, the report states, "the number of unemployed job losers not on temporary layoff grew by 518,000 over the month and has increased by 1.4 million since last December." The rise in the newly unemployed reflects the grim picture of a contracting economy as businesses shed workers, either due to declining demand for goods or services, the need to cut back excess production, or both.

The report also gives the tally for "total employment," which dropped in October 2001 by 619,000 to 134.6 million. What this shows are fewer people in the work force.

Another employment statistic I like to look at is average payrolls, which is broadly watched for signs of "wage inflation." What this statistic shows is the rise or fall in average hourly earnings of production or nonsupervisory workers. For example, in October 2001, average hourly earnings rose by 2 cents to $14.47, seasonally adjusted. This followed a revised gain of 5 cents in September. Wage inflation is part of the overall inflation picture that the Fed watches closely. Thus, if wage inflation were a problem, one would be on the lookout for the Fed to take action to slow an overheated economy with at least a "tightening bias" if not an actual rate hike.

JOBLESS CLAIMS

While the "Employment Situation Report" is a comprehensive look at employment nationwide, it is by its very nature a lagging report subject to revisions. A better snapshot of what is happening now (or at least as close to "now" as an economic report can be) is the weekly "Jobless Claims Report." Equally important is the fact that the jobless claims reflect the number of people standing in line at state unemployment offices filing for benefits the first time or continuing to file for benefits.

This is not a percentage or a calculation of how many people are working (or not working) based upon an estimated labor pool. This is the number of people standing in line, right now. For example, in late 2001 when corporate layoffs were in the headlines, it was important to look at the jobless claims to see if these announcements were affecting the number of those filing for unemployment. Company X may announce it is going to lay off 5000 people, but if the layoffs will occur over a period of months, then the impact is not going to be seen on the "grass roots" level of the unemployment line.

Taking a recent report as an example, initial jobless claims during the week ending December 1, 2001, dropped by 18,000 to

475,000. At first glance, this shows that the number of people filing for unemployment for the first time dropped, which would appear to bode well for the economic pickup that, at that time, people were looking for. Further, the report stated that the 4-week moving average continued to trend downward to 460,750 from a peak of 505,750 on October 20, 2001. This 4-week moving average is closely watched by many economists, since it tends to smooth out the blips and aberrations that can be caused in a week's data. For example, when auto plants cut back production seasonally, it's common to see an uptick in jobless claims, as these workers file for unemployment. But viewing this over a 4-week time horizon, you can see the general trend without the weekly fluctuations.

Another important statistic is the number of continuing claims. In our sample report from the week ended December 1, 2001, the number of continuing claims dropped by 349,000 to 3.6 million, the largest decline in 18 years. That could be good news, since a decline in continuing claims may reflect that people who have been out of work and actively looking are finding jobs. However, continuing claims remained at an elevated level. It may also mean they have given up looking or have left the work force.

The "Jobless Claims Report" does not preclude the more detailed "Employment Situation Report"; in many ways it is a precursor to it. But the employment situation could be compared with the National Weather Service's forecast for the entire country, with rain in the Northeast, unseasonably warm in the South, and snow in the Rocky Mountains. But when it comes to fluctuations in the barometric pressure, you'd better take a closer look than just the weather map from coast to coast. In the world of employment reports, jobless claims act as that barometer.

HOW LOW IS TOO LOW?
Now that I've dissected an "Employment Situation Report" and addressed the weekly "Jobless Claims Report," the question arises: Is it always good to have low unemployment and bad to have high unemployment? This seems to be the kind of "common sense" question that you shouldn't ponder for too long. Of course it's good when the unemployment rate is low! People want to have jobs! They have jobs, earn

money, and buy stuff, which creates more demand for more goods and services, and then that creates even more jobs! Therein lies the potential bad news, too.

When unemployment is too low, some economic smarty-heads think this can be a problem if left unchecked. When everyone is working and making money, spending goes up. If production doesn't keep pace with all the new workers in the work force who are making money every week, then shortages can be created. This results in more money chasing fewer goods, and if you were awake at all in your Econ 101 class, you'd remember that is the formula for inflation. Further, in a state of low unemployment, demand for workers is such that individuals can demand more money for their services. That raises labor costs, which already make up a large percentage of the cost of producing goods. This is not only inflationary because of the wages earned by these workers, but it means higher product costs and higher costs for consumers to buy products. That can also mean smaller profits for the company, which may not only translate into a lower stock price but spark layoffs down the road as well. And thus the downward cycle begins.

While the Fed's policies are aimed, at least in part, at creating "full employment," there will be times when the Fed will respond with caution to a low unemployment figure by taking an anti-inflationary stance, which is a very important Fed objective (see Chart 6-4).

This brings us to another point called worker productivity. The amount of output per worker is almost as important to the health of the economy as the rate itself. The Bureau of Labor Statistics defines productivity as a "measure of economic efficiency which shows how effectively economic inputs are converted into output." In plain English, that means it measures how efficient people, plants, and production are when it comes to taking stuff and making other stuff. This is more than just how "hard" people are working. It also takes into account a variety of efficiency factors, from technology to the rate at which factories are operating.

In economic terms, productivity measurements are important because they gauge the ability of the U.S. workplace to produce more with the same or less input. This is vital not only for businesses, but also for the country as a whole. "The U.S. economy has been able to

CHART 6-4 Comparison of Unemployment Rate (% SA) and Fed Funds

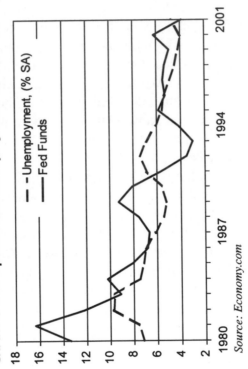

Source: Economy.com

produce more goods and services over time, not by requiring a proportional increase of labor time, but by making production more efficient," the BLS explains.

Overall productivity is measured by comparing the amount of goods and services produced with the "inputs" used in production. Labor productivity is the ratio of goods and services produced compared with the labor hours devoted to that production. Labor productivity is the most commonly used gauge of productivity, and it's one of the most important components. In the United States, labor costs represent some two-thirds of the value of output produced.

Now, as we know from business cycles discussed in Chapter 3, when the economy is in a trough—and just as it starts its upswing into expansion—workers will automatically be more productive than before. They are, in general, working harder and faster. The work force that was cut back when demand was declining now has to produce more goods as inventories are built and demand picks up. Productivity really shows. You've got five workers producing 15 widgets instead of their usual 10 (or 3 widgets per worker instead of 2). Therefore, the unemployment rates may remain comparatively high just as the economy goes into recovery. When demand looks like it's sustainable, the company calls back one of the workers who was laid off. Now you've got six workers, but they are producing the same 15 widgets (or even 20 widgets) because demand has picked up. But on an "output per worker" basis, productivity increases faster than employment.

Referring back to the employment report for October 2001, BLS stated that the average workweek for production or nonsupervisory workers on private, nonfarm payrolls "edged down by 0.1 hour in October to 34 hours, seasonally adjusted." In other words, those who were still on the job were working slightly less than previously. The trough at which the workers typically work more hours is not yet evident, raising some concern for the future employment picture.

This is an important statistic to watch during a contracting economy (read: recession), as it generally can signal that things are getting better. Enough fat has been trimmed from the operational side, while demand for products has increased. Once a corporation sees incremental increases in revenue and profits, it will hire more workers.

Now, let's take a look at the overall employment situation the way most of us view things: from the perspective of our own lives. Consider the story of this hypothetical family: David and Lisa are married with two children, Olivia and Ava. They live in a house in Chicago with David's parents, whom we'll call Jerry and Bay. David works at a steel tubing manufacturer, while Lisa has exited the work force to take care of Olivia and Ava, as well as her in-laws. Jerry retired from the same steel tubing company where David works, and Bay was only in the work force for a short time, many yeas ago. Now, let's look at how their individual employment histories could (theoretically) impact the employment situation—both accurately and inaccurately.

Before Olivia and Ava were born, both David and Lisa worked. But when Lisa became pregnant, she quit her job and stayed at home. In other words, Lisa voluntarily left the work force. The month that Lisa left her job, the unemployment figures did not count her as "unemployed" and actively seeking another job, and it didn't include her as a member of the work force. However, the nonfarm payroll number hypothetically should have gone down by one when Lisa left her job. If the company she was working for did not replace her with another worker yet still maintained its production level, worker productivity would increase.

Now, let's say that over time the economy slows down to the point that the steel tubing company sees a drop in demand. There is less output, which means that worker productivity declines. To offset this, the steel company lays off David. The unemployment rate goes up, as David is out of work and looking for another job. Meanwhile, the steel tubing company lays off employees until worker productivity reaches a point at which profits improve. When the layoffs began, Jerry decided it was time to exit the work force. He had been laid off back in the recession of the early 1990s, and he decided it was time to hang up his hard hat. After all, he had worked for the steel tubing company for 30 years, and he could retire with a good package.

At this point, even though the labor force has declined, the unemployment rate has not gone up a commensurate amount. Lisa, David, and Jerry have all stopped working, but only David is actively looking for another job. Thus he gets counted in the unemployment figures.

It's important to note, from the steel tubing company's perspective, that the need to trim its work force is a vital part of its effort to return to profitability. As I've said, a company will continue to reduce its work force through layoffs, attrition, and so forth, until it reaches the point of profitability or it goes out of business. Therefore, spikes in the unemployment rate prior to an economic turnaround are common.

Then one day, David, an ingenious, entrepreneurial kind of a guy, decides that it's time to start a consulting business to tap his experience with steel tubing manufacturers. He recruits many of his co-workers—most of them laid off—to join him in the new venture. They land a consulting gig at their former employer's biggest competitor. David is working again, and he's making more money than before. However, he does not show up in the employment statistics. Technically, because he's self-employed, he's not part of the work force that gets counted.

This is the same phenomenon that we saw in the late 1980s and early 1990s as a result of corporate downsizing. Employees were laid off, and the upswing that followed is often referred to as the "jobless recovery." More people were back to work, but their employment was not in traditional firms, and thus they did not hit the "radar" of the employment statistics.

Let's assume that by taking the advice of David's consulting business, the steel manufacturer has become so efficient and so productive that it comes up with a new and improved product that's in hot demand. The company can't keep this new product in stock and needs to hire more workers, preferably experienced ones. The steel company offers such a great employment package that Jerry comes out of retirement to work at the steel company.

When this occurs, the labor force goes up (Jerry is back to work), but the unemployment rate remains the same. Why? Because Jerry wasn't among the workers looking for a job. He wasn't counted as "unemployed" when he retired, but he is part of the work force again when he returns to work. When he gets his first paycheck, nonfarm payrolls go up.

The economy, of course, moves in cycles. Eventually the economy turns down, and the steel company must cut back production and reduce its work force. So Jerry is laid off. He's happy to go back to retirement. So while he is initially counted in the layoffs, he is not part of the unemployment rate because he's not looking for another job.

What's the moral of this story? Many variables can impact the employment rate and make the statistics convoluted. Retired workers coming back on the job will increase the work force, but not reduce the unemployment rate. Outsourced workers and temps are not counted as part of the labor force.

This isn't to undermine the importance of the employment situation, but rather to show that this—like GDP—is best viewed as a kind of index. Look to see what's going up or down, or the general trend. Don't assume that 4.4 percent unemployment means that 4.4 percent of all eligible workers are looking for work. The number could be significantly more or less than that 4.4 percent.

As with many things economic, it is the comparison of statistics— one month to the next, one year to another—that tells the real story.

Employment Chat with Paul L. Kasriel, Senior Vice President and Director of Economic Research, Northern Trust Co.

Imagine you're tuning into your favorite financial news network. On the screen are four intelligent-looking people dressed in gray, navy, and the occasional red tie. The commentator introduces them as economists who will talk about the economy. Now, you may ask yourself how many economists it takes to figure out the economy (like that old light bulb joke). The fact is that economic indicators are best discussed from a variety of opinions. Nothing is clear-cut in economics, even when it looks as simple as "the unemployment rate is higher. More people are looking for jobs." There are as many variations of gray as there are variations of gray-suited economists. To discuss the employment situation, I talked with my friend and fellow economist, Paul L. Kasriel, who is also the author of Seven Indicators That Move Markets: Forecasting Future Market Movements for Profitable Investments.

> ROB: When it comes to the economic statistics, the employment situation/nonfarm payroll is certainly at the top of my list—along with GDP—for measuring the strength of the economy and gauging the Fed's policy.

PAUL: Employment is very important to Fed policies. In fact, you can almost track Fed policy in tandem with the employment situation report. That was certainly the case in the early 1990s when the Fed kept lowering rates as the unemployment rate was increasing—in spite of the fact that the United States was officially out of the recession in the spring of 1991. Yet the Fed continued to cut rates.

ROB: This raises the issue of the employment situation being a lagging indicator, albeit an important one.

PAUL: That's just it. And the Federal Reserve, for all its talk of being a forward-looking organization whose actions today have an effect on the economy down the road, pays attention to coincidence and lagging indicators. The employment report is certainly one of them.

There is a political aspect to this as well. When the unemployment rate goes up, it's plastered across the headlines across every newspaper in America. And the Fed, for all its talk of being independent, is somewhat like Finland during the Cold War. Finland was officially neutral, but unofficially it paid a lot of attention to the wishes of the Soviets. The Fed is technically independent of the administration and Congress. But the Fed, like the Supreme Court, reads the election returns.

ROB: That's why I believe the employment statistics reflect the economic "mood" of the country. I think of GDP as if it were the medical report on the economy, how well does it do what it's supposed to do. Employment, on the other hand, certainly reflects how the economy is performing, but it also has a huge psychological impact.

PAUL: Right. Certain aspects of the employment situation are a proxy for the output of the economy. It's a combination of the number of people working and the number of hours that they're working. It takes into consideration productivity gains. In a recovery stage of the economy, for example, you would expect the workweek to start getting longer before a lot of new hiring took place. You would also be on the lookout for wage pressures that could contribute to inflation.

ROB: The "old school" of economics used to consider low unemployment as a precursor to inflation. When I was in college, I think 6 percent was the threshold. Below 6 percent unemployment you had to begin to worry about the possibility of inflation, as companies competing for available workers would offer higher compensation, and workers earning more money would bid up the prices of goods that were in short supply. Now that percentage is around 4 percent. What are your thoughts on the correlation between low unemployment, the economy, and inflation?

PAUL: We have seen a pick up in unit labor costs and nominal wage growth with a decline in the unemployment rate this time, although it seemed to kick in at a lower rate. It used to be that 6 percent or 5.5 percent was the magic line of demarcation. When unemployment dropped below that level, you could see higher labor costs and inflation. I think that rate is definitely lower now.

ROB: There were also certain changes in compensation packages that changed the traditional relationship between low unemployment and inflation. Back when the market was very, very strong, there were people who told their bosses, "Forget the 4 percent raise. Give me 500 more shares of stock options." That took some pressure off the traditional wage equation.

PAUL: You're absolutely right. That's still captured in the productivity cost, but it doesn't show up as a direct salary increase.

ROB: Another phenomenon, especially in the late 1990s, was the growth in outsourced labor. Temporary workers, outside consultants, and so forth all contributed to a company's productivity, but they never were part of the payroll.

PAUL: To the degree that manufacturing firms hire temporary workers, they are not counted as manufacturing workers, even though they are doing the same thing as regular employees.

ROB: But in the service sector, temporary workers and consultants were certainly a factor in productivity, while not being officially part of the payroll. Despite all the drawbacks of the employment report—its nature as a lagging indicator, the revisions that can be made months later, and even the ambiguities about who is part of the work force and who is not—it's vitally important to determine just how well the economy is doing and how we are "feeling" about the economy.

To conclude, the employment numbers may have their limitations as calculations of who is working and who is part of the work force. Nonetheless, they certainly give insight into the overall health and psychology of the economy. With two-thirds of the economy consisting of consumer spending, it is important for these consumers to get their paychecks. Additionally, labor costs are a significant factor to businesses.

In its simplest form, the health of the economy is based upon investors and companies who invest capital to produce goods and services. Workers invest their labor. Together they create output. As output increases and profits are made, more investment is made—both capital and labor to create more output.

From an investor perspective, it's important to keep an eye on the employment data, first by looking at average hours worked, then at nonfarm payrolls, and finally at the overall employment rate. This will give clues to the condition of economy. As the economy starts to contract, average hours worked will decrease, which is normally followed by layoffs and payroll reduction, which in turn results in a rising unemployment rate. This can be one of the first signs of economic trouble ahead. Conversely, when average hours worked begins to increase, resulting in the hiring of more workers and a decline in the unemployment rate, then it's a sure bet that good economic times are ahead—not only measured in increased production, but also in increased consumer spending.

7

The Consumers

The United States is a consumer-driven economy. As you recall from Chapter 4, consumer spending makes up 67 percent of GDP. When the consumer spends freely, the economy grows. When the consumer tightens the purse strings, the economy shrinks. Consumer spending—whether for retail goods, houses, cars, or trucks—is what impacts the economy. While consumer psychology, consumer sentiment, and consumer opinion are interesting as indications of what the consumer might do, they really don't offer much beyond the anecdotal.

That brings us to our first sets of data: Consumer confidence, published by the Conference Board, and consumer sentiment, which is put out by the University of Michigan.

The "Consumer Confidence Report" is based upon a "representative sample" of 5000 U.S. households surveyed monthly. This yields an index, with the base of 100 equal to 1985, which supposedly measures the relative change in how confident consumers are about the economy, their jobs, and spending in general. Looking at a recent report, The Conference Board's Consumer Confidence Index fell in November 2001 to 82.2 after it had already "declined significantly" in the previous 2 months.

The Present Situation Index fell to 93.5 from 107.2, while the Expectations Index increased from 70.7 to 74.6. In other words, consumers were more pessimistic in the here and now, but were more hopeful about the future. The report went on to say that consumers' appraisal of the current economic conditions in November 2001 was "more pessimistic" than the previous month. Further, 21.4 percent of consumers rated current business conditions as "bad," up from 20.7 percent the previous month. The percentage of consumers who thought conditions were good declined, and the percentage of those who thought jobs were "hard to get" increased. Those who thought jobs were "plentiful" (who apparently were living under a rock, since the news headlines had been full of unemployment statistics and rising joblessness) fell to 17.0 percent from 20.9 percent.

While I don't want to criticize the "Consumer Confidence Report," it's important to understand what it actually is. It is a measure of sentiment, of feeling. It seeks to gauge how pessimistic or optimistic people are about the economy and the state of employment. In all fairness, The Conference Board is a highly respected organization that Alan Greenspan, himself, once was associated with, and many of its reports on the economy are truly insightful. The Conference Board also adds an important private-sector analysis of the economy, complementing government statistics.

Let's take a look at another sentiment number: the University of Michigan's "Consumer Sentiment Survey," an index with the "100" reading set to the first quarter of 1966. Again, looking at a recent survey from December 2001, the Michigan Sentiment Index stood at 85.8, up two points from the previous month. Economic pundits seeing this report said it offered some hope that the economy might be recovering from the dark days of the late third quarter and early fourth quarter of 2001. Further, the apparent recovery evident in the Michigan Sentiment Index was contrary to the increased pessimism in The Conference Board's Consumer Confidence Index. This divergence confused retailers who were hoping for a holiday miracle to produce a profitable fourth quarter.

These reports often conflict with each other in any given month because of the sample size of 500 versus 5000, the types of questions asked, and most importantly the time of month the surveys are conducted. While I contend that the actual economy doesn't change from day to day or even week to week, sometimes events, such as rate hikes, or reductions, or newsworthy events, can change the perception about the economy. Therefore, consumers' feelings about the economy could change from one week to the next. However, despite these shortcomings and contradictions, the overall direction of the indicators does tend to be consistent.

The "Michigan Sentiment Report" was initially commissioned by the auto industry to get a read on demand for new cars. The data was analyzed to help auto companies smooth out production schedules. The leap from this to evaluating the overall economy is a large one. Buying a car can have many factors associated with it, which may not reveal a consumer's true feeling about the overall economy. For one, if your 1985 Olds Cutlass is on its last leg and you need it for work, or to take the kids to school and to soccer, or to help you care for a loved one, then this purchase might have a priority over other purchases. As a result, you might make this car purchase instead of another that is nearly as significant, or instead of making a lot of other little purchases.

The question remains just how accurate, and therefore significant, are the sentiment or confidence reports? While it may be a good hint at how people are feeling, and therefore an indication of how they may act, their actions are far more important. In fact, there is a bigger correlation between increases in actual consumer spending foreshadowing a more positive consumer confidence/sentiment reading, than the inverse. That's why, while many economists place a lot of significance in these reports, it is hard for me to put much credence in them. These reports are created based on interviews of people who answered the phone in a random poll, and there is no assurance that this represents a valid cross section of consumers.

Additionally, many of the responses generated by these surveys clearly reflect recent headlines in the media, whether gloomy or euphoric. Economists like to say, with tongue in cheek, that consumer confidence numbers have predicted something like six of the last two recessions. Further, the trend in consumer confidence is also less effective because the surveys poll different consumers each time.

That being said, there are some good data in these numbers. This is particularly true when it comes to future expectations, which is most likely less impacted by recent market moves and headlines and therefore may give at least some sense of how the average Jimmy and Amy feel about the future.

Since consumer spending is such a driving force for the U.S. economy, it is important to take a look at how and in what ways we can measure this. While sentiment has some meaning, the proverbial actions speak louder than words. Income levels have the highest impact on consumer spending, since the average consumer spends almost 95 cents for every dollar earned.

The reports that yield more meaningful data about consumers—the "beef" of the hamburger, as it were—are those that measure activity. Retail sales, home sales (new and existing), and services—which includes everything from day spas to medical service and is reflected in the PCE (Personal Consumption Expenditures)—and auto sales. These reports reflect the kind of consumer action that drives the economy. Further, the relative level of interest rates affects them all, because many of these purchases are financed. Let's take these reports one by one.

RETAIL SALES

The "Retail Sales Report" measures consumer activity. Nondurable goods make up 60 percent of sales, while durable goods account for 40 percent. Retail sales on a whole make up almost 50 percent of all consumer spending. Trends in this report are very meaningful to economic activity. However, as we break down this report into the two major categories we see many areas of extreme volatility. There are the durables, which are goods built to last 3 years or longer (not to be confused with durable goods orders for manufacturing), and there are the nondurables. On the nondurable side of retail sales, the report has the least long-term impact, because it reflects disposable income, unlike durable goods, which, after their purchase, may trigger further purchases (i.e., accessories). Also, food and energy prices, such as for milk and gasoline, are usually factored out of the report because of their extreme volatility in both demand and prices.

Further, the total retail sales number is quite volatile, and therefore shouldn't be viewed as a one-time snapshot but rather in the context of several months. A strong retail sales number followed by a comparatively weaker one means very little, as a sale in one month (due to promotions, holidays, and so forth) can pull sales away from the subsequent month. I mean, how many Gap sweaters (which would show up in the nondurable side of retail sales) do you need? If you bought two this month, are you going to buy two more next month? By the same token, factors such as extreme weather conditions can defer sales from one month to another, leading to statistical aberrations.

The durable goods side of retail sales, which includes furniture and appliances, is mostly made up of the very volatile auto sales number. But since this is almost always factored out as retail sales "ex-autos" (meaning retail sales excluding autos), that leaves very little on the durable goods side. Thus, the report's significance to long-term spending trends and long-term indications of the direction of the economy are much less supported by this report. It is a nice snapshot, however, of how the consumer is feeling today and certainly of how he or she felt about last month's income. This, as you probably gathered by now, is important to our analysis as we make assumptions that the status quo will continue until new factors arise to change it.

Let's take a look at some recent "Retail Sales Reports" for the kind of information that they can yield. The report for November 2001 showed a dramatic drop, with retail and food service sales falling 2.9 percent—the worst monthly performance in at least 9 years. This decline followed strong sales in October, which showed a 6.4 percent increase. The "Retail Sales Report" for November 2001 was closely watched for a couple of important reasons: For one, economists and savvy investors alike were looking for evidence of whether consumers were going into full-blown holiday shopping mode. The fourth quarter of the year is when retailers reap most of their sales and, as a result, make most of their money. But for that to happen, consumers have to flock to the stores and buy.

Consumer behavior is always closely watched, since it accounts for two-thirds of GDP, which brings us to the second reason why retail sales were scrutinized in late 2001. After September 11, consumer spending became even more of a focal point given the state of the U.S. economy and the economy of the world at large. If consumers are too nervous about their jobs or worried about national security issues to spend, or at least to spend freely, then that spells trouble for the economy.

Still, a month does not provide the entire picture. A notably good or bad report still has to be viewed within the context of what was actually happening. For example, vehicle sales dropped considerably in November 2001. October 2001 retail sales were strong largely due to auto sales, which were the direct result of dealer incentives. With "0 percent" financing offers, which resulted in interest-free loans to buy a new car, truck, or SUV, auto dealerships were busy. Dealers needed to move inventory, even if the resulting sales price was not as economically favorable to them as it was to the consumer. Car shoppers, being no dummies, saw it made much more sense to buy a new car for essentially the same monthly payment they were already making on the 2-, 3-, or 4-year old vehicle they were driving. Of course, this left the auto dealers with a growing inventory of used cars at time when they were aggressively pushing new vehicles.

Meanwhile, if you factor out motor vehicle and parts sales, November's retail sales were about flat. As you can see in Chart 7-1, retail and food services, excluding autos, showed a 0.2 percent change in November 2001 from October, which were up (ex-autos) 1.1 percent from the previous month. The previous drop, ex-autos, occurred in September 2001, when sales declined 1.3 percent. The decline was expected given the disruption to consumers' lives and to businesses due to the terrorist attacks.

Looking at the categories in the retail sales charts, we can see that motor vehicle and parts sales were off about 10 percent compared with October. Thus, even though 0 percent financing brought consumers to the dealerships in October, the immediate demand was satisfied, and the pace of those incentive-driven sales had slowed.

Further, clothing and accessories dropped 1.9 percent from the previous month, which is not the kind of performance that retailers

CHART 7-1 National Retail Sales (month-to-month % change, SA)

	Nov-01	Oct-01	Sep-01	Aug-01	Jul-01	Jun-01	May-01	Apr-01
Retail & food services	-2.6	6.2	-2.1	0.3	0.2	0.0	0.2	1.4
Ex-autos	0.2	1.1	-1.3	0.3	0.1	-0.2	0.3	0.9
Motor vehicle & parts dealers	-9.7	22.6	-4.5	0.1	0.6	0.6	-0.1	2.9
Furniture & home furnishing stores	3.4	1.2	-3.0	0	-0.2	0.2	1.0	-0.6
Electronics & appliance stores	5.0	1.9	-1.4	1.2	0.3	1.3	0.5	0.3
Building material dealers	-0.2	2.3	-1.9	-0.1	0.1	-0.2	-1.4	3.0
Food & beverage stores	0.5	0.3	0.6	0.2	0.4	-0.2	0.7	-0.1
Clothing & accessories stores	1.9	5.8	-5.1	-0.7	1.5	-0.3	-1.3	0.2
General merchandise stores	1.0	1.5	-0.3	0.4	0.5	0.4	-1.2	2.6
Food services & drinking places	0.7	0.4	-2.4	0.7	0.2	0.7	1.0	0.0

Source: Economy.com

want to report a month before Christmas. Curiously, unseasonably warm weather was reported to be hurting Christmas shopping. I know that in places like Chicago a few flakes of snow do help to produce that "holiday feeling." But instead, if it's 60 degrees in December, are you not going to buy your kids any Barbies, Nintendoes, GI Joes, or Legos? You may not be dreaming of a white Christmas, but eventually you'll have to make your trek to the mall to shop regardless of the weather conditions. If retailers, concerned about inventory levels, slash prices *before* Christmas, then consumers will have no excuse to be Grinches—that is, unless consumers are concerned about the economy in general and about their jobs in particular and keep spending to a minimum.

One bright spot in the November report was furniture and home furnishings, which showed a 3.4 percent gain in sales. However, this may be a result of a strong housing market in the summer.

With food services and drinking places showing a mere 0.5 percent rise in sales in November, perhaps more of us were staying home, which enabled us to see just how tacky that sofa in the living room looked. This, in turn, might have sparked a little home-improvement boomlet. Who knows! Kidding aside, economists and financial journalists love to hypothesize about the numbers. While that may make for some interesting TV chatter, the fact remains that the numbers measuring consumer sales say it all. Shoppers are buying or they're not. Consumers are spending or they're not. No matter the reason, rhyme, sentiment, or confidence level, when consumers take out their wallets, that's when things really getting interesting, as well as economically significant.

If there is one thing that a study of consumer spending will show, it's that you should never underestimate the power of a person with a dollar in his or her pocket to spend. We saw this throughout 2001 as aggressive rate cuts by the Fed did not spur the economy, which slipped into recession officially in March. Rather, attention turned quickly to consumers who were either going to make or break economic recovery.

This was a lesson we had learned some 20 years before when the virtues and vices of "Reaganomics" were hotly debated. The challenge was how to stimulate the economy without sparking inflation. The answer from the Reagan administration was to put more money in consumers' pockets through tax cuts. But before that step was taken, the case had to be made that cutting taxes would result in more money being pumped into the economy. A study of consumer spending and saving habits overwhelming showed the connection. For every $1.00 in tax rebate, consumers could be expected to spend $1.10! That means that the tax savings not only would go into the economy in the form of purchases, but that consumers (particularly high-income ones) would be more than willing to take on additional debt to buy a little more.

Thus, the Reagan administration saw that to spur $1 billion in spending, they didn't need to cut $1 billion in taxes. Rather, they could enact, say, $900 million or so in tax cuts, and they'd get their $1 billion in additional spending. But the money had to go into the "right" pockets in order for that spending rate to occur. In general, high-income consumers are more apt to spend $1.10 for every extra $1.00 in their pockets, while those in lower-income brackets would likely spend 90 cents of every dollar and save 10 cents. This is a prime example of one of the laws of a consumer economy: 20 percent of the population spends 80 percent of the money.

VEHICLES SALES

If a retailer marks down merchandise, you might be tempted to buy two sweaters instead of one. Or you could be so enticed by the sale prices that you buy one in white, one in black, and one in blue. After all, you wear clothes every day and you probably like a little variety in your wardrobe. But when it comes to a new car, are you going to be so motivated by 0 percent financing that you decide to buy two? Not likely. Hence, the story that was revealed in vehicle sales reports for November 2001. While sales were comparatively strong in November, as incentives continued to pull in buyers, the results were down from October's blockbuster levels. November vehicle sales amounted to 18 million units, down from 21.3 million in October (see Chart 7-2).

Looking at the vehicle sales breakdown in the chart, you can see that light trucks outpaced cars. As anyone who has driven or ridden on a highway lately can tell you, consumers are enamored with the "light truck" concept, even if they're only hauling kids and groceries.

CHART 7-2 Vehicle Sales (in millions, SAAR)

	Nov-01	Oct-01	Sep-01	Aug-01	Jul-01	Jun-01	May-01	Apr-01
Total vehicle sales	18.0	21.3	15.9	16.5	16.5	17.3	16.5	16.6
Autos	8.6	10.2	7.7	8.1	8.1	8.4	8.3	8.5
Light truck	9.4	11.1	8.2	8.5	8.4	8.8	8.2	8.2

Source:Economy.com

That's also a factor of lower gasoline prices, since it takes more fuel to fly down the highway in your SUV than in a two-door coupe.

Taking these vehicle sales into consideration—with 2 strong months posted back to back in October and November 2001—you would have to ask yourself the important question: What would the impact be on demand next year? If you bought a new car or truck in November 2001, would you turn around and buy another one in February 2002? Unlike those Gap sweaters or Old Navy sweatshirts, if you like your new blue SUV, are you going to go back and get a red one? Vehicle incentives that moved inventory in late 2001 just displaced sales that would have occurred in 2002.

HOUSING SALES

One of my favorite "consumer behavior" statistics is housing sales. While much is made about the correlation between mortgage rates and housing sales, I think that this connection is sometimes too simplistic. While favorable mortgage rates might spur some new-home buying, I don't think people automatically decide to move because they can get a 6¾ percent rate instead of the 7½ percent rate they now have. Rather, I believe that low mortgage rates spark refinancing of the homes that consumers already own. The only direct link between mortgage rates and buying a new or existing home is that consumers may be more inclined to buy "up." In other words, if your budget is for a $200,000 house, with mortgage rates low you might be inclined to look at $250,000 houses, since your monthly payment would be about the same.

I believe housing sales are the result of consumers overall willingness to buy a first home or a bigger or newer one. This willingness comes from only one thing: a sense of security about the economy and one's own job. If you fear being laid off next month, you're probably not going to buy a bigger, more expensive house this month. Or if you're renting an apartment, you probably won't take that next big step toward home ownership until you feel confident that you can afford the payments. In other words, if you're looking for a direct reflection of overall consumer attitude toward the economy and their employment, look at housing sales. Further, housing sales typically spark a rise in sales of related products, including durable goods such as appliances, furniture, electronics, and lawn and garden products.

That being said, let's take a look at a recent report for existing home sales for October 2001, which showed a 5.2 percent increase from September's drop. As Chart 7-3 shows, October's existing home sales amounted to 5.27 million units, up from 5.01 million units in September and more in line with the levels seen earlier in the year.

October's rise from September's level (as shown in Chart 7-3) clearly illustrates the concept of home sales as a barometer not only of real estate activity, but also of consumer confidence and sentiment. Even if you are not in danger of losing your job, economic uncertainty would likely lead you to "sit and wait" a little while longer. In September, the emotional as well as the economic upheaval from the terrorist attacks impacted home sales. As life went back to normal (or as close to normal as could be expected given the magnitude of the tragedy), home shoppers went back to business.

New home sales, meanwhile, also showed an increase in October 2001 compared with September levels. October 2001 sales of new homes rose to 860,000 units from 854,000 in September. Further, October new home sales were in line with levels seen earlier in the year (see Chart 7-4). In general, most regions of the country, with the exception of the Midwest, showed higher sales where one might presume that a concern over manufacturing, transportation, and airline jobs could have put a lid on demand.

Looking at the new home sales over the course of several months (as shown in Chart 7-4), you can see that demand has been brisk. No doubt mortgage rates in the 7 percent area did entice buyers who were already thinking of buying a new home to take that step. But the housing market moves in cycles. While we might trade in our cars fairly frequently, most of us don't buy a new house every year or every few years. Thus, it would make sense that at some point the housing market will slow as demand wanes and the inventory of houses declines.

There is another important factor when it comes to the housing market: For most of us, our home is our largest asset and our largest debt. Think about it. The biggest debt you have is probably your mortgage. And the biggest asset you have is the equity you carry in

CHART 7-3 Existing Home Sales (in millions, SAAR)

	Oct-01	Sep-01	Aug-01	Jul-01	Jun-01	May-01	Apr-01	Mar-01
Units	5.27	5.01	5.49	5.30	5.30	5.36	5.22	5.43
Monthly % chg.	5.2	−8.7	−3.6	0.00	−1.9	2.7	−3.9	4.6

Source:Economy.com

CHART 7-4 National and Regional Home Sales (in thousands, SAAR)

	Nov-01	Oct-01	Sep-01	Aug-01	Jul-01	Jun-01	May-01	Apr-01
National	937	860	854	871	871	889	882	899
Northeast	67	64	52	64	70	61	55	71
Midwest	176	150	162	150	150	170	152	163
South	483	433	429	426	426	423	439	424
West	211	213	211	231	231	235	236	241
Fixed Mortgage Rate	6.66	6.62	6.82	6.82	7.13	7.16	7.14	7.08

Source: Economy.com

your home. Take the example of Albert and Susie, a two-income Brooklyn family that has $140,000 in equity in their home due to rising housing values in the area. This is 8 to 10 times what they have in savings (excluding their retirement and 401(k) accounts). This is the wealth effect from the housing market that has been closely watched, particularly by Greenspan's Fed.

In the Fed's report entitled "Economic and Financial Developments in 2000 and early 2001," it was noted that "real outlays for residential investment declined about 2¼ percent, on net, over the course of 2000 as construction of new housing dropped back from the elevated level of the previous year." Housing investment, the Fed noted, was influenced by a "sizable swing in mortgage interest rates" as well by slower growth of employment and income and a downturn in the stock market. Keep in mind that this report, released in February 2001, was well before the recession of 2001 officially hit (which was pegged at March 2001) and some 7 months before the terrorist attacks.

"But even as homebuilding activity was turning down, conditions in mortgage markets were moving back in a direction more favorable to housing," the report added. "From the peak in May (2000), mortgage interest rates fell substantially over the remainder of the year and into the early part of 2001, reversing the earlier increases."

This contributed to an increase in household borrowings. "For the year 2000 as a whole, consumer credit is estimated to have advanced more than 8½ percent, up from the 7 percent pace of 1999," the report added. "Households also took on large amounts of mortgage debt, which grew an estimated 9 percent last year, reflecting the solid pace of home sales."

The Fed's attention to housing sales and household debt is obvious. The consumer's willingness to make the commitment to purchase new housing or an existing home reflects, as I stated earlier in this chapter, a confidence about the economy and the consumer's own employment situation. Further, the level of debt is watched carefully by the Fed, since the specter of consumer loan default or credit card debt could spell trouble down the road.

As Fed Chairman Greenspan stated in his February 28, 2001, testimony before the Congressional Committee on Financial Services, consumer confidence will require close scrutiny in the period ahead, especially after the steep falloff of recent months.

"But for now, at least," Greenspan noted in the February 2001 comments, "the weakness in sales of motor vehicles and homes has been modest, suggesting that consumers have retained enough confidence to make longer-term commitments..."

This evidence of consumer willingness to make "longer-term commitments" was vital given the fact that the stock market had already turned down sharply. As Greenspan put it in his testimony, "Even consumer spending decisions have become increasingly responsive to changes in the perceived profitability of firms through their effects on the value of households' holdings of equities. Stock market wealth has risen substantially relative to income in recent years—itself a reflection of the extraordinary surge of innovation. As a consequence, changes in stock market wealth have become a more important determinant of shifts in consumer spending relative to changes in current household income than was the case just 5 to 7 years ago."

Later in 2001, when the recession, rising unemployment, and the events of September 11 took their toll on the economy and on consumer spending, the Fed kept a close watch on the housing market. While the stock market decline did take a bit off the "wealth" (at least on paper) reflected in investment portfolios, the housing market kept its value. Given the size of this asset, the retention of value in housing was vital to give any spark of hope for consumer spending, which would, in the end, be the life preserver that a sinking economy was grasping for.

Evaluating the confidence of consumers and their spending patterns is important to monitoring the well-being of the economy. Retail sales, particularly the nondurable goods side, illustrate how the consumer is feeling today. Consumer confidence numbers actually tell us how the consumer felt yesterday, but they give us little insight into what they will buy or how much they will spend in the future. Interestingly, consumer sentiment goes up after big purchases are made, but usually not before.

The durable goods side of retail sales, along with housing starts and home sales, carries a larger message for the economy moving forward. These larger purchases require a feeling of stronger financial security and, when made, lead to more purchases and increased consumer spending, which in turn leads to further growth and productivity.

Watch consumers' big purchases and little ones, because you, the consumer, have a greater impact on the economy than most market analysts and economists do. Maybe you're more important than even the Fed itself. After all, it can lower rates, but it can't make you buy a home microwave and stereo. You can lead a horse to water, but you can't make it buy a barn.

8

The Producers

ECONOMIC FAIRYTALE, VERSION 1

Once upon a time, in a tiny kingdom isolated from the rest of the world, the people were largely self-sufficient. They raised their own crops and livestock, made their own clothes and shoes, and gathered firewood from the forest. Then one day, while dragging their carts of hay and vegetables along the ground, one of the villagers named Paul got the idea that a round object attached to the cart could help it roll along. The more he thought about it, the more he decided that this would make life a lot easier. So he cut down a tree, sawed the trunk crosswise to yield wooden discs. He mounted four of these wooden discs on the bottom of his cart, using a pole to connect them, two across, which also let them turn freely. When Paul pulled his cart through town, he created quite a stir. All the other villagers clamored for these wooden disc things until the point that demand was so strong, the villager began to make them for other people.

Moral of the story: The consumers created the demand and the producer responded with the product.

ECONOMIC FAIRYTALE, VERSION 2

Once upon a time, in a tiny kingdom isolated from the rest of the world, the people were largely self-sufficient. They raised their own crops and livestock, made their own clothes and shoes, and gathered firewood from the forest. Then one day a stranger named Dennis came to town, peddling goods brought from far away. He saw the villagers dragging their carts along the rocky and hilly ground. His peddler's cart, however, moved easily along the ground because of these wooden disc things he had mounted on the bottom. If he could make more of them, the villagers would buy all he could make.

So Dennis set up his Ye Olde Wooden Disc Shop, sawing trees, cutting the discs, and shaping the poles to connect them to carts. Then he waited for the villagers to come along and buy. No one came. They were so used to dragging their carts along the ground that they didn't see the need to change things. Dennis, however, was a visionary. He knew that if the villagers would just give these wooden discs a test drive, they'd be hooked. He cut his prices in half and had Saturday specials. But no one came. Undaunted, he offered a promotion to bring the villagers in—a pound of headcheese and a dram of grog for every test drive. Being no fools and being particularly fond of headcheese and grog, the villagers flocked to Ye Olde Wooden Disc Shop. They tested the wooden discs, and they were hooked.

Moral of the story: The producer had vision and anticipated demand.

* * *

In economics, sometimes the producer is the chicken, and sometimes the producer is the egg. Consumers can create demand to which producers respond, or producers entice consumers, which results in demand. The important thing to remember is that for every product, there must be a producer and a consumer. You can't have one without the other. Additionally, it helps if the product is adding value or in some way is making life easier or more efficient for the consumer, and at a price that is fair. After all, no matter how much consumers are enticed to buy "X," if there were never a true need or demand for "X" it would become a collector's item. (As a case in point, one of the most notable flops in automotive history—the Edsel—has a Web site devoted to Edsel collectors, fans, and devotees.)

Moreover, everything—whether it's an Edsel, an egg carton, or the ergonomically correct chair I'm sitting in—requires an input of capital and labor, which ends up as output of finished goods sold to the consumer. The consumer is able to buy it because he or she has converted labor or capital into spending power. And so the wheel goes 'round.

As discussed in Chapter 7, there are many factors that influence consumer purchases, from pent-up demand to price incentives. Clearly, the consumer is king. But without the producer, the consumer would still be using flint tools (or dragging a wheelless cart along the ground). In economic terms, if consumer spending represents two-thirds of economic activity, then producers are fulfilling two-thirds of that output for consumers.

It comes down to what I call the economic family tree. Producer efficiencies and profit margins directly impact the price they charge, which in turn plays a role in spurring demand. Equally as important is the selection of products made available, which is why retailers, in particular, spend so much time surveying consumers to find out why they bought, what they did buy, and why they didn't buy something.

When I'm looking at producer numbers—such as the Institute for Supply Management (formerly the National Association of Purchasing Management or NAPM) report—I'm trying to measure producers' impressions of demand based upon the consumer activity that they see. Further, I'm also looking to gauge the actual demand they are measuring. Just as in the consumer numbers, impressions may be helpful to predict activity, but actions are far more important.

Producers perform two vitally important tasks: they produce because there is demand for what they are making. Or, as we saw in 1999 and 2000, they produce because it has become economically advantageous to do so. In other words, it made more sense to produce than not to produce because certain efficiencies and other factors had reduced the cost involved. For example, back in late 1999 and early 2000, based on demand alone, there was no reason to ramp-up production of DRAM. But DRAM (dynamic random access memory, the heart of all computer hard drives) prices were heading down. At the same time, the labor market was very tight, which put a premium on keeping workers on the job. The Mr.

companies can focus on selling their excess inventories. Thus, when the inventory levels get to a low enough level and demand begins to pick up, production increases, workers are hired (or rehired if they were laid off), and the economy picks up steam.

While the reports did not show the U.S. economy to be in a state of recovery, given the evidence of the reduction in inventories, hopes were raised for an eventual recovery.

For investor/consumer and economist alike, there are two important questions that sum up most economic analysis: If the economy is doing well, how long will it last? If the economy is doing poorly, when will things get better? At the risk of oversimplifying, I think most economic analysis can be reduced to the pursuit of answers to those two questions. Certainly through the 1999-early 2000 bubble, any economist worth his or her salt would have been asking the question "When is this runaway economic train going to slow down?" We know that the Fed was pursuing a tightening policy only to have the bubble burst, the market plummet, and the economy slip into recession.

INDUSTRIAL PRODUCTION AND CAPACITY UTILIZATION

Looking at the economy from an "output" standpoint, two factors come into play: how much is being produced and what does it take to produce it? Those answers are found in the "Industrial Production and Capacity Utilization Report" from the Federal Reserve. The issue is how much of our resources, including labor and industrial capacity, are we using to make what we need. In layman's terms, do we have the pedal to the metal cranking out goods as fast as we can, or is the industrial engine idling a bit? How much capacity being utilized is a direct reflection of what we're producing. What we're producing is, by and large, a direct reflection for the amount of demand that's in the marketplace (or perceived in the marketplace). Even when inventories are being built, as we saw in 1999 because it's cheaper to produce than not to produce, it's still a reflection of demand because if inventories build to excessive levels, the production spigot will have to be turned off or at least turned down.

Capacity utilization, as one might guess, is expressed as a percentage. Optimum capacity—full power and all pistons firing—is in the mid- to high-80s. According to Federal Reserve statistics, the average of capacity utilization for 1967 through 2000 is 82.1 percent. The high was 85.4 in 1988-89. Conversely, the low was 71.1 percent in 1982. At this rate, some 30 percent of capacity was unused, meaning factories and production facilities had production lines idled and equipment and workers functioning at a slow and often inefficient rate.

At first glance, it may surprise the average person that 85 percent-plus is considered full capacity. If you were filling, say, a canteen and declared it full at 85 percent, you might find yourself 15 percent thirsty somewhere down the trail. But capacity utilization should not be thought of as something that's half empty or half full. A better mental picture is the tachometer that measures how fast your engine is going. When the tachometer needle is comfortably in the low numbers, then you know your engine is humming along regardless of whether you're doing 25 miles an hour down a residential street or 55 on the highway. When you "floor it" and the tachometer needle jumps into the red at the far right of the gauge, your engine is probably roaring—and potentially sounding pretty strained. That's not the kind of "engine utilization" level you want for the safe and smooth operation of your car.

Similarly for industrial facilities and factories, the mid-to-high-80 percent level is an efficient, optimum level at which most demand is met—but there may be some additional demand to reach for if conditions persist. And, usually by the time a company gets to and sustains capacity utilization in the mid-to-high-80 percent level, plant engineers and company management are looking to add something to the capacity equation—more labor or a new production line or entire new facility. When that's added, the percentage of capacity being utilized will automatically drop.

Industrial production, on the other hand, measures output as an index set at the 1992 average. As production increases or decreases, the output index rises or falls. (For example, in November 2001, industrial production was at 137.1 percent of its 1992 average, down from 137.6 in October and off 5.9 percent from the year before.)

Another factor in industrial production and capacity utilization is the role that productivity measures have played. With better technology, automation, and inventory management tools, productivity has increased. More output can be produced with the same or even less utilization (see Chart 8-1). Throughout the 1970s and 1980s, for example, a lot of older, less efficient manufacturing capacity was "retired" and newer, advanced production capacity and technology was employed. As a result, output increased, but at lower levels of capacity, which is an advantageous position for a company to be in.

Producers seem to be either cutting back production to an extreme, thinking the demand is gone forever, or else they are ramping up for some sort of insatiable consumer demand and then cutting back again. This ramp up or cutback in production cycles reminds me of a game one of my professors had his economics students play back at the University of Michigan. We were divided into teams of four and were instructed to market and create a production schedule for beer. The professor represented the consumer. At first, he demanded one beer for $1. We could produce beer in our hypothetical brewery for 50 cents, and at this demand rate we did not need to keep any inventory. Since the cost of keeping inventory was 10 cents, we could pocket 50 cents for every beer we sold fresh out of our "supply."

Then the professor increased his demand to two beers. We decided to ramp up production, and many of us thought we were smart when we started to warehouse the beer. Then suddenly, he was only willing to pay 90 cents for a beer. My team sold it to him happily because we had it in stock and we had to move our inventory. The other teams, trying to cut in on our action, decided to sell beer at 80 cents. The price-conscious consumer showed no loyalty.

Then without warning, our consumer decreased demand to only one beer. My team responded by cutting prices to 70 cents (we had to move inventory), only to have another team cut prices to 60 cents. To make a long story short, there we were with our hypothetical breweries operating at full capacity, inventories building, and a price war erupting all because the professor increased consumption temporarily by one bottle of beer. None of us had waited to see if the increase in demand was sustainable, or even to consider the cost of building inventories versus not producing. All we were focused on was selling that one extra bottle of beer.

When it comes to a real-world example of this kind of short-sightedness, you don't have to look any further than the technology

CHART 8-1 Comparison of Industrial Production, Capacity Utilization, and Gross Domestic Product (in hundreds)

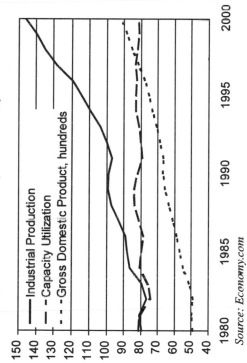

Source: *Economy.com*

production bubble of the late 1990s. As discussed in Chapter 6, when it was cheaper to produce rather than scale back and risk losing experienced workers, that's exactly what many companies did— build inventories that would later contribute heavily to an economic slowdown. Thus, it's not much of a stretch to see how changes in capacity utilization and industrial production can be a prelude to changes in GDP, and then in turn to changes in employment. If capacity utilization declines, output will also drop, and then it probably won't be long before layoffs occur. Conversely, with increases in capacity utilization, industrial production also rises, which usually leads to more hiring.

SUPPLY MANAGERS' REPORT

The Institute for Supply Management (ISM) publishes an "ear to the ground" report that is based upon a survey of supply managers who report on the activity at their businesses and their near-term prospects. Like consumer spending numbers, the "ISM Report" is important because it measures actual activity, not just what is anticipated to happen. The no-nonsense report measures things like production levels, orders, exports, and so forth, giving a snapshot of industrial and business activity across the country. Not surprisingly, there is a close correlation to what we see in GDP statistics and what the ISM indicates as actual output.

As always, the best way to evaluate an indicator is to take a look at a sample report. For the month of November 2001, the index rose to 44.7 percent, showing a recovery from October lows at 39.5 percent. However, this continued the trend (see Chart 8-2) of an index reading below 50 percent, a level that is considered critical to indicating recovery. ISM is a diffusion index, meaning levels below 50 show contraction and levels above 50 indicate expansion. While 42 is better than 32, both show signs of contraction. A reading of 65 is better than a reading of 55, but the importance is that manufacturing is expanding.

Manufacturing is less important to the U.S. economy today than it was a generation ago. Further, this sector can be in a recession while the overall economy is still expanding, as was the case during most of 2000. However, if manufacturing stays below 50 or contracts for extended periods of time, generally the rest of the economy will slow dramatically or even go into a full recession.

As Chart 8-2 indicates, there was recovery in several areas measured by ISM, including new orders, production, and backlog of orders. Inventories ticked up slightly from October to November, while employment held roughly steady. While new export orders also increased by more than four percentage points, it, too, was below the 50 percent level due to weakness in the world economy.

ISM surveys also yield semi-annual forecasts that project trends for the upcoming 6 months. While it is important not to "bet the farm" on forecasts based on sentiments and projections, do not discount them either. They provide a "heads up" of what may lie ahead, although for my economic analysis and investment model I'd rather base decisions on actual data.

In its *62nd Semiannual Economic Forecast* released in December 2001, the ISM projected that "economic growth in the United States will resume in 2002." While that sounded good to those awaiting heralds of the recovery, there was a caveat: "Expectations for 2002 are higher in the non-manufacturing sector, but both sectors are less optimistic about the coming year. While this is somewhat of a mixed message, the overall prediction is for resumption of economic growth after the downturn experienced in 2001."

Mixed message, indeed! Things are going to get better, but maybe not as good as we had hoped. As with every economic report, you have to look beyond just the headline that may overstate or oversimplify the prediction. Just as in Chapter 7, we saw that auto sales could sway the "Retail Sales Report," which means that most of us look at this number ex-autos.

Since the "ISM Report" is based upon a survey of supply or purchasing managers, the actual results are included. As the report stated, "Looking forward to 2002, 59 percent of survey respondents expect revenues to be greater than in 2001, when 66 percent expected revenues to be greater than in 2000." In other words, slightly over half of those surveyed expect a rise in revenues in 2002, which compares with about two-thirds who had expected a rise in revenues for 2001. Given the recession in 2001, those two-thirds were wrong. However, the panel of purchasing and supply executives expects a

CHART 8-2 ISM, (Index, SA)

	Nov-01	Oct-01	Sep-01	Aug-01	Jul-01	Jun-01	May-01	Apr-01
Purchasing Managers' Index	44.7	39.5	46.2	47.9	43.9	44.3	42.1	43.2
New orders	48.4	38.0	49.0	53.1	47.3	47.9	45.5	45.9
Prices paid	32.0	33.3	36.6	35.0	39.9	42.8	45.2	48.9
Production	48.2	40.4	49.7	52.3	46.2	45.6	42.7	42.9
Backlog of orders	38.5	36.0	43.0	44.5	42.5	42.0	40.0	43.5
Supplier deliveries	47.8	48.7	46.8	46.6	47.1	47.6	45.7	47.4
Inventories	37.9	37.3	38.6	37.6	36.6	40.2	38.7	39.6
Employment	35.7	34.9	40.8	40.8	37.1	36.6	35.0	38.1
New export orders	48.6	45.3	46.1	51.7	48.2	45.7	45.6	47.3
Imports	49.9	45.8	49.9	49.5	48.0	48.1	46.6	47.2

Source: Economy.com

3.2 percent net increase in overall revenues for 2002, compared to an actual decrease of 2.3 percent reported for 2001. Just as with the consumer sentiment and confidence numbers discussed in Chapter 7, what is projected may not be borne out. What is always more important is actual activity.

CHICAGO PURCHASING MANAGERS

While the "ISM Report" provides a national "barometer reading" for business and industry, there are important regional reports. The Chicago Purchasing Managers' Index (PMI) is important largely because it is released ahead of the ISM and may be a predictor of what the national report will read. Like ISM, the Chicago PMI is a regional survey of purchasing managers.

For example, the Chicago PMI in November 2001 fell to 42.7, its lowest level since July 2001. Unlike the ISM, the Chicago index did not show a recovery from October to November. However, since ISM had already dropped dramatically in October (to 39.5 from 46.2 in September), the national survey had not been expected to decline even though the Chicago index continued to soften (see Chart 8-3).

Like its national counterpart, the Chicago PMI remained well below the 50 percent level, showing the continued weakness in manufacturing, as you can see in Chart 8-3. In fact, with readings between the upper 30s to low 40s for several consecutive months, the report yielded little hope of a manufacturing or an industrial recovery in the near term.

Looking at the Chicago PMI readings, the weakness in manufacturing and industrial activity is evident since early 2001. While much attention has been paid to the economic slowdown that occurred after the September 11 terrorist attacks, a glance at the Chicago PMI shows that the industrial and manufacturing sector was weak for much of the year.

"BEIGE BOOK"

Named presumably for the color of its cover, the Federal Reserve's "Beige Book" is officially known as "Summary of Commentary on Current Economic Conditions." The most important thing about the "Beige Book" is that it provides a survey across various business sectors,

CHART 8-3 Chicago Purchasing Managers Index

	Nov-01	Oct-01	Sep-01	Aug-01	Jul-01	Jun-01	May-01	Apr-01
Index	42.7	44.6	44.9	43.6	38.1	42.6	39.2	38.9

Source: Economy.com

as well as across several regions. The November 28, 2001, "Beige Book" Report, for example, noted that "economic activity generally remained soft in October and the first half of November, with evidence of additional slowing in most regions outweighing signs of recovery in a few districts.

"Manufacturing activity weakened further, with declines in production, new orders, and employment widely reported," it added. "Consumer spending was mixed—aggressive financing incentives drove automobile and light truck sales to exceptional levels, but tourism remained weak and non-auto sales were spotty, with stronger sales growth in some areas offset by weaker sales elsewhere. Retailers' outlook for spending during the upcoming holiday season was also mixed."

Does that all sound familiar? It should, since many other economic reports, from GDP to ISM to retail sales to consumer confidence, yielded many of the same types of comments. Economic data when reviewed as a whole does produce some overlap, but, more important, it builds a consensus. What we're making and buying or not making and not buying as a nation may fluctuate. But when consistencies yield trends and those trends can be studied over a period of weeks or months, then the real "activity" is revealed.

As an investor, you don't want to make a snap decision to sell a particular stock out of your portfolio just based on one comment that the economy may be doing this or that. But a view based upon economic data that clearly indicates what part of the business cycle we're in and what industries may or may not be favored could lead you to an investment decision regarding, say, growth stocks or more defensive issues.

PHILADELPHIA FED

Another closely watched regional survey is the Business Outlook Survey put out by the Federal Reserve Bank of Philadelphia, better known as the "Philly Fed Report." This regional index looks at business conditions and manufacturing activity in Pennsylvania, New Jersey, and Delaware. Unlike the scale used in the ISM and Chicago PMI, the "Philly Fed Report" has a "general business condition index" that shows expansion when the index is above zero and contraction when it is below zero. Like the Chicago PMI, the Philly Fed is considered a predictor of what the "ISM Report" will show for the nation.

The Philly Fed Survey in the fall of 2001 also showed contraction in the manufacturing sector, with a reading of minus 18.5 in November (well below the zero line of demarcation for expansion), although it was improved from the October level of minus 28.5. This mirrors what was later reported for the ISM for November, with manufacturing still down but somewhat improved. And as was seen for all the purchasing manager surveys, the contraction was evident from early 2001.

What will we be looking for? Clearly, the first solid signs of hope will be dramatic up ticks in readings for the Chicago PMI and Philly Fed, which will lead to much improved readings for the ISM national index. With the U.S. economy officially in a recession since March 2001, according to the NBER, the low readings were not a surprise. Sustained indications of recovery will be eagerly awaited by economists, investors, and consumers alike.

CONCLUSION

Producers are clearly a vital part of the economy, both in the goods that they supply in response to demand and for the demand that they create with innovative products (that are cleverly marketed). But it's important as an investor to keep production in perspective. You can never count on production levels to be a hard-and-fast indicator. Increased production, as we saw in late 1999, may not be a harbinger of rosier economic times ahead. It could be that we're building inventories instead of supplying consumers who have increased their spending. At the same time, low production levels may not mean that the economy is in for a long recession or slowdown. It could be that low production levels are chipping away at inventories that will soon lead to production increases that are backed by real demand. But until that happens, producers must find a way to move that inventory, whether it's with "0 percent" financing for a new car or a "free monitor" with every Pentium IV computer sold. Then eventually, the economy will move out of one cycle and into the next, bubbles and bumps along the way notwithstanding. The bottom line is not to overlook the production numbers, but rather to look at them in a context of what else is happening in the economy.

   Also keep in mind that with most economic data, especially those expressed in a diffusion index (levels above 50 indicate expansion, and below 50 a contraction), the weaker the data appears in previous periods the more likely the data will look promising on a comparative basis. This is similar to when it's 10 degrees outside in the middle of a Chicago winter, then it "warms up" to 20. That may feel balmy, and you might be tempted to drive down Michigan Avenue with your window open. But the fact is, at 20 degrees, it's still freezing cold and a far cry from 65 and sunny! In economics, it is nice to be improving from weak levels, but getting to the economy's full potential still may be a long way off.

9

Inflation Indicators

Inflation is probably the most talked about, but least understood economic statistic. It is so important to financial planning and investment decisions that it is included in legal contracts, life insurance policies, and annuity purchases. Inflation is so important that it was one of the causes of World War I; sparked political upheaval in South America; led to the devaluation of currencies; and contributed to the destruction of not only financial systems but political systems as well, including the former Soviet Union.

Yet, what exactly is inflation? It is the incremental change in prices paid for goods and services over a period of time. It is caused by two factors: either too much money chasing too few goods, or shortages in supply compared with the demand for the good or service. Both have similar effects in the short run of decreasing the value of assets in relative terms (constant dollars) and decreasing one's purchasing power. The long-term effects, however, are different, as are the remedies taken and the side effects suffered.

First, let's take a look at what is called monetary induced inflation. This can be caused by several factors, but most notable is the government printing press. When government spending gets out of hand as it did in the late 1960s and early 1970s, Uncle Sam has no choice but to print more money. This is good for the government and debtor alike because they can pay back old debts with cheaper dollars. As inflation moves up, your dollar's purchasing power declines. This is far more important than whether a dollar bill can buy a loaf of bread anymore. Let's say you borrowed a dollar a few years ago and now you're paying it back. If the interest rate did not outpace inflation, then the lender is actually getting back less money in terms of purchasing power. You, the debtor, received a dollar with more purchasing power than the one you have to give back—even with interest!

When the government wants to buy something really big like a B-52 bomber or a new highway from New York to Los Angeles across the Rocky Mountains, it needs to pay everyone involved with these projects today. In other words, the project is paid for before revenue from the assets is realized. When the government borrows from the Treasury, this basically turns on the paper-money printing press in order to pay all the workers and suppliers on the government project. This increases the money supply, putting more dollars in the system. When productivity doesn't increase at the same rate, suddenly there are excess dollars in the system. With too many dollars chasing the same amount of goods, prices rise and, *voila*, the result is inflation.

Another way inflation is caused is when the Federal Reserve lowers the fed funds rate or the reserve requirement, meaning that banks have to hold less in reserve. This allows banks to loan money more freely with the same amount of deposits, which increases the money supply or the monetary base. When money is cheap, people are encouraged to borrow, which adds to the supply of dollars. If production doesn't go up, we again have more money chasing fewer goods, which will cause prices to go up, and you know what happens next: inflation! As you might expect, monetary and fiscal policies are the most effective when it comes to curbing monetary-induced inflation, at least in the short run.

The other type of inflation reflects imbalances in supply and demand. "Demand-pull inflation" is caused by sustained or continued increases in overall demand. "Cost-push inflation" is caused by sustained or continued decreases in overall supply. For our purposes, the important thing to consider is that this type of inflation is due to an imbalance of some kind in supply and/or demand. This is far different and harder to control than the other type of inflation that is caused by an increase in monetary supply.

Further, it's important to note that inflation caused by supply and demand imbalance can be confined to one pocket of the economy rather than across the whole economic vista. For example, if a $1 Beanie Baby is priced at $10 on some collector's Web site, does that really represent inflation? Or is it only a factor that 5-year-olds across the country are crying for the Beanie Babies that are in limited supply. Likewise, if you were in the desert and a bottled-water salesman had only one bottle left, what is the chance that the price of that water would equal the $50 in your pocket? That doesn't reflect the whole economy.

But supply and demand inflation can ripple through the broader economy when an important commodity, such as oil, is in short supply or if demand is stronger than the existing supply. That's when it is much harder to control this type of inflation. For example, when oil prices spiked up in the 1970s due to shortages caused by the oil embargo, there was very little the Fed could have done with interest rates or money supply to stop prices from rising. This was a basic supply and demand function, not a monetary policy issue. Supply-and-demand-induced inflation typically is not as big of a shock to the financial system as one might think, since supply and demand imbalances generally work themselves out. Either capitalists try to exploit the higher prices by producing more goods, hoping to sell at higher prices (and more profits as a result), or some producers loosen up supplies they may have been holding back—such as some OPEC countries that cheated on their production quotas in hopes of selling more oil at a higher price. That's exactly what happened in the 1970s during the oil embargo.

At the same time, other remedies to the supply and demand energy crisis were also applied during the oil embargo. For one, conservation measures and efficiencies actually cut back on demand. Further, soaring gasoline prices helped to spur commercialization of alternative sources, such as diesel fuel and solar power. With demand created for alternative products, the result was lessening demand for the commodity (oil) that was in short supply. Adding to the supply and demand solution, automakers saw this as an opportunity to make lighter, more fuel-efficient cars, which in reality were cheaper to make, thereby further reducing the demand for energy.

The real problems exist when supply and monetary inflation happen simultaneously, or when monetary policy is used to fight supply and demand inflation, which ends up causing monetary-induced inflation. Price controls not only don't work, they also exacerbate the problem. Remember WIN—Whip Inflation Now? The Ford administration's campaign to "whip inflation" was to keep a lid on prices. In reality, price controls only create pent-up demand. The best medicine for monetary inflation is to tighten the money supply. To combat supply/demand-induced inflation, the market will find its equilibrium.

There is one other type of inflation that is the most economically deadly: "hyperinflation." Wheelbarrows full of currency to buy a loaf of bread are vivid images from the hyperinflation days in Germany during the early 1900s. Dramatic currency devaluations cause daily changes in the price of food and basic commodities, which is reminiscent of South America during the early 1980s. Shopkeepers had to change the price of goods on their shelves just to keep up with the currency devaluations and the reality of what it would cost to restock those shelves.

Under former Chairman Paul Volcker, the Federal Reserve sought to fight back against inflation following the hyperinflation during the Carter administration in the late 1970s. The weapons in this battle were a tightening money supply and higher interest rates that were cranked up to almost 20 percent. This was painful medicine, but ultimately it allowed us to get inflation under control. Granted, it nearly stalled the U.S. economy during the recession of 1980-81, but this was the only way to get inflation under control and put the economy back into a position to expand. With the greatest tax changes in a half century, inflation under control, and worker productivity rapidly increasing along with a minitechnology boom, the stage was set for the beginning of the next and so far one of the greatest periods of expansion this country has ever seen.

The fight against inflation is such a primary and important goal of the Fed. Yet we almost never look at the problems that result from it. But the fight against inflation can produce periods of deflation or, worse yet, disinflation.

Deflation, according to the dictionary, means lower prices over a period of time. On the surface, that may not sound so bad. But the reality is many forecasts, projections, and budgets are made with some degree of inflation factored in, even if it is a slight amount. If these budgets and forecasts are consistently wrong because of a miscalculation of inflation, then that can cause problems. On the surface, it may sound like a good idea to be under budget if you end up with a reserve because something cost less than you expected. But what if workers are expecting a raise based on an inflation index? Or what if a landlord is willing to make property improvements based on the amount of rent he will likely receive, which reflects some amount of inflation. If the ability to raise rents to cover inflation is not there, the landlord will effectively overspend and can suffer the consequences.

Unfortunately, I have some firsthand experience on this one. My brother, David, and I owned an apartment building in Chicago. We were anticipating being able to raise rents based upon some improvements we were going to do and the fact that property values had been going up. The problem, which we did not foresee, was that our apartment-improvement plan preceded the 1990-91 downturn in the Chicago real estate market.

Confident that we would be able to recoup our investment, we took out a home equity loan on the building. To do a proper job, the current tenants had to leave so that the apartments would be vacant. No matter, we told ourselves. We'd be able to charge more rent for the fixed-up apartments, which would not only repay the home equity loan but also improve the cash flow from the building.

The problem was that the leases for the building were tied to an inflation-price index, and inflation was declining at the time. Unfortunately, so was the value of Chicago real estate. Thus, regardless of the improvements we made, we ended up renting out nicer apartments for less money. This is good for the new tenant, but bad for the landlords.

In the next scenario—disinflation—there is not only less inflation-driven price growth, but also "negative price growth," which is an economically complicated way of saying that prices are going down. The prices paid for things today are less than the prices paid last year. This impacts your absolute buying power and your overall wealth. It is challenging enough investing and earning more each year to keep pace with inflation, let alone trying to preserve capital and income despite disinflation. This is a concept most people are not comfortable with—earning lower rates of return today compared with inflationary times because prices are declining. Thus, capital preservation is better than losing money.

At first glance you, the consumer, might think that lower prices would be better for you. You might like the idea that, say, a double-mocha-skim-no-whip-latte declined in price to $2.50 from $3.00, saving you 17 percent on the surface. But what would happen if disinflation resulted in your *income* going down 25 percent because your employer, needing to cut back on expenses, reduced your wages. Then on a comparative basis, that mocha would actually cost you more.

Similarly, let's say you are on a fixed income earning interest from bonds and money market savings. If the rate of interest goes down, you will make less money. And if the rate of return on those fixed-income investments declines more than the decrease in the cost of goods, the net result is higher expenditures and lower income. That is what occurs during disinflation. The prices of most goods are somewhat inelastic to the down side meaning they have less room and are less likely to move down. Thus, when income levels and investment returns decline because of disinflation, your buying power is less.

STAGFLATION

The term "stagflation" was coined in the 1970s to describe a very unusual economic condition of high inflation and high unemployment. As noted previously in this chapter, two forms of inflation exist: monetary-induced inflation and cost-push/demand-pull inflation, which is caused by disparities in supply and demand. In stagflation, the supply and demand levels are so out of whack that even high levels of unemployment do not reduce demand. While the economy may be stalling or even contracting, the demand for certain goods—such as oil and gasoline—are so strong in certain sectors that prices remain very high. If the commodity or service is so vital to the overall economy that very few alternative products exist, the result will be stagflation. Fortunately, this condition cannot be maintained for very long, but while it is happening, it is sure a mind game for traditional Keynesian economists who believe that high unemployment and high demand cannot possibly coexist.

This brings us to the indicators that will reveal if we are experiencing inflation, hyperinflation, deflation, or disinflation. The first indicator I look at is the Consumer Price Index, or CPI. The next indicator, which is slightly less relevant than CPI, is the Producer Price Index, or PPI. The third indicator, which ties as the most important, is the deflator used in the GDP report.

CONSUMER PRICE INDEX (CPI)

The CPI measures changes in the prices of goods and services, such as food and clothing, that are directly purchased in the marketplace. While we tend to regard the CPI as a "cost-of-living index," it does fall short of that definition. For one thing, in order to be a true cost-of-living index, the CPI would have to take into account changes in governmental and environmental factors that affect consumers. Further, the CPI does not reflect changes in buying or consumption patterns that consumers probably would make to adjust to relative price changes. Nor does it reflect substitution of purchases among items (from high-priced goods to lower-priced substitutes) as a true cost-of-living index would. Rather, the CPI measures the cost of purchasing the same basket of items month after month.

The fact remains, however, that the CPI is a good benchmark for prices paid and for sniffing out any telltale signs of that old demon—inflation. For example, let's take a look at a recent CPI report, this one for November 2001 with a reading for the index of 177.5, which was roughly in line with October levels. That produced a headline of "-0.1." With CPI, the focus is always on the month-to-month change and not on the absolute index reading. As Chart 9-1 shows, this followed a steady decline in the CPI headline rate from September. Why would this be important? Keep in mind that throughout 2001 Alan Greenspan and the Federal Reserve had been on a rate-cutting campaign to stimulate the economy. But as discussed earlier in this chapter, the monetary actions of the Fed to lower rates and increase money supply can have an inflationary effect. One of the places that inflation could be detected would be in the CPI report.

The goods news in the chart is that based on the headline rate (all items), inflation stood at a modest 1.9 percent reflecting the year-to-year change in the CPI. But as with many economic reports, when certain data is extracted, a clearer picture is revealed. In the case of the CPI, looking at the statistics ("ex-food and energy"—meaning excluding food and energy) shows an inflation rate of 2.8 percent compared with a year ago. This is also known as the "core rate." Typically, a core rate of less than 3 percent is considered to be a relatively low level for the economy.

Another standout feature in the chart is "gasoline, unleaded regular," which showed a 22.3 percent year-to-year drop. Gasoline prices plunged in late 2001, largely due to ample supplies and weaker demand reflecting a slower economy and the fact that many consumers were staying closer to home. Oil prices declined by an even greater degree, contributing to the lower gasoline prices.

PRODUCER PRICE INDEX (PPI)

A sister report to the CPI, the PPI, measures prices for finished goods. I consider the PPI to be less important than the CPI, because the impact of higher prices at the producer level is not always an indication of higher prices for the consumer. Many times producers, in an attempt to keep or increase market share, will not pass along higher costs in the form of higher prices to the consumer. It may be economically beneficial overall to keep prices the same or even to lower them a bit when producer costs are rising. The reason is that a smaller profit on the same amount of goods, or potentially more goods, is better than selling fewer goods at a higher price. Companies that have well-established brands, products, and services usually can sustain their businesses during slowdowns, while competition from weaker producers can be reduced or eliminated if they require higher prices to generate cash and stay afloat.

The intangible element of these producer business decisions will affect consumer prices, thus making the PPI less meaningful than the

CHART 9-1 Consumer Price Index

	Nov-01	Oct-01	Sep-01	Aug-01	Jul-01	Jun-01	% change mo. ago	% change yr. ago
All items	177.5	177.6	178.1	177.4	177.3	177.9	-0.1	1.9
Ex-food & energy	188.1	187.4	187.1	186.7	186.3	186.3	0.7	2.8
Health care	277.5	276.3	275.2	274.1	272.9	272.7	1.2	4.9
Energy	116.7	122.7	130.5	127.0	129.5	136.5	–6.0	–9.9
Gasoline, unleaded regular	102.2	114.9	129.4	117.7	120.9	135.8	–12.7	–22.3

Source: Economy.com

CPI when it comes to measuring the overall impact of inflation. Nonetheless, it is worth taking a look at the PPI to gauge the price and cost pressures that producers are facing. Taking a look at a recent report (see Chart 9-2), also from November 2001, we see that producer prices in November fell 0.6 percent from the prior month, which followed a 1.3 percent drop in October.

As with the CPI, the core rate excludes food and energy. In the case of the November 2001 PPI report, this showed a 0.11 percent rise from October. What this report shows clearly is that producers are having difficulty raising their prices, a "good news" scenario for those who were looking for the Fed to make more rate cuts, but a "bad news" scenario for anyone looking for short-term economic recovery.

DEFLATOR

Unlike the CPI and the PPI, which are measures of prices paid, the "implicit price deflator" is an actual number that is used to calculate the value of something in constant dollars. The most obvious examples are the deflator used in GDP and Personal Consumption Expenditures (PCE). In Chart 9-3, you can see the deflator that is used to convert nominal (meaning today's dollars) values into real or constant dollars. But this deflator is more than just a multiplier; it's a very important benchmark for inflation in the current economy. The Federal Reserve, in fact, has stated that it no longer uses the CPI as its primary inflation indicator and instead uses inflation deflators.

As you can see in Chart 9-3, the implicit price deflator for the third quarter of 2001 was 2.3, which was greater than the deflator of 2.1 in the second quarter of 2001 but less than the 3.3 deflator in the first quarter of 2001. But what does that mean? It means the bigger the deflator, the more inflation there is to contend with. In other words, if a deflator increases from one quarter to another, it means there was more inflation to factor out of the equation to convert into real, constant dollars.

The question often arises why the GDP deflator is less than the core rate for the CPI? The answer is that the GDP deflator is being applied to things that are less expensive than the "basket of goods and

CHART 9-2 Producer Price Index

	Nov-01	Oct-01	Sep-01	Aug-01	Jul-01	Jun-01	May-01
M to M % Chg.	−0.6	−1.3	0.4	0.4	−1.2	−0.5	0.1
Ex Food & Energy	0.1	−0.4	0.1	0.0	0.1	0.1	0.2
Y to Y % Chg.	−1.1	−0.3	1.6	2.0	1.4	2.6	3.9
Ex Food & Energy	0.9	0.9	1.4	1.5	1.7	1.6	1.6
Index Value	138.3	139.2	141.1	140.6	140.0	141.7	142.4
Ex Food & Energy	150.1	150.0	150.6	150.4	150.4	150.2	150.1
Intermediate materials	126.7	127.6	129.3	129.2	129.5	131.0	131.3
M to M % Chg.	−0.7	−1.3	0.1	−0.2	−1.1	−0.2	0.1
Crude materials	102.9	98.1	107.6	112.5	113.3	119.6	130.1
M to M % Chg.	4.9	−8.8	−4.4	−0.7	−5.3	−8.1	−2.2

Source: Economy.com

CHART 9-3 GDP Implicit Price Deflator

	01Q4	01Q3	01Q2	01Q1	00Q4	00Q3	00Q2	00Q1
Implicit price deflator	−0.1	2.3	2.1	3.3	1.8	1.9	2.2	3.9

Source: Economy.com

services" measured by the CPI. When trying to measure inflation, the question often arises as to which indicator to use. There are inherent problems with each indicator, which may underestimate or overestimate inflation. The deflator, which is used in the GDP report (see Chapter 5), tries to smooth out the impact inflation to enable comparisons from one period of time to another. The deflator, however, does not account for deficiencies that can be created over time.

Remember, the first VCRs and cell phones offered on the market cost more than $1,000. Today, a cell phone may be free in return for signing up for cellular telephone service for a specific period of months or years, while a basic VCR may cost about $100. That being said, it is not a good indicator of inflation, or in this case of deflation, to compare or try to even out the prices of these products to a constant level because the high initial price would reflect development costs and not the mass production efficiencies that followed.

While the deflator is a good tool for gauging inflation, it is far from perfect. In fact, the deflator may understate inflation because it does not take into consideration things like changes in spending patterns as they relate to a consumer's standard of living. Further, the deflator in the GDP report deflates things that consumers don't pay for directly, such as certain medical costs.

Nonetheless, you can see that if the CPI tends to overstate inflation and the deflator tends to understate it, the truth (or at least the perceived truth) lies somewhere in the middle. Just as economists don't rely on one report to tell them the whole economic picture, you can't judge inflation solely by one number. A wiser approach would be to look at the CPI and the GDP deflator and judge the rate of inflation based on the two figures.

INFLATION: WHY YOU SHOULD CARE

Put eight quarters in your pocket. That small, $2.00 allowance is all you have to spend today for coffee, a Snickers bar, whatever. Now, give me one of your quarters. Now, you're down to $1.75. Do you feel the pinch in your purchasing power? Sure you do. And that is precisely what inflation does. It effectively takes money out of your pocket by decreasing the purchasing power of your financial resources. No, inflation doesn't take money out of your wallet, but it does make your money worth less. Put another way, inflation makes the same stuff you always bought cost more and also reduces the real value (as opposed to the nominal value, which may in fact be higher) of your investments.

In the U.S. economy in recent times, inflation has not taken too much of a bite out of your spending power. Whether you spent 75 cents or 80 cents for candy, or $1.95 or $2.05 for coffee didn't really matter much. You had less change in your pocket, and you had no choice but to pony up for the increased price. But consider the impact of inflation over time on something really big, say, your retirement account.

Our grandparents' generation, which thought the stock market was a form of gambling, and maybe which, post-depression, didn't trust banks very much, wanted to keep their money "safe." In other words, they generally shied away from investment schemes that put their money at risk. In the most dramatic cases, they may have hoarded cash in a box or in a sock under the bed rather than entrust it to a bank. But the fact of the matter is that cash under the bed, while a potential "windfall" to some house-cleaning heir, will be worth less in years to come than the day that Grandpa hid it under the Sealy Posturepedic. The culprit is inflation.

Today's investors have drummed into their heads the importance of staying ahead of inflation. They're not trying to swim the English Channel; they're trying to keep their heads above economic waters. Consider the fact that a savings account could be paying around 2 or 3 percent interest. But the core inflation rate is at 2.8 percent. That sounds like treading water to me.

Thus, the challenge—and the opportunity—is to devise some kind of savings and investment strategy that will keep you at least one step ahead of inflation. In other words, people who are retiring today (and who may very well live longer than their parents and grandparents) will need more and more income every year that they're retired just to maintain a lifestyle.

Consider the Rule of 72: Divide 72 by the inflation rate, which is currently around 3 percent. That's how many years (in this case 24) it will take for costs to double. So if something costs $20 today, in approximately 24 years it will cost $40 assuming that inflation stays about where it is right now.

Retirees today typically have three sources of income: their investments, Social Security payments, and personal savings. Social Security, as it now stands, has a cost-of-living adjustment (COLA) to help benefits keep pace with inflation. But defined-benefit pension plans probably don't carry the same adjustments, since those benefits are fixed. Therefore, it is important to adjust your portfolio, taking into account various levels of inflation over your investment time horizon.

Various investment strategies have proven valuable during times of high inflation, while solid saving strategies have proven successful during low inflationary periods. Over the long run, however, only stocks have outpaced inflation (see Chart 9-4), as fixed income investments have only matched or slightly outperformed the rate of inflation once capital appreciation is factored in. The caveat, of course, is the term "long run."

At any given point in time, the economy could be in the midst of a business cycle that would be more or less favorable for your investment portfolio. If this should occur at the time you need your capital, then timing will likely be the biggest factor in your investment results. Therefore, when choosing investment strategies, it is important to have some expectation about inflation, the knowledge of what varying degrees of inflation can do to your portfolio, and, of course, what stage of the economic cycle we're currently in.

It was once thought that gold was an effective hedge against inflation, since the price of this commodity would rise in sympathy with inflation. In reality, there was nothing further from the truth. The fact that gold enjoyed a terrific rally at about the same time that the United States was experiencing hyperinflation is the only correlation I can cite to hypothetically support this fact. While many market strategists and economists recommend some small percentage of assets be held in gold, gold stocks, or a gold fund, I strongly believe that the correlation between gold and inflation is merely a coincidence at best.

Nearly any hard asset—whether it's a tanker of crude oil or a bushel of wheat—would be a better hedge against inflation than gold, which has no store of value and no longer backs currencies. Gold is not consumed in any significant industrial uses, and

CHART 9-4 Relative Performance of Equities, U.S. Government Bonds, and Inflation over the Past 25 Years (figures rounded)

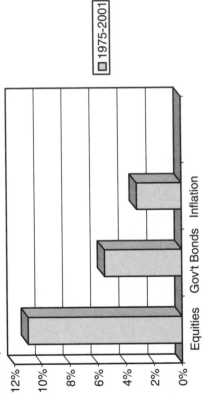

therefore its supply and demand fluctuates to the whims of pro-ducers and producing countries. Clearly, there are many better financial instruments that hold their value during times of hyper-inflation, such as Treasury inflation-adjusted notes. Some vari-able annuities also make variable payments based upon some benchmark of inflation, and almost all hard real assets such as real estate often serve as excellent hedges against inflation. Even stocks, whose values deteriorate during inflationary times, usu-ally rebound, once the inflation surge abates, to levels that are greater than before they began to deteriorate due to inflation. Fur-ther, these stocks tend to perform so well during times of eco-nomic growth and low inflation that they more than offset any depreciation during inflationary times, making their return over the long run well above inflation.

The key is to make sure that during times of inflation you are fully invested. Staying in cash or cash-equivalents is like throwing money out of the window, or stashing it under the mattress, thereby allowing your buying power to deteriorate. During periods of low inflation or even disinflation, cash is king. Having liquidity and buying power as other assets are depreciating is advantageous to making sound investments and buying undervalued assets that will appreciate in the future. Understanding the different types of infla-tion and how inflation impacts your portfolio and your buying power will allow you to make better investment decisions for today and the future.

When you see prices increase, try to assess the reason. Is it because of shortages, or is there too much money around due to sus-tained low interest rates and low levels of unemployment, making it seem like everybody has an extra $100 bill in his or her pocket? This brings to mind a phrase my good friend, Paul, coined. Told that he would have to wait 6 months for the renovation of his kitchen but pay the full cost of the project now, he balked at what he saw as "repent prosperity." Pay now and wait.

If it appears that the cause of rising prices is too much money, then be on the look out for inflation. Check the CPI and the deflators in the GDP report to see if there are steady month-to-month rises. Make an assessment of your own costs. Are your living expenses notably higher than a year or so ago? Are you making comparatively more money? How are your investments doing? The answers to these questions will help you determine if the economy is starting an inflationary cycle and thus prepare you to make smart investments that will appreciate along with inflation.

10

The "Out of Favor" Indicators

In economics, as in life, things go in and out of favor. Take the bell-bottom pants you wore in the 1970s. If you kept a pair in the attic, you'd be back in style again. Similarly, there are economic indicators that were once hailed as the great predictors, which then fell out of favor, and are now back in vogue. For example, GDP that in its GNP days was dismissed as a lagging indicator, today is considered by many (including me) to be one of the best gauges of current economic activity. Mr. Greenspan, himself, is well known for reanalyzing economic and statistical data—looking at old numbers in new ways to determine the economy's potential. But there are some things that, like Earth Shoes, just never seem to have quite the same appeal again.

From inflation measures and growth indicators to early warning recession detection, so much information is available that it's hard to pinpoint which reports are really telling the story. This is particularly true these days when the economy is so diverse that strengths and weaknesses can coexist in different sectors. There can be inflation in one part of the economy that can be offset by contraction in another. Data that show growth in one sector may be misleading or downright erroneous for the economy as a whole.

So what do you do, today, with what I call the "out of favor indicators" that were once gospel and now are paid little heed? These indicators are like the "one-hit wonders" of rock 'n' roll, making a big splash for a moment and then ... nothing. Do you ignore them now, or do they warrant a passing glance just in case they have something to say? As an economist, I take note of most economic reports, giving some a cursory review while studying others more closely. While they are likely singing the "same old song" about the economy, which I already know from GDP and employment, it's always good to listen to, or at least be familiar with, the report. Old economic reports, just like rock 'n' roll classics, don't really go out of style. They just lose their broad audience until they make a comeback.

Moreover, looking at the breadth of indicators also serves as a "reality check" for the number mania that exists in the market. Short-term speculators, and even some otherwise levelheaded investors, can get caught up in the frenzy caused by the "indicator of the moment"—be it employment, or consumer confidence, or whatever. Just when you think that some indicator, forecast, survey, or poll is "it," the out-of-favor indicators remind you of all the "it" that has come before. In investment, as in life, a little perspective goes a long way. That being said, let's take a walk down the economic memory lane and revisit some of the indicators that once made our hearts beat faster in the market, and which may come back.

THE FED WATCHER

Whatever the real job titles were, we all knew what they did. They were the "Fed watchers." Employed most by commercial banks, as well as some brokerages and other financial institutions, their main job was to watch and interpret what the Fed might be doing. The Fed watchers included traders who managed the balance sheet of the bank, buying deposits with excess funds or borrowing for cash reserves. These decisions were in response to what they thought the Federal Reserve was doing in the open market. Fed watchers scoured the market for signs of "repos," as the Fed bought Treasuries to pump more money into the market or had "reverse repos" to sell Treasuries to tighten up money supplies. A repo is an obligation to repurchase securities from the markets and replace them with cash. Conversely, a reverse repo is selling securities and taking cash out of the system. Terms like "overnight system repos," "2-day repos," "Fed buying all bills," and "Fed selling bills" were common terms heard around money market desks back in the 1970s and 1980s.

These were the days when the Fed watchers would try to determine what the Fed's stance was on money supply, short-term interest rates, and, by extension, the economy. That would account for about the first 45 minutes of the business day. The next time the Fed watchers would look up from their newspaper crossword puzzles would be around 3 o'clock on Thursday afternoons when the Fed would issue its all-important money supply figures.

Today, a Fed watcher at a bank is as out-of-date as a blacksmith at a downtown garage. For one thing, the Greenspan Fed has been a much more transparent organization than the Fed of the past. Rather than leaving it to the market to interpret what the Fed is doing, the Fed issues statements regularly and then releases the minutes of its meetings about a month after they are held. These statements and minutes are scoured not only for statements of what the Fed has done or is now doing, but for hints and indications of what it may do in the future. Furthermore, the Fed actually makes an announcement at the end of its regular meetings as to whether it increased or decreased rates, or if it left policy unchanged. Now the only thing left up to conjecture is guessing what the Fed will do, which is a popular sport not only among analysts but among financial market commentators as well.

IN AND OUT OF STYLE

It is common knowledge that the PPI and the CPI (see Chapter 9) as well as the deflators are good indicators of overall inflation. Whatever one you choose may signal more or less inflation at a specific time and give more specific details. In general, however, if inflation exists, it will show up in one of these indicators. To gauge inflation, the Fed has flip-flopped over the years, considering some data more relevant at times than others. We know, for example, that Greenspan looks at the Commodity Research

Bureau's CRB Index, which measures the price movements of 22 basic commodities, for early indications of changes in economic conditions. The Fed, which once relied heavily on the CPI, also uses the GDP deflator. Whatever the measure, clearly the Fed is keeping its eye on inflation.

Other indicators that have stepped into and out of the economic limelight include the various consumer confidence numbers, including The Conference Board's Consumer Confidence Survey (see Chapter 7). Originally this report was not given much attention; in fact, you had to search to find out when it was released. Then suddenly in the 1990s, everyone was paying attention to the consumer as the excessive consumption of the 1980s was ending. We started looking not only at consumer confidence, but other surveys of consumer behavior—sort of a mixed bag of psychological indicators to measure the economy. Today, as stated in Chapter 7, the consumer's feelings about the economy are far less important than what the consumer really does. For me, consumer confidence has taken the backseat. However, the market lately does respond in the very short run to this report. Perhaps in the future there will prove to be tighter correlation between what the consumer thinks, feels, and spends, and how the economy is doing.

INTERNATIONAL TRADE

Another "oldie but goodie" from the 1980s are the international trade figures, which had a perceived impact on currency rates, as well as on the balance of trade. It was widely viewed that the state of international trade would not only reflect the strength or weakness of the U.S. dollar, but it would also reflect in part on the health of our economy and business sector. If we suddenly developed a widening trade deficit, buying more from overseas, such as from Japan, it didn't take much to assume that a strong dollar needed to come under pressure against the yen to help the trade imbalance.

What the market was too short-sighted to see, however, was the fact that companies—particularly manufacturers—were becoming increasingly multinational in their operations. A U.S.-based company could easily source raw materials from one continent, ship them to another for processing or basic manufacture, and then send components or the finished product to the United States. This was a reflection of everything from tariffs to labor costs. The world was no longer a patchwork of competing marketplaces. Rather, the world was a map of the supply chain from raw material to end users, and companies were becoming more adept at crossing borders.

As companies become multinational, trade figures become less meaningful. Nonetheless, it does no harm, and potentially a little good, to consider the international trade reports. A recent report serves as a good example. In October 2001, the U.S. trade deficit rose to $29.6 billion (see Chart 10-1), after shrinking to $19.4 billion in September. This was more in line with readings earlier in the year.

What exactly does that mean? Clearly the increase in the trade deficit in October had more to do with a resumption of normal business after the disruptions in September than it did with a fundamental business shift. Further, the trade balance decline in October compared with April levels showed something else that should be taken into account: the slowing of the U.S. economy in terms of consumption of imported goods.

EMPLOYMENT COST INDEX

Mr. Greenspan, those in the know used to say with a wink and a nod, watches the Employment Cost Index (ECI) very carefully. If you said that at a dinner party with one or more economists in attendance, you could be the smarty-pants for the night. It is true that the ECI is useful in analyzing things like the change in wages and benefits as they relate to productivity and inflation. Obviously, if the labor market is tight and companies have to "pay up" to hire and retain good workers, this is going to color the inflation picture. That's why when U.S. unemployment levels were under 5 percent, it was widely believed that the Fed was keeping a close watch on the ECI.

But the ECI has some definite drawbacks. For one thing, many companies have dealt with rising labor costs in ways other than paying out more wages, such as granting stock options that are tied to the company's performance. Another drawback is that benefits, such as health insurance, are part of the ECI, but such insurance is really not an optional offering for companies. In fact, it's practically mandated. Thus, one of the components of the ECI is something over which companies have little control. Further, there is the change in "climate" that we saw in the last half of 2001. With rising unemployment and a

CHART 10-1 Trade Balance (in billions of dollars)

	Nov-01	Oct-01	Sep-01	Aug-01	Jul-01	Jun-01	May-01	Apr-01
Balance	−28.5	−29.6	−19.4	−28.4	−30.7	−29.8	−28.9	−31.8
Goods	−34.3	−35.1	−35.6	−34.1	−35.9	−35.6	−34.4	−37.7
Services	5.8	5.5	16.2	5.7	5.2	5.7	5.6	5.8

Source: Economy.com

slowing economy, the inflation detection capabilities of the ECI were not as important as they once were. Some day the ECI may come back into favor, but as of this writing it garners only mild interest.

LEADING INDICATOR INDEX

Then there is the Leading Economic Indicators Index(LEI), or as an economist friend of mine likes to call it, the "misleading indicator index." The LEI used to be the crystal ball of economics. What a name! Leading Economic Indicators Index! Who wouldn't pay attention? But the name belies what the index really is. The LEI is really a basket of indicators that gives some irrelevant information and a few nuggets. But those nuggets tend to be myopic in their view. Knowing that one particular industry in one particular region looks like it might see an increase is fine, but it is nearly meaningless when you're trying to assess a broad picture. In other words, it's not a true barometer of where the economy is going, or is going to be going.

JOBLESS CLAIMS

As we discussed in Chapter 5, the weekly jobless claims do provide a quick glance at the state of employment in the United States. There are so many variations from week-to-week, however, that they do little to counter or confirm a trend. This renders the jobless claims to be of little value on their own. When viewed in the context of a rolling 4-week average or as a prelude to the monthly nonfarm payroll report, the jobless claims have some value. But on their own, they're not much to talk about.

IN AND OUT OF FAVOR

What will come in or out of favor from here is really anyone's guess. To some extent, we will always need and use GDP as a gauge for what the economy is doing now. The employment report packs a big psychological wallop when it comes to how the U.S. investor/consumer feels. That "feeling," while not important as it is surveyed and gauged, becomes important as it relates to action—meaning spending and saving. For these reasons, I doubt we'll ever push GDP and employment to the back burner. At the same time, I think it's vital to keep in mind that any economic report is just that—a report. It's the same way your medical chart at the doctor's office is not your health, it's a recording of your health. The state of your blood pressure, your arteries, and your cholesterol reside in your body. The chart is only what someone has observed, tested, and reported.

While this may sound simplistic, it's important in today's information-overload environment to keep the patient separate from the chart. Turn on the financial television news on any morning and you can see the latest economic report disseminated, debated, digested, and discounted. This happens live in front of a national audience. Reports that were the purview of a few and understood perhaps by even fewer are now widely broadcast to the public just like the weather report is. Don't get me wrong. That's a good thing, especially in today's markets when it's every person, and his 401(k), for himself! Seriously, as individual investors become increasingly savvy about the markets, and increasingly responsible for their financial futures, there needs to be more education about how the economy functions and how to gauge its health. Indeed, if nothing else, that is the premise of this book. But at the same time, we all need to take a little healthy distance from the economic flavor of the month, be it trade figures, inflation, or factory orders.

This fact is brought home, as I recall, by a typical springtime evening out in Chicago back in the 1980s. My colleagues and I were the guests of a major Chicago-based consumer products company that had box seats at Wrigley Field for one of the few night games for the Chicago Cubs. This company did a lot of foreign-currency business with the bank I worked for, and we were the currency traders on the desk in Chicago.

I remember it was a Thursday night, about 7:30, and we were relaxing and watching the game. That's when one of the top financial executives of the company pulled me aside. He was an older gentleman, especially compared to me at 20-something years of age. "I don't know how you do it," he said, shaking his head. "You've had a couple of beers by now, and it's getting late. How do you guys do this all the time and then make it into the office by 7:30 in the morning for the next number? What do you do? Decide which numbers are important and then sleep in on the mornings when the unimportant ones come out?"

The short answer to his question was "yes." There were times when we were all rushing in because some "hugely important" number was going to move the market. As traders, we were looking for the market to move—even momentarily—in order to make a trade. We didn't need nor have a long-term attention span for this. The market was going to move in one direction or the other when report "X" came out, regardless of its long-term impact.

I can remember there were traders who did not go out at all on the Thursday night before employment report Friday. They were home resting and getting ready for the big morning. Today there is far less of that. Sure, there are still "big numbers" like GDP and employment that are watched by traders and investors alike. But those of us who've been around for a while look beyond the knee-jerk reaction of the market. By the time the stock market opens, the employment report will be an hour old, and it will be sliced and diced 16 different ways by a dozen economists and pundits on numerous Web sites and financial news stations. This all comes after at least a day of anticipation and speculation about the number, which means you—and the market—may be sufficiently desensitized by the time the report is released.

Economic reports are important as a means to gauge what is going on, but they shouldn't be confused with the actual events. The state of the economy is reflected in a GDP that is growing or shrinking and an unemployment rate that is rising or falling. Don't confuse that with thinking that the report is the economy.

That was the topic of conversation with my friend and fellow economist Peter Corona, who writes and publishes the Diametrix newsletter, which examines and discusses cycles and patterns in the market and the economy. Peter is also a bit of an historian when it comes to political and economic events. There have been many times when we have sat down over a drink and a cigar to discuss topics ranging from Winston Churchill's politics to international trade policies. The topic of this particular conversation was the relevance—or, shall I say, irrelevance—of certain economic indicators that we once watched so closely and but that today we hardly pay attention to.

ROB: When it comes to economic reports, the world has changed, Peter. The things we thought were so important years ago—money supply, for example—is not even paid attention to anymore. Obviously, this reflects greater visibility of policy and opinion at the Fed. But I also think that it reflects a greater dissemination of economic data.

PETER: People are always looking for something to hang their hats on, to gain that edge in the market. That was no different then than it is today. Today, in the information age, we all have the same weapons and the same ammunition. The only edge to be gained is by the one who can fire first. Now, we're not spending our time with money supply figuring out what the Fed is doing, we're trying to figure out what the Fed is going to do.

ROB: Our understanding in general has changed to be sure. We would watch trade patterns because of the impact on currency moves, thinking that there would be an economic impact. But the fact was economics weren't going to change based on currency moves. Companies were building plants in one country or another because of certain cost and currency advantages. Companies also became much more sophisticated in their use of currencies, whether they were hedging their dollar-yen exposure or they were borrowing in Spanish pesetas. We were watching trade numbers, thinking that they would have an impact on the economy or on the companies that had exposures to currency shifts. In reality, companies were reacting the other way. They didn't respond to currency shifts. They made currency changes based on economic shifts.

Today, there are indicators that are more important than others. As I've said, GDP once took a backseat because it was such a lagging indicator, which was subject to revision. Today, it's back in style because it gives such a broad picture of the economy in terms of what we're producing.

PETER: Frankly, I view all indicators the same way. They are bits of information that are released, and what people are trying to do is use that information to gain some kind of edge. I mean, if they thought they could use the news about the death of Bill Clinton's dog, they would! It's true that we do look at GDP more than we used to. But what's crucial to keep in mind is not that the report is more important than it used to be, but that our "microscopes" are more powerful. It's the same indicator, but we are looking at it differently. This is a process that I do not think will ever end. We'll replace an old indicator with an altered old indicator, and then we'll try to see what we can make out of it for production and consumption and all these things.

At the same time, everything is happening in a split second. You have the information and I have it, and we're all trying to figure out what it means. We're trying to see into the future for one important reason: We want to know how the market is going to react to this information.

ROB: Isn't it funny that when we go through all these economic and business cycles, we forget what went on before—until we're done completing the cycle. That's what is happening right now. When the economy turned down, we forgot that this had happened before and that it will happen again. All we could focus on was that the economy was slowing down and could be headed into a recession.

PETER: What doesn't change is human nature. When the human is attacked, it will defend itself. We saw this in 1998 with the Far Eastern financial crisis that shook the world. In an economic sense, what happened on September 11, 2001, was the same thing. Now I'm not saying that they were the same sort of event. What happened in September was tragic. But if you can view them both as crises, regardless of the cause, then what you focus on are the reactions. From this perspective, the events are similar enough in market reaction. Then you can see that what the Fed was most concerned about after September 11 was how the public would react and how market participants would react. That brings us to the heart of the matter: What we are trying to focus on is the Fed's perception of our perception. How is Mr. Greenspan going to judge what the American consumer/investor will do in reaction to a particular event or situation?

ROB: I find it interesting that in July 2001 you wrote in one of your newsletters that we were trading like we were in a "war market," based upon the association of past patterns and cycles. That was certainly very interesting to read in retrospect since, a few months later, we were actually in a "war market." It brings home to me how short our attention spans are. We see thunder and lightning and forget that the last time this happened there was a flood. Only after the flood happens do we remember that the last time it occurred there was also a flood.

PETER: We could safely say we were trading like we were in a "war market" because of certain similarities in patterns and cycles.

ROB: The Fed was already lowering rates, and there was evidence that the economy was heading toward a recession. That's what was being done at the time. That makes you wonder if the reason Mr. Greenspan was lowering rates aggressively was because he was seeing the same patterns—GDP contracting, inventories building up …

PETER: And what he's trying to do is anticipate how the market will react. And sometimes he has to step in when he sees the public's perception going the wrong way.

ROB: Ah, yes! "Irrational exuberance!" That's my favorite quote of his, which he used to describe the rise in the stock market in 1996. The result was that the average investor thought the market was going to the moon. The stock market was an inflated balloon, and Greenspan was holding a pin.

PETER: You see, Greenspan is like a responsible parent. And what child agrees with his parent when he's being disciplined?

11

The Big Picture

There's an old joke about five blind men who try to describe an elephant. One picks up the elephant's trunk and, thinking that's the whole elephant, says confidently, "It resembles a snake." Another touches the ears and decides the elephant has wings like a bird, and so on. But when this composite of descriptions is put together, there is a very accurate verbal picture of an elephant.

That elephant is like the economy. For 10 chapters, we've dissected different parts of the economy—from growth as measured by GDP to employment to the roles of consumers and producers. At each step I've given you, the investor, tools with which to judge the relative strength or weakness of the economy so that you can recognize the patterns and plan your investments accordingly. Now it's time to step back and consider the economy as a whole, a living organism, if you will, that functions not in a bubble, but within a global structure that is impacted by everything from geopolitical forces to severe weather, a favorite excuse of economists.

Add to that the dynamics of individual investors. In the past two decades, there has been a proliferation of mutual funds for long-term investment that has opened up the stock market and other markets to retail clients. Prior to 1980—before the days of widespread profit-sharing plans, individual retirement accounts (IRAs), and 401(k) retirement plans—the largest holders of stocks were institutions and pension plans. Today, for the first time in U.S. history, more than 50 percent of households own stock either as outright investments or through their pension and retirement plans.

As the retail investment market has exploded, indexing and benchmarking have become the standards by which everything else is judged. Mutual funds are regularly gauged by how well or poorly they match up with major indices such as the Standard & Poor's 500, which, as the name implies, is 500 stocks of large corporations across a variety of industries. Other indices that have become household names include the Nasdaq 100, the 100 largest stocks in the technology-dominated Nasdaq market; the Russell 2000, which tracks the performance of 2000 small companies; and the Wilshire 5000 Total Market Index, which measures the performance of all equity securities of U.S.-based companies with readily available price data.

Indeed, many investors consider mutual funds that seek to match and track the performance of various indices to be very attractive. As investment managers use indices, benchmarks, and other market averages to measure the relative performance of their funds, the performance of the underlying index becomes more important. And, as more and more investors look to professional fund managers to invest their money, the performance of the underlying index or benchmark becomes the investment objective.

The popularity of investing in indices among retail investors has created its own ripple effect in the market. As fund managers try to keep their portfolios in line with various market indices and averages, they have increased their use of derivative products such as futures and options.

The use of these derivative products has given the fund managers the ability to make broad market decisions and implement them more quickly than in the past. For example, in the past if a manager discovered information that might affect a portfolio, he would have to sell several different stocks at various prices, which would take a lot of time and effort. Now, to hedge a portfolio against an adverse market condition, all the manager would have to do is use futures and/or options to hedge.

Remember, a futures contract is a way in which to speculate on the future movement of the price of the underlying security or commodity. For example, S&P futures contracts trade based upon what the marketplace of traders, speculators, and professional money managers believe the future value of the S&P Index will be. In the simplest of terms, futures contracts have given professional money managers a kind of insurance policy to hedge, or protect, their portfolios. If a manager wants to protect the profits of his stock portfolio, he or she can sell—or go short—futures contracts, which will make money if the market goes down. Thus, if the market does go down, the value of the stock portfolio is less, but the profit on the futures contracts helps to offset that decline. Conversely, if the market does go up, the value of the stock portfolio is greater, which is trimmed somewhat by the loss on the futures contracts.

In reality, professional money managers use a variety of sophisticated hedging strategies across a number of markets to protect their portfolios, offset losses, and maximize gains. The result has been a shortening of the duration of market corrections, but the swings have also been more severe. Through the use of these derivative products (futures and options), managers can hedge, liquidate, or short a market in hours or minutes, whereas years ago a move of that magnitude could take days or weeks to complete. The effect of this will make the positive slope of markets more pronounced, while making corrections in markets deeper and shorter in duration with snap backs faster and more aggressive. Because of the relative ease of using these derivative products, managers now take an active role in hedging and benchmarking their portfolios. As a result, managers are in and out of the market more quickly than before. Thus, when conditions change again to a positive stance, and the protective hedging is no longer needed, the hedges will need to be "unwound." This creates an even bigger rush getting into the market, causing more swings.

In other words, there has been a dramatic climate change in the market. With more retail investors, there is more participation, or liquidity. While increased liquidity is generally good for the investor, it is not without its cost, which is increased volatility. Volatility—sharp up-and-down movements—can be tough to stomach at times.

This brings us to the next topic: the role of the stock market in the economy. As I stated emphatically in the opening chapter, the stock market is not the economy. But the stock market does play a role in the economy, particularly as a means to view the collective opinion about the economy. The level of stock prices has relevance to economic well-being and sheds forward-looking light on the picture of the economy. This is significant given the fact that most economic data—even the all-important GDP—is lagging. That lag doesn't matter much, given the fact that a $10-trillion-plus economy isn't going to turn on the proverbial dime. Yesterday's trends are important to determine what tomorrow is likely to hold, and impact today's price.

Yet the stock market is all about perception and expectation: Buy today because tomorrow that investment is going to be worth more. Sell today because tomorrow it's going to be worth less. Sometimes the stock market provides a clear picture of expectations: How often did you hear in late 2001, for example, that the stock market was "pricing in a recovery"? In other words, with the economy still in recession or at best just pulling out of it, the stock market was already reflecting the recovery that it expected, or hoped for. But stock market expectations are often like kids before Christmas. Their expectations are for the entire inventory of FAO Schwartz under the Christmas tree. The reality of Christmas morning, while not without its bounty, is far less.

And there are times when the forward-looking stock market is just plain dead wrong when it comes to judging economic activity and corporate activity. Take a look at early 2000. Weakness had started to set in the economy, even while the stock market was making all-time highs in March of that year. The weakness in the economy wasn't recognized until late 2000 as the Fed shifted its stance from seeing the risk of inflation and overheating of the economy to easing rates—and bypassing neutral altogether. Then in the first week of January 2001, there was a surprise rate cut by the Fed, the first of what would be 11 rate cuts in 2001 (see Chart 11-1). These

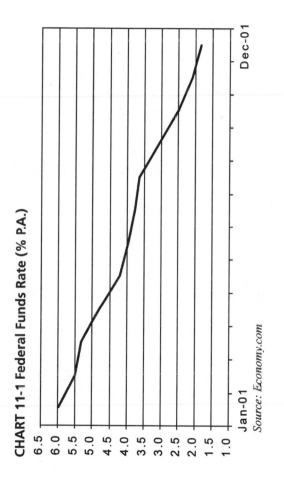

CHART 11-1 Federal Funds Rate (% P.A.)

Jan-01   Dec-01

Source: Economy.com

cuts, in response to economic weakness, were the most in any calendar year since the Fed began targeting its fed funds rate in the 1970s.

The market's response to the surprise rate cut was one of the greatest 1-day rallies on record—with the Dow rising some 300 points—even though there were clear signs that the economy was weakening, a fundamental fact that should not bode well for stocks. However, the market eventually succumbed to the reality that the economic expansion had run out of steam. While the Januuary 2001 Fed rate cut propped up the market that month, by February it had begun a sharp sell-off.

So what caused the recession and slowdown of 2001 and the corresponding bear market? What should we have been looking at? What data gave clues about the downturn that might provide indications about a future recovery? To figure that out, let's take a trip in the "Wayback Machine" (for all you fans of Peabody & Sherman cartoons, a favorite from my childhood) to 1998. That was a good year by many measures, from the ushering in of widespread telecommunications spending to broad use of the Internet. The market embraced the new technology, capital spending soared, and money poured into stocks.

The initial public offering (IPO) market was so hot that companies with fluffy names like "takeashot.com" or "intelecommunication.com" and, of course, the ever-popular "wirelessliving.com" all went public with mind-blowing valuations despite little or no revenues. Urban legends were spawned about 23-year-old whiz kids serving mocha lattes at Starbucks one day and then becoming CEOs of multibillion-dollar companies the next. Never mind that these ventures had no earnings and little revenue. They had lots of ideas, promise, and marketing plans. Curiously, that was not the start of the bubble, but the end. Granted, worker productivity was accelerating at a record pace, which helped to keep inflation low and went a long way to support greater stock valuations. But as time progressed, high price-to-earnings (P/E) ratios needed to be supported by earnings. The high market valuations that were based upon hopes and speculation outpaced even the most optimistic expectations for growth. What was really going on here?

If we break the economy down to its simplest form, we see that capital and labor come together to produce output. This output represents the total value of the economy. While Wall Street tries to measure this value in terms of profit forecasts that are expressed in share prices, I just say that if output is increasing, then it's a sure bet that company profits are also increasing. Otherwise, they would not continue to produce for very long. Likewise, if unemployment is decreasing, it's safe to assume that more workers are finding jobs to make more stuff, along with additional capital. Otherwise, capital would stop being invested, which would automatically lead to a drop in the demand for labor. Therein lies the clue to the 2000-01 slowdown. Unemployment remained low, as did inflation. With low unemployment, consumer spending remained strong since the vast majority of us had a paycheck to spend. But when profits and revenues did not materialize to support the overvaluation of stocks, the return on investment started to decline. Company inventories were built up as manufacturers continued to produce, in part, to take advantage of production efficiencies and to keep workers on the job in a tight labor market. This contributed to the appearance—on the surface anyway—that the economy was still expanding. Inflation was low, unemployment was very low, and production remained high.

Then investment stopped not only in the stock market but also in terms of capital investment and business expenditures because of the uncertainty that a return could be realized. In fact, all the money that went into the "hot" telecom sector looked like it wouldn't produce anything. After all, investment seeks some return, and investors' patience was wearing thin. The first evidence of a problem came in the decline in the rate of growth of GDP in the third quarter of 2000. Not only was output growing at a much slower pace, inventories were piling up and capital expenditures by corporations were all tapped out. This was on the back of a 50-basis-point rate *increase* by the Fed, which wanted to sidestep an overheating economy. Even Greenspan, in retrospect, got it wrong. But at least the Fed was the first to see the problems and reverse course about as abruptly as anyone has ever witnessed.

Again, the consumer stayed strong and unemployment remained low. After all, as long as there was consumer spending, the economy should continue to grow. Right? Wrong. Like a car that is made up of hundreds of moving parts that weigh thousands of pounds, the car won't go very far unless you continue to put a few gallons of gas in it. The same is true of the economy. The consumer can keep spending and keep the economy treading water, but for real expansion to occur you need corporations to spend and invest. This investment is the gasoline that propels the economy. These expenditures do things for the economy like create jobs, build factories, and enhance efficiencies. New products and services come from these expenditures, which fuel further investment and so on.

The point is, all of us, including Mr. Greenspan, had our economic vision clouded by the contented pace of consumer spending and the building up of inventories that had looked like GDP growth. So once GDP growth stalled and inventories had swelled, it was obvious that investment would stop. After all, investment chases returns, and the returns had dwindled. This was the sign that 2000 and, more specifically, 2001 would not be a good year for the economy or the stock market. During the slowdown of 2000 and the recession of 2001, the great inventory buildup and decline in capital investments were the major culprits. This is unlike the recession of 1990-91, when the consumer ran away. In the economic slowdown (the so-called recession) of 2001 and into 2002, the consumer has remained relatively strong. Therefore, when monitoring the economy, consumer spending–related data, such as retail sales and housing sales, had little significance to my strategies as long as they continued to show healthy signs or at least minimal signs of deterioration. Far more important this time were inventory levels and the export and import levels of GDP, as well as capital spending outlays and business spending and investment.

There is no magic formula for which data to watch, and no magic level that will trigger investment decisions. As we've seen in the conflicting economic data for early 2000 (at a time that the stock market was making all time highs) there were good elements that one thought supported a higher market. The negative economic data, however, actually pointed to the real conclusion in this scenario. Focusing on one particular set of data can be as dangerous as ignoring all the data. A far better approach is to define the business cycle and then let the data support or refute that view.

As you remember from Chapter 3, the four stages of the business cycle are expansion, peak, contraction, and trough, with each stage lasting from several months to several years, with expansions lasting about three to five times as long as contractions. Characteristics of each of these phases show up in the economic data that we've discussed, and may become obvious to the economically awakened investor. While expansions and peaks are the desired results, let's not lose sight of the fact that contractions and troughs—while painful—are valuable to the business cycle as well.

Defining the stages of the business cycle may be pretty obvious even without the ability to decipher large amounts of boring economic data. The harder part is to determine what caused the current cycle we are experiencing. Why did GDP decline or unemployment rise? Was it political or caused by inflation? Was it caused by the consumer or large corporations? Within that framework, let's go back even further in time and look at recessions and recoveries.

As stated earlier, the economic slowdown and recession of 2001 was unusual in that consumer spending remained strong during the contraction. Thus, as one viewed the economic data focusing on housing numbers, retail sales, and other consumer-related spending, it appeared as if everything was still okay.

Now let's consider the employment picture. The unemployment rate bottomed in 1999 and in early 2000, at which point we started adding fewer jobs to the economy (see Chart 11-2).

Eventually, we started losing jobs. Contractions in GDP meant that we were making fewer goods. Therefore, we needed fewer workers. This drop in job creation and the subsequent rise in unemployment was the sign we had been looking for. The economy was truly in a contraction (see Chart 11-3).

As Chart 11-3 shows, GDP growth slowed at the end of 1999 and the growth rate decelerated precipitously through 2000 and into 2001. It would be hard to explain stocks going up during this time period, since unemployment was rising and growth was contracting. How could companies increase revenues with fewer workers making less stuff, let alone make profits, which are the key to higher stock prices? The short answer is they couldn't. Yet as stated earlier, housing and retail sales remained strong in this period, which added to the confusion of both the Fed and the mainstream economist, who were betting on the consumer to keep us out of a recession.

CHART 11-2 Employment: Total Nonagricultural (year-to-year % change)

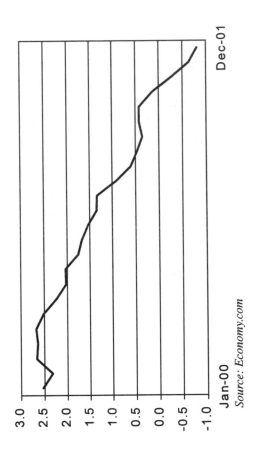

Source: Economy.com

CHART 11-3 Gross Domestic Product (year-to-year % change)

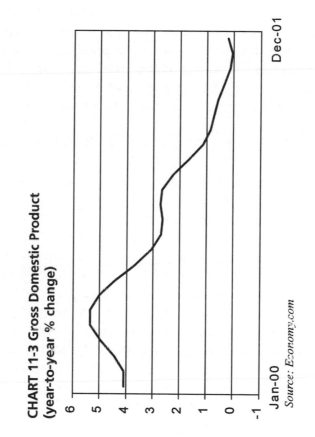

Jan-00

Dec-01

Source: Economy.com

While housing data is very volatile due to seasonality and lag times of purchase, the overall housing market remained strong during 2000 and 2001 (see Chart 11-4), as did retail sales. Remember that retail sales tend to be very volatile and need to be smoothed out by looking at several months, because sometimes a purchase in one month offsets a purchase in another month. As you can see in Chart 11-5, despite a weakening labor market, declining GDP growth, and a depreciating stock market, retail sales remained positive.

So what does this tell us? Since the problem was not the consumer, the recovery wouldn't come from that camp. Rather, we needed business spending to increase and inventories to decrease in order for the rebound to occur. It's important to keep an eye on retail sales and the housing market, which were both robust during 2000-01, to make sure that declines in these areas don't stall a recovery. However, for a recovery to take hold, we would need to see capital investment and reduced inventories. When these two areas turn around, expect an expansion in both employment and GDP.

Fed Chairman Greenspan, meanwhile, was between a rock and a hard place. In late 1996, Greenspan uttered his now infamous words "irrational exuberance," referring to asset prices and equities. He was not saying it was overdone or overbought. Rather, he was just noting that investors need to create more diversified portfolios, and financial leaders as well as political leaders need to support policies that could lead to some sad faces in the short run because it's healthier in the long run. The investing public in its "irrational exuberance" needs to have the benevolent firmness of a parent who takes away a second dessert in favor of some fruit, knowing that the fruit is healthier and there will be plenty of time for cake later. This was a message investors did not want to hear.

Mr. Greenspan was observing how investors were responding to economic conditions at a time when they held an unusually high concentration of stocks as opposed to a more balanced portfolio of stocks and bonds. In fact, risky, unproven stocks comprised the core holdings of many mainstream portfolios. On a more positive note, home ownership was soaring and so were home values, which helped to even out the wealth effect in light of the decline in equity prices. Clearly, home ownership helped to cushion the contraction

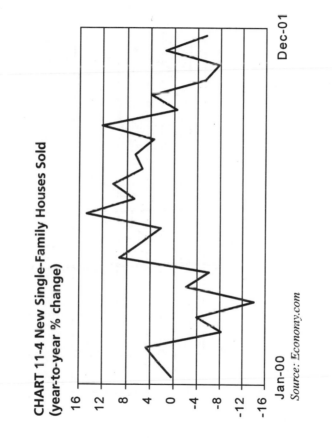

CHART 11-4 New Single-Family Houses Sold
(year-to-year % change)

Jan-00

Dec-01

Source: *Economy.com*

**CHART 11-5 Retail Sales and Food Services
(year-to-year % change)**

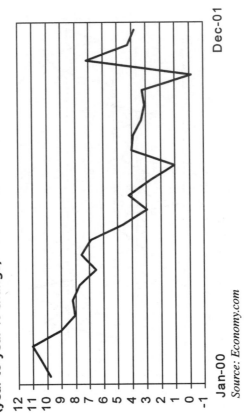

Jan-00   Dec-01

Source: Economy.com

of 2000-01 and to encourage consumer spending, the backbone of the economy.

Still, back in 1998, it felt like the booming economy would never come to an end. Enter the Latin American currency crisis and Russian debt problems that plagued the world. Greenspan, despite his caution on the market speculation and concerns of an overheating economy, had no choice but to act as central banker to the world and lower rates. He lowered them three times: 25 basis points in September, 25 basis points in October, and 25 basis points in November, which moved the fed funds rate from 5.5 percent to 4.75 percent. This brought rates well below the appropriate target levels. Knowing that the U.S. economy was in good shape already, the lower rates were a very volatile ingredient in an explosive market. This was like gasoline leaking steadily near an open flame. With lower rates pumping more liquidity into an expanding economy, where was the liquidity going to go? You guessed it—the roaring stock market!

The Fed had hoped it would be able to provide liquidity to the world, and then by acting quickly would be able to avert an overheated economy and speculative bubble here in the United States. It took the usual 6 to 12 months for monetary policy to work through the system. And work it did! It created an even bigger bubble in asset values, particularly stocks. The Fed needed to retract the rate cuts without upsetting the very fragile bubble that had been created. They started with a 25-basis-point rate hike in June 1999, using the shield of a higher CPI report that warned of possible inflation. After all, Wall Street had to understand that all the extra liquidity could induce some monetary inflation. The Fed continued to see signs of overheating in the labor market and raised rates again in September, and finally in November 1999 it raised rates by another 25 basis points, which brought rates to the level of "neutral" from the stimulus of 1998. In the meantime, Wall Street seemed to understand that fighting inflation and slowing things down a bit would be good in the long run for both the stock market and the economy.

Enter the problem of the unknown. Specifically, Y2K. The scenarios of possibilities seemed endless, including a run on cash that could compromise the financial system and lead to a breakdown in the world as we knew it. The Fed, which had stopped providing liquidity that year by hiking rates, needed to add immediate liquidity into the banking system for the unknown. So it added a little extra liquidity to the system for safekeeping.

As we all know now, the world as we knew it was just fine on January 1, 2000. (The only possible exception was a bomb threat at the Ritz-Carlton in West Palm Beach, Florida, which forced me and some other New Year's revelers into the parking lot at 11:30 p.m. to listen to synthesized rock 'n' roll and a very funny comedian named Rita Rudner, whose set was staged on top of a car using its headlights as floodlights.) The new millennium was not a big event in any sense of the word.

In the economic world, though, the flow of money to guard against Y2K Armageddon added to flood waters that were rising. The Fed needed to shore up things, so in May 2000 the 50-basis-point rate increase brought things back in line. But the timing proved wrong. The economy started to slow down and head into what we would later determine was a recession. The excessive liquidity had created the final stage of a bubble that needed to be popped. The Fed, in the form of that May 2000 rate hike, provided the pin.

Then the slowdown in the economy that followed caused the Fed to shift gears quickly from tightening to easing, while bypassing neutral. One easing after the other played some mind games with the market, which didn't know whether to grasp the conventional wisdom (lower rates are good for equities) or the reality that the economy was in the dumpster. Ultimately, the slowdown created a loss of production, jobs, and wealth, which rate cuts alone could not help. Inventories remained high through 2001, and, with rising unemployment, the question was who was going to buy all the stuff that we made? More important, companies stopped spending.

The solution employed by the Fed throughout 2001, and with more intensity following the events of September 11, was extra liquidity. But it was like adding gas to a sputtering engine—not to an already well-oiled machine. What remained to be seen was whether this fuel boost from extra liquidity would help the economy pull out of recession and then into another bubble, or if the right amount of liquidity had been applied to get us moving on a track of higher productivity and greater growth. After all, even with the broad market averages down by double-digit percentages for 2001, valuations still remained high by historic standards. What we saw clearly was that interest rates alone cannot help an economy that needs to contract and shed excesses from inventory to personnel.

For now and the near future, if the economy ends up recovering from all this stimulus and if earnings growth actually does support market valuations, then it will show up in the data. Conversely, if the economy starts overheating as a result of the stimulus, that also will be evident in GDP, inflation indices, and the unemployment rate. Whatever the outcome, it will show up in the data.

THE LATE 1980S—FROM CONSPICUOUS CONSUMPTION TO PINCHING PENNIES

Data are like footprints that show where the economy has been and most likely where it's headed. This data trail can be seen in all periods of time, especially notable ones. Let's take the "Wayback Machine" to the next economic era of note: from 1988 to the recession of 1990-91. It was the end of the Reagan decade with Bush Sr. finishing the Republican reign and setting the stage for the first baby-boomer president, Bill Clinton. Rap music had not become mainstream yet (thankfully) and punk rock was on its way out (finally). Cellular technology was exploding, but the Internet and the dot-com world were known to only the "supergeek," if at all.

The markets had finally recovered from the Crash of 1987, and the economy was strong. The great merger and acquisition boom, however, was causing a different type of decline in the job market than was seen in the past. This time, the middle-management layer was being hit. "Corporate downsizing" was the term *du jour*. Middle management wasn't "fired" or "laid off." Rather, the terms used were "getting downsized" or that their jobs had become "redundant." Whatever the terminology, the fallout from this change in the labor market was a sharp decline in consumer spending. After all, this had been the generation of conspicuous consumption. Buy now, pay later, and worry about saving even later than that! "Hey, didn't Mom and Dad put anything away for me?" became the battle cry of Generation X.

Massive corporate restructuring during this time resulted in increases in unemployment and the taking on of huge amounts of corporate debt. The result was not only a slowdown at the end of the decade, but a full-fledged recession that took hold in 1990 and 1991. This was a typical, garden-variety recession: a slowdown that followed a period of excess. There had been too much of everything: too much consumption, spending, corporate acquisitions, and the like. But what was most interesting, which would earn the recession of 1990-91 a place in history, was how we recovered from it. True, it was mild as recessions go. In fact, we didn't know we were in the recession until, a few years later, the National Bureau of Economic Research (NBER) told us we were.

Though the 1990-91 recession was a mild one, those who were "downsized" in the middle of it felt the pain. These were the kind of middle managers who are normally spared the job cuts felt by their blue-collar work force brethren. Many of those in collars of white had never been out of work before. They were used to a high standard of living. But in the midst of the 1990-91 recession, they had to convince themselves that changing from Neiman Marcus to Target was somehow chic. It was suddenly "cool" to be thrifty and get a deal on a $200 pair of Ray Ban sunglasses.

The curious thing about this recession was that the recovery did not show up in the data. Even Mr. Greenspan was a bit flummoxed by it. Here's what did show up: Unemployment was not going down, but capital spending and new orders were going up. As we discussed in Chapter 3, there was a recovery going on somewhere, but the traditional businesses were not adding workers. What happened in the midst of this "jobless expansion" was that the middle-manager yuppies were going out on their own. This new wave of consultants and small-business owners was proliferating—and it was real.

These entrepreneurs were ordering equipment—new phones, computers, printers, desks, and the rest of the accoutrements—at a record pace. It was these orders that caught Mr. Greenspan's eye, and he knew that something was happening, and he knew that new growth and productivity were just around the corner.

Of course, Mr. Greenspan was right. This new, aggressive entrepreneurial worker ignited the greatest and most efficient expansion that we have ever seen. This expansion was forecasted by increases in business orders and technology. Once it ignited, GDP increased, unemployment declined, and worker productivity increased at a rate not seen since the Industrial Revolution. As wealth was being created at record levels, consumer spending kicked in, and the economy was a rocket ship bound for Mars.

THE 1970S—DISCO, AFROS, EMBARGOES, AND INFLATION

Let's take the "Wayback Machine" to another notable time—the 1970s, when it seemed everything was happening at once. It is not very often that you get to see a period of time like the 1970s, when you have so many psychedelic colors to look at. The 1970s had it all: low unemployment, high unemployment, political uncertainty, embargoes, monetary inflation, supply shortage inflation, declining worker productivity, tax hikes, and investment incentives to try to keep the ship afloat.

The 1970s started off with the Vietnam War. Political uncertainty at home started to undermine our economy. Inflation, which was relatively low during much of the 1960s, was headed above 5 percent. Unemployment, which had remained low in the 1960s at 3 to 5 percent, was also on the rise. However, major changes were occurring regarding the work force, as women played a more significant role, making measuring the work force more difficult. Thus, the overall unemployment rate was higher than stated. During the 1970s, the government started running large deficits. Government deficits during inflationary times meant the Treasury was printing more money, which caused the inflation rate to jump even further, to more than 14 percent in the second half of the 1970s. Added to this situation was the financing of the increasingly unpopular Vietnam War, which was putting a strain on the U.S. economy and society as a whole.

Inflation was cutting into wealth and spending. This came at a time when the average investor was still uneasy about hyperinflation, and many could still remember the Great Depression. The result was the average investor/consumer pulled in the reins. Slower spending and increased savings gave way at times to actual hoarding. Consumer spending collapsed in the wake of political and economic uncertainty. This fear all but dried up investments as well, which turned out to be a fiscal fiasco for anyone trying to stay one step ahead of the inflation monster. The oil embargo caused a spike in gasoline and other energy prices that wreaked havoc on the economy. The United States was already printing dollars to fund the debt from the war. Then supply shocks from oil shortages were starting to really push the inflation button. The problem was the Fed's inability to restrict the money supply because of the great amount of U.S. debt. The answer? Government-instituted price controls.

What a big mistake that was! I've said it before, and I'll say it again. Price controls don't work because they create excess demand at the higher prices and exacerbate the problem. Fortunately, cartels don't really work either and rarely survive, since greed usually leads someone to cheat and loosen up supplies. Or capitalists take advantage of the profit potential and enter the market with like goods and products. Remember, short-term supply shortages have little long-term impact. But before this happened, there was a good deal of consumer fear of the OPEC cartel. The American consumer was convinced the world was running out of energy and that substitute products just weren't available. The result was panic-driven price controls and rationing, which in turn caused huge drains on resources. Government and private business alike reallocated resources to address the energy problem, which caused a sharp decline in productivity. What an economic soap opera this turned out to be!

At this point, the 1970s—in addition to sideburns, afros, and disco music—was marked by low worker productivity, high inflation created by excess money in the system and supply and demand imbalances, plus high unemployment. With the misunderstood condition of the oil embargo, fighting inflation, increasing productivity, and trying to grow GDP was going to be a tough job. If only we had understood that high energy prices, if left alone, would result in a rush to exploit that opportunity in the form of either more supply or technology and new products.

The increasing deficit, which was backed by the printing of more money, turned inflation into hyperinflation. Inflation, let alone hyperinflation, is a rare occurrence during a slowdown. This resulted in the coining of a new term, "stagflation." Stagflation is slow growth with inflation, and this was bewildering economists everywhere. If the economy is not growing by much or hardly at all, then how could prices be rising? The answer was the shortage and significance of energy, plus the fear of the OPEC cartel that helped create this situation—albeit temporarily. On the positive side, opportunities from these events also presented themselves. Investors took advantage of long-term yields on government-backed securities in the mid double digits. When it became apparent that the cure to these economic ills would be a self-induced recession and contraction in the money supply, investors took advantage of some of the highest yields ever on U.S. government bonds, which are some of the safest securities around. This contraction in the money supply and the reining in of inflation created a terrible recession in 1979 and again in 1981-82. But the seeds were set for great economic expansion in the years to follow.

POSTWAR BOOM FOR THE ECONOMY . . . AND BABIES!

After World War II, the U.S. economy experienced what might have been easily predicted for the years and even the decades to follow. The United States depleted all inventories during the war years. In addition, war-time rationing and subsidies created pent-up demand. An educated, skilled work force came home ready to produce and to consume. Government spending, favorable interest rates, and an eager work force combined to create large increases in GDP, creating a terrific economic environment. Granted, there were slowdowns in the 1950s, as the economy rested to absorb the benefits of these conditions, but the result was the decade of the 1960s. This remains a perfect example of the potential of our economic system. The hallmarks of the system are an educated work force eager to produce and consume, low interest rates to spur capital investment, low inflation, and smart monetary policy to spark sustained growth without unnecessary intervention. In other words, if it's not broke, don't fix it!

During the postwar era, particularly the 1960s, the U.S. economy experienced a protracted period of low inflation, a sharp contrast to the decade that would follow when double-digit inflation would become an American nightmare. In the 1960s, no one watched the Fed, and the Fed chairman was certainly not a household name (unlike Mr. Greenspan of today). The prime rate was little changed during the post–World War II era and didn't budge at all between 1960 and 1966.

These were great years for the U.S. economy. The nation's standard of living improved steadily, measured in both personal income and consumption. This was a period of rapid fixed investment and tight labor markets. From 1962 through the end of the decade, the unemployment rate held fast at 4.5 percent. Confidence was through the roof, and the markets loved every bit of it.

Amid all these economic good times, there were lessons to be learned. The wonder years ended rather abruptly because of unpopular political action (namely, the war in Vietnam), combined with a fiscally irresponsible government. This ushered in the 1970s nightmare. You can see the similarities between the 1960s and the 1990s that go beyond the coincidence. To quote Yogi Berra, it seemed like "*déjà vu* all over again."

THE BIG ONE—1929

As our economic journey back in time continues, let's take a look at the mother of all crises: the stock market crash of 1929 and the depression that followed. So much has been written about this era that the basic events hardly need to be reviewed. For our purpose here, we'll take a look at some of the highlights.

The early 1900s were an important time for the U.S. economy with the end of World War I and the formation of the Federal Reserve. More important, the U.S. economy was transforming itself from an agricultural base to an industrial one. The consumer was playing an ever-increasing role in the U.S. economy. With victory in World War I, the U.S. economy started to create jobs and increase production while Europe was strapped by huge debts from the war and found it difficult to expand economically.

Without much guidance on such matters, the U.S. government—viewing ours as a closed economy—restricted trade with Germany. The rationale was that it would be better for U.S. companies and their workers if this country built and consumed its own goods. While these restrictions, particularly after the war, may have been beneficial to the United States in the short run, they were not helpful at all to Germany. How could the Germans repay their war debt and rebuild their economy if that country could not trade with the United States, the largest economy in the world? The result was total economic chaos in Europe, which would in time affect the U.S. economy as well. There may have been some benefits reaped in the United States from the trade embargoes, but the overall result was a disproportionate distribution of wealth here in the United States. Further, it created a bubble supported by an overleveraged economy. The economy and society as a whole seemed out of touch with reality. Consider that the majority of cars on the road in those Roaring Twenties were American-made convertibles. Or was it just that the weather was better back then? There were some engineering advancements being made abroad that we were not part of. It was no joke, though, when the bubble burst in October 1929 with the crash that ushered in the Great Depression.

This era teaches economists and politicians alike many lessons, ones that we still follow today. From unreasonable trade restrictions we learned that sometimes the punishment brought on our neighbors can also hurt us as well. Conversely, we learned that supporting other nations economically actually helps build not only a trade partner, but develops another consumer who will eventually buy some of our goods. Call it the Economic Golden Rule: Do unto others so that someday they'll be able to buy from you.

The other lesson was a painful, but important one about the absence of monetary policy and at least some guidance on interest rates, trade, securities, banking, and loans. Without the proper structure and policies to oversee banks, markets, and the monetary system in general, the result is economic havoc.

When the stock market crashed in 1929—unlike the crash that would follow 68 years later—there was no government body or nongovernmental body in a position to add the appropriate stimulus or to instill confidence that could have headed off the depression. As times grew bleaker, unemployment rose from 3.2 percent in the beginning of 1930 to 8.7 percent by the end of that year, and later to 24.6 percent in 1933 as industrial production collapsed. At first, raising taxes seemed like a good idea, as it would put more money in the hands of the government so that Uncle Sam could increase spending. Bad idea. Higher taxes actually produced lower tax revenues as the economy shrunk even further, unemployment increased, and corporate profits dwindled.

The depression was feeding upon itself in the 1930s, and no one, it seemed, could figure out how to stimulate the economy. Then came Franklin Roosevelt's "New Deal." The concept was to get people working again. Building infrastructure from highways to parks would create output, help spur demand, and jump-start the economy. It wasn't until the onset of World War II that the United States truly pulled out of and away from the depression. Regulation started to create some order in the banking and financial services arena with the Securities Act of 1934 and the Investment Act of 1940.

Increased government spending to support the war effort and returning industrial capacity utilization to higher levels was the medicine that an ailing economy needed.

The rest, as they say, is history up to the present day and into the future. If history is our great teacher, then the lesson to be learned here is that cycles repeat themselves. If we learn our lessons well, however, we will be better prepared and avoid the same mistakes. Sometimes those lessons are in the form of what *not* to do, such as the flawed tax increase policies of the 1930s, which hurt the economy instead of giving government more money to spend, and the price controls that we employed in the 1970s, thinking they would fight inflation.

Regardless of what we may hear about a new economy that can expand indefinitely, about technology that can solve anything, and about business cycles being dead, the reality is that we continue to face—and will continue to face—the same problems, although the symptoms may be different. Certain cycles, such as expansion, may be longer, and others, such as troughs, may be shorter. That still does not change the basic ebb and flow of the economy, from expansion to peak to contraction to trough. The challenge for us now is to try to create smoother transitions from cycle to cycle, employing the best of solutions that history can teach us.

Wealth and You

I am often asked what to look at when making investment decisions. Is now a good time to buy stocks, or is it a good time to purchase real estate? Should I buy bonds now, or is it time to refinance my mortgage? The real answer to all of these questions is a qualified "it depends." It depends on variables from your investment time horizon to whether the economy is pulling out of a recession or steaming ahead, with a nod to your financial goals and objectives as well. Despite these variables, let's examine these questions.

By now, you've gotten the message about the business cycle: expansion, peak, contraction, and trough. Identifying what stage the economy is in will go a long way toward answering many of your investment questions. In a nutshell, here's a guide to investing according to the current stage of the business cycle.

- **Expansion**. This is the easiest time to invest, as the prevailing economic conditions are good for most investments. The expansion phase usually produces a bull stock market and a steady bond market. Stocks typically outperform fixed-income investments, so during this phase, one would be better off with a higher weighting of stocks. Beyond increasing holdings in your favorite mutual funds and stocks, it would also be prudent to create an equity portfolio that includes the larger mutual funds and broader market averages to ensure that you benefit from the expanding economy overall and not just from a few sectors (which may or may not grow in line with the overall economy). Bonds are a great diversification tool. During this phase, however, while their performance tends to be stable because of low inflation, they are usually outperformed by equities.

During the expansion phase, taking on increased equity risk makes sense. This means not only increasing your exposure to equities, but throwing in some riskier issues as well. You might even dabble in some speculative new issues (e.g., IPOs) and private equity deals that have the potential to bring in some substantial returns. The expansion environment is likely to yield a higher probability of success, so taking on a bit more risk can pay off. However, the one negative that expansion can bring is inflation, which is the killjoy of many investments. As inflation may lead to higher interest rates, lower bond prices and lower stock prices can follow. Thus, as you invest during the late stages of the expansion, you must be on the look out for inflation. Investments in hard assets, other than gold, or in companies that produce commodities, such as oil, tend to do well during inflationary periods. Another possible investment is "TIPS," or inflation-adjusted securities.

- **Peak**. If inflation doesn't kill the economic expansion (and sometimes it doesn't), then the peak will. With everything and everyone clamoring to invest, consume, and buy assets at any price, it's no wonder that the peak is characterized by irrational investment behavior with little regard to valuations. Producers, meanwhile, increase supply because it looks like the economic party is never going to end. Even Wall Street increases the number of IPOs because demand appears to be so hot for everything. The Fed may try to stop a peak or slow down the economy by raising interest rates a few notches. Nonetheless, the result of the overzealous investor and overoptimistic business is a peak.

The best place to be in a peak is in cash or very liquid, short-term securities such as money-market securities and funds. Granted, there are some stocks and sectors of the stock market that will hold up very well during peaks, such as real estate investment trusts (REITS) and stocks of large multinational consumer products companies, or even companies that sell staple goods. Still, the overall volatility and inability to calculate appropriate valuations makes investing at these times not only difficult but less lucrative. The best investment advice for a proactive investor during the peak stage is to sell. Take advantage of overvalued assets to raise cash levels in your portfolio. Cash is king if a bubble has been created and is about to burst.

- **Contraction**. The contraction stage is the most difficult to manage. Some contractions turn into full-blown recessions, in which case patience is prudent. Certainly investment in fixed-income securities can not only preserve capital, but achieve capital appreciation as the Fed lowers interest rates in response to the contraction. As rates decline, the price of bonds goes up.

  During a contraction, the value of assets may appear "cheap" compared with the overvaluations at the peak, but still may get cheaper. It is important, therefore, to wait for clear evidence that the contraction is ending and that the groundwork is being laid for the trough—and the expansion to follow.

- **Trough**. When the economy "hits bottom," it's time to get ready for expansion. Keep in mind the economy is still in a contraction during the trough, although in its latter stages will show improvement. While the contraction trough phases will be ripe with business and investment opportunities, the market is typically very volatile during these times, as uncertainty and capitulations linger. As the economy pulls out of the trough and heads to the next phase—expansion—equities will be the place to be.

Knowing how to invest your money during an economic cycle, as you can see, is half the battle—and quite frankly it's the easier half. The more challenging part is to judge just what economic cycle we're in. This can be made all the more difficult by the fact that some indicators may contradict others, depending upon what they're measuring—whether it's industrial output (which looks good for the economy) or the building of inventories (which is usually a negative sign).

That's the benefit of hindsight. As an investor, don't be dismayed if you don't hit the "trough" or pick the "peak." Being able to identify and act upon the longer-term phases of expansion and contraction will serve you well even if your timing lags.

With the benefit of hindsight and by anyone's definition, it's clear that the U.S. economy was in a phase of great expansion during most of the 1990s. During this phase, a portfolio that was heavily weighted toward stocks produced the best results (once the recession of 1990-91 was behind us). At the end of 1996 and during 1997, Fed Chairman Greenspan issued his now famous warning about the "irrational exuberance" of the U.S. investor, particularly as it related to investing in the stock market during this time period. Mr. Greenspan saw a bubble being created, and the peak cycle was not too far behind. The question was how to manage the bubble so that, when it inevitably popped, the ensuing slowdown would not become too devastating and wipe out too much wealth.

There were stories galore in the late 1990s of people who had made a "killing" in a stock that they bought just before it really "popped." There were "lucky" stock picks that doubled or tripled in value. There were astute investments in emerging sectors. There were mailroom clerks whose employers went public and now they were worth many, many times more than their salaries—on paper. Doctors made more money in part-time stock speculation than they did in their practices, which were certainly nothing to sneeze at when it came to revenue-generating businesses. I know of "somebody's wife's cousin" who became a multimillionaire, at least on paper, because of the stock options she held in a company whose shares traded well over $100.

In the light of these stories, no wonder Mr. Greenspan was concerned about irrational exuberance. I don't think he was purposefully raining on our investment parade. Rather, Mr. Greenspan saw what was behind us, and he knew what was ahead of us.

The solution to the "exuberance" problem? Diversification—not only from stocks to bonds, but to hard assets as well. Home ownership needed to be encouraged, as well as diversification into fixed-income instruments. Diversification is such an overly used term that most of us can overlook the power of its meaning. We may even hear "diversification" as a punitive term, one that means, "eat a salad with that steak" or "take your vitamins and no more dessert!" From an investment standpoint, diversification may make us think, erroneously, that we're not "smart" enough to pick the "right" investments. Nothing could be further from the truth. In reality, diversification is hanging multiple lines in the water to increase your chances of making a good catch.

Thus, when the signs became clear at the end of the 1990s that the expansion was becoming a peak, or in early 2000 that the peak was becoming a contraction, then diversifying into fixed income and reducing exposure to stocks would have been prudent. Not only would you have preserved capital that you reaped during the expansion, but you would have profited from the peak through the contraction as fixed-income investments appreciated during the period of aggressive rate cuts by the Fed.

Let's take this a step further. As an aggressive investor myself, I do not just pare back my equity holdings from peak to contraction and add a few more bonds to my portfolio. I get totally out of equities when the data indicate that the economy is slowing. And then, anticipating the slowdown that will cause a contraction in stock prices, I take a short position in the stock market. Conversely, when economic data indicate to me that we've reached the trough cycle and are headed for expansion, I will not only cover my short position in equities, I will also go long. Using this strategy, I will (thankfully) miss the ultimate peak with a long position as I will also (thankfully) miss the final bottom with a short position. I say "thankfully" because trying to pick the exact top or bottom is not as productive compared with identifying the overall trend.

Of course, my aggressive strategy is certainly not for everyone. In fact, it may be too aggressive for many investors. But even my extreme strategy is based on the same premise as the more conservative approach: Use the economic data to identify the cycle and invest accordingly. Simply stated: When the economy is contracting, you will profit from fewer equities and more bonds; when the economy is expanding, you will profit from more equities and fewer bonds.

As an investor, you have limited choices of where to place your capital. You have individual stocks, stock mutual funds, real estate, hard assets, bonds (fixed income), and of course, cash. Over the long term, the stock market is an expanding, appreciating asset. As the U.S. economy continues to grow over time, so does the value of the stock market. Of course, the economy—and the market—also contracts and goes down. But the overall objective is to increase value. Now achieving that goal is another story.

The bond market or fixed-income market is actually a loan, either to the federal, state, or municipal government, or corporations. These bonds produce a yield or a return on your investment. Unlike stocks, interest rates over time fluctuate in a range, albeit a wide one. Granted, rates can go up as high as 18 percent or as low as 1 percent, but over time they will be somewhere within this range and most likely a smaller range than this. Thus, investing in fixed-income instruments to generate capital appreciation has its limitations. However, bonds fulfill another objective and produce a steady return on your money if capital preservation is more important to you than appreciation. This is in sharp contrast to stocks that, theoretically, can go up forever.

The point is that bonds can be used for diversification, and while they are generally less risky than equities, they actually require more active attention than stocks. Assuming that credit quality is not an issue, if you hold the bond to maturity, you will get your capital back, along with some interest that has been paid to you or accrued over time. However, your capital investment before maturity fluctuates with the current interest rate, making your original capital worth more or less before maturity. An individual stock, no matter how long you hold it, may never return your original investment if the price plummets the day after you purchase it. If you bought 100 shares of a high-flying technology stock that was trading at $200 a share, and over the next year it plummets to $5, there is no guarantee that you'll get your original $20,000 back.

Looking at stocks as a whole, however, they do have a higher return overall. This is the risk premium you pay for owning stocks. Since as an investor in stocks you have to face more risk, you are rewarded for it with the possibility of capital appreciation.

So you should be 100 percent in stocks all the time, right? Wrong. Remember that word "diversification," which implies a strategy not just for today, but for the long haul. Given the returns implicit in stock investment over time, this is the focus of your investment. Granted, there are personal variables that must come into consideration. For example, if you're 25 years old and a lifetime and a half away from retirement, you are likely to be more heavily weighted in stocks than, say, a 75-year-old on a fixed income. But even that 75-year-old, with the prospect of living to the age of 85 or 90, still needs some capital appreciation along with the overall goal of capital preservation.

The need for your funds will govern how much risk will be prudent for you. If you need your money in 5 years, then you would be more risk averse (Read: you need to preserve your capital more) than someone with a longer time horizon, such as 10 or 20 years, who can a take few of the market's roller coaster rides. Nonetheless, if you are 60 and you want your money at the age of 65, I would be hard pressed not to tell you to have some exposure to stocks. And don't forget that while someone may retire at age 65, his or her prospects for living 10, 20, or more years is usually quite good. Thus, when it comes to capital appreciation at any age, the tool is stock investment for some portion of your portfolio.

In other words, make your allocation into stocks based upon the business cycle that we're in and your time horizon and investment parameters. Then invest the remainder into bonds. Don't do this the other way around and invest first in bonds and put the rest in stocks because, as investors with time horizons beyond 3 to 5 years, most of us want to have at least some exposure to stocks. Perhaps our stock portfolios take a more conservative look during economic slowdowns, but most of us don't want to be in all bonds just because GDP is growing at a slower rate and unemployment is starting to rise.

While it's true that buy-and-hold strategies have their merits, you may further improve the performance of your portfolio through diversification and changing asset allocation. If this is done within the context of the economic cycles, I believe you'll be pleased with the results.

Thus, the ebb and flow of the economy is matched by the ebb and flow of your own portfolio, with greater or lesser use of fixed-income instruments as a diversification tool—depending upon whether the economy is chugging along or decelerating.

Stocks and bonds, as I alluded to at the opening of this epilogue, aren't the only "investments" available to us. Back in the "irrational exuberance" days, in fact, Mr. Greenspan was very pleased by one thing in particular during this economic peak: Home ownership was increasing rapidly. The wealth of our country was naturally being diversified into home equity. Thus, the Fed's rate cuts could produce real results as homeowners refinanced and put extra dollars in their pockets—and into the economy. This phenomenon would make rate cuts even more powerful during consumer-led slowdowns.

Of course, the slowdown in the new millennium was not led by the consumer. As stated previously, the slowdown was the direct result of a decline in corporate spending and the buildup of inventories. That may raise the question in your mind about what you can do about any of this. It's really a great question. Because of the way that the slowdown occurred and how the Fed responded, the fear of inflation was overstated. With the 10-year Treasury note in January 2002 yielding about 5 percent and the annual inflation rate under 2 percent, it would appear that 300 basis points is a pretty high risk premium for inflation—if, in fact, we do get inflation.

Everywhere you look, prices are lower than they were a year ago—cars (thanks to dealer incentives), gasoline, electronics, air travel, hotel, stocks, and even real estate and homes, although not as much as with other assets. It looks as if inflation is well under control.

With the unemployment rate on the rise, it would be surprising to see wage inflation pick up. However, health care costs and insurance have seen significant price increases, and their impact cannot be ignored. To that end it still appears the economy is contracting. We can't get too overly excited about a bounce back in activity and in the

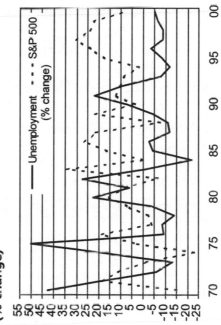

Comparison of Unemployment Rate and S&P 500 (% change)

markets since September 11, 2001. After all, the economy was effectively shutdown for a period of time and the stock market became extremely oversold.

Thus, for the first half of 2002 I remained out of the stock market (in fact I had a short equity position on) during the continued contraction. However, it would be wise to be on the alert for signs of expansion in the manufacturing sector, as well as business investment picking up across many sectors. Then, when the final sign occurs, when unemployment stops its acceleration and GDP expands, I would move into equity-related investments. When this will happen is anyone's guess.

With the tools you have to make interpretations of the various economic reports, it's time to take off your water wings and jump into the economic and investment pool. There is no set of rules or circumstances that should elicit your investment decisions. Rather, a steady approach of information gathering, research, and evaluation should be your objective.

Buy-and-hold in the long run has advantages, and time has proven this approach to have a high degree of success. The question is, how "long" is the long run? But if you want to be more proactive than passive and shorten the timeframe to achieve your goals, then you should make investment decisions according to economic conditions. To accomplish this, you need to be proactive. This will give you flexibility to make financial decisions on *your* terms. You don't have to wait for the next bull market or economic expansion to do things like retire or make big purchases. You have your destiny in your own hands.

SUMMARY OF KEY ECONOMIC REPORTS

ABC NEWS/MONEY MAGAZINE CONSUMER COMFORT INDEX

Source: ABC News/Money Magazine

The ABC News/Money Magazine Consumer Comfort Index represents a rolling average based on telephone interviews with about 1000 adults nationwide each month. Each week's results are based on about 1000 interviews conducted in the prior 4 weeks. The margin of error is plus or minus 3 percentage points. Field work is done by ICR—International Communications Research of Media, Pa.

Survey participants are asked to rate the national economy, personal finances, and buying climate. There are four possible responses, two negative and two positive. The negative response to each index question is subtracted from the positive response. The three resulting numbers are then added and divided by three. The index can range from +100 (everyone positive on all three measures) to –100 (all negative on all three measures).

AGRICULTURAL PRICES
Source: National Agricultural Statistics Service, USDA
Agricultural Prices is a broad release containing prices received by farmers for principal crops, livestock, and livestock products; indices of prices received by farmers; feed price ratios; indices of prices paid by farmers; and parity prices. Primary sales data used to determine grain prices are obtained from probability samples of 2600 mills and elevators. These procedures ensure that virtually all grain moving into commercial channels has a chance of being included in the survey. Generally, states surveyed account for 90 percent or more of total U.S. production. Livestock prices are obtained from packers, stockyards, auctions, and dealers, and data from AMS-USDA, private marketing organizations, and state commodity groups and agencies. Interfarm sales of grain and livestock are not included since they represent very small percentages of total sales. Grain marketed for seed is also excluded. Fruit and vegetable prices are obtained from sample surveys and market check data from AMS.

"BEIGE BOOK"
Source: Federal Reserve Board
Commonly known as the "Beige Book," the "Summary of Commentary on Current Economic Conditions" by Federal Reserve District is published eight times a year. Each Federal Reserve Bank gathers anecdotal information on current economic conditions in its district through reports from bank and branch directors and interviews with key businessmen, economists, market experts, and other sources. The "Beige Book" summarizes this information by district and sector. The "Beige Book" does not represent the views of the Federal Reserve Board or the Federal Reserve Banks, but summarizes comments from businesses and contacts outside of the Federal Reserve System.

BUSINESS INVENTORIES
Source: Bureau of the Census

- **Monthly Retail Trade.** Retail firms provide data on dollar value of retail sales and sales for selected establishments; a subsample of firms also provides data on the value of end-of-month inventories.

- **Monthly Wholesale Trade**. Companies provide data on dollar values of merchant wholesalers' sales and end-of-month inventories.

- **Manufacturers**. Data on manufacturers' current production levels and future production commitments. Information includes value of shipments; new orders (net of cancellations); end-of-month total inventory, materials and supplies, work-in-process, and finished goods inventories.

CHAIN STORE SALES

Source: Mitsubishi Bank-Schroder Wertheim

The Mitsubishi Index is one of the longest running chain store indices. It tracks spending at major chain stores that fit in the broad "general merchandise, apparel, and furniture" category. This distinguishes it from the Redbook Survey that focuses on department stores. The Mitsubishi Index includes only same-store sales (sales from stores that have been in business for at least a year). Because the index is a same-store sales index, retail industry expansion is not immediately captured in the index, and the result is that the Mitsubishi Index tends to underestimate sales growth. The index is reported as a percentage change from 1year ago and covers the following specialized retail groupings: apparel, building supply, department, discount, drug, electronic, footwear, furniture, and wholesale clubs.

CHICAGO FED NATIONAL ACTIVITY INDEX

Source: Chicago Federal Reserve Board

The Chicago Fed National Activity Index is a coincident indicator of broad economic activity. It is released monthly by the Chicago Reserve Board. The index value is set such that a value of zero indicates that the economy is growing at its long-run potential growth rate. A value above zero indicates that the economy is growing above potential, while a negative value indicates that the economy is growing below potential.

The index is a weighted average of 85 indicators of national economic activity. These indicators are drawn from 5 broad categories of data: (1) production and income; (2) employment, unemployment, and hours worked; (3) personal consumption and housing; (4) manufacturing and trade sales; (5) inventories and orders. The main purpose of the Chicago Fed selecting these indicators is to provide a tool for forecasting inflation pressure caused by the economy growing too quickly. An additional benefit of this goal is the creation of a coincident index of broad economic activity.

CHICAGO PMI
Source: National Association of Purchasing Management—Chicago
The National Association of Purchasing Management—Chicago releases a monthly composite index based on surveys of more than 200 purchasing managers regarding the manufacturing industry. Index values above 50 indicate an expanding economy, while values below 50 are indicative of contraction. This so-called diffusion index is seasonally adjusted for the effects of variations within the year, differences due to holidays, and institutional changes. The index is a composite of seven similarly constructed indices, including: new orders, production, supplier delivery times, backlogs, inventories, prices paid, and employment.

CONFERENCE BOARD'S CONSUMER CONFIDENCE
Source: The Conference Board
The Consumer Confidence Survey measures the level of confidence individual households have in the performance of the economy. Survey questionnaires are mailed to a nationwide representative sample of 5000 households, of which approximately 3500 respond. Households are asked five questions that include (1) a rating of current business conditions in the household's area, (2) a rating of business conditions 6 months in the future, (3) job availability in the area, (4) job availability in 6 months, and (5) family income in 6 months. The responses are seasonally adjusted. An index is constructed for each response and then a composite index is fashioned based on the responses. Two other indices, one for an assessment of the present situation and one for expectations about the future, are also con-

structed. Expectations account for 60 percent of the index, while the current situation is responsible for the remaining 40 percent.

CONFERENCE BOARD'S HELP-WANTED INDEX
Source: The Conference Board
The Conference Board surveys help-wanted advertising in 51 major newspapers across the nation. Since the index has been maintained, the same 51 newspapers have been sampled. The Conference Board then constructs an index based on the volume of advertising. An index is created for the nation, covering the nine census divisions and for the 51 metro areas in which the newspapers are published. The year 1987 is the base year, with a value of 100. The index is seasonally adjusted.

CONFERENCE BOARD'S LEADING INDICATORS
Source: The Conference Board
The composite leading index is constructed as a weighted average of 10 key economic data series designed to predict economic conditions in the near term. The index generally turns down before a recession and turns up before an expansion. The indicators that comprise the index are listed in order of importance as follows: spread between the 10-year Treasury and the fed funds rate, M2 money supply, average work week in manufacturing, manufacturers' new orders for consumer goods, S&P 500, average weekly initial unemployment claims, vendor performance component of the ISM Index, housing permits, consumer expectations, and manufacturers' new orders for nondefense capital goods. A simple rule of thumb often used is that 3 consecutive months of decline in the index are a sign that the economy will fall into recession.

CONSTRUCTION SPENDING
Source: Bureau of Census
Construction Spending, also known as "Value of Construction Put in Place," reports the dollar value of newly completed structures. Individual data series are available for several residential building types; nonresidential private building types; public buildings, and other public and private structures, such as roads and utility lines. Both current

dollar and inflation-adjusted estimates are available. This release is used directly to estimate the investment in the structures component of the expenditures estimate of GDP. Since a building is not recorded in the data series until it is completed, this series is a lagging indicator of construction activity. Permit issuance available from the Bureau of the Census for residential structures and proprietary databases of nonresidential construction starts are more useful as leading indicators of activity.

CONSUMER CREDIT
Source: Federal Reserve Board
Consumer Credit represents loans for households for financing consumer purchases of goods and services and for refinancing existing consumer debt. Secured and unsecured loans are included except those secured with real estate (mortgages, home equity loans and lines, etc). Securitized consumer loans, loans made by finance companies, banks, and retailers that are sold as securities are included.

The two categories of consumer credit are revolving and nonrevolving debt. Revolving debt covers credit card use whether for purchases or for cash advances, store charge accounts, and check credit plans that allow overdrafts up to certain amounts on personal accounts. It accounts for about 43 percent of consumer installment debt outstanding. The nonrevolving category was created in 1999 by combining the old categories "auto" and "other." It includes auto, personal, student, and other miscellaneous loans such as recreation vehicle loans.

CONSUMER PRICE INDEX
Source: Bureau of Labor Statistics
The Consumer Price Index (CPI) is a measure of the average change over time in the prices paid by urban consumers for a fixed market basket of consumer goods and services from A to Z. The CPI provides a way for consumers to compare what the market basket of goods and services costs this month with what the same market basket cost a month or a year ago. The CPI reflects spending patterns for each of two population groups: All urban consumers (CPI-U) and

urban wage earners, and clerical workers (CPI-W). The CPI-U represents about 80 percent of the total U.S. population.

The CPI represents all goods and services purchased for consumption by urban households. The CPI reports price changes in over 200 categories, arranged into eight major groups. The CPI includes various user fees such as water and sewerage charges, auto registration fees, vehicle tolls, and so forth. Taxes that are directly associated with the prices of specific goods and services (such as sales and excise taxes) are also included.

CURRENT ACCOUNT
Source: Bureau of Economic Analysis
The Current Account Report reflects the movement of noncapital items in the balance of payments account. The report breaks out the balance on goods, services, and income. Changes in the Current Account balance are a useful barometer for the state of U.S. foreign trade as well as the flow of investment to and from the United States. The United States has held a deficit on its Current Account for the last 2 decades (excluding the period of the Gulf War). A widening deficit on the Current Account is typical when the United States is purchasing excessive imports. The Current Account provides a good measure of the performance of the United States in the international markets.

DURABLE GOODS
Source: Bureau of the Census
The Durable Goods release is the advance release of overall factory orders and shipments. Durable goods are industrial products with an expected life of 1 year or more. They include intermediate goods, such as steel, lumber, and electronic components; finished industrial machinery and equipment; and finished consumer durable goods, such as furniture, autos, and TVs.

Data are reported for seven different industry groupings, plus the total. New orders are the dollar volume of orders for new products received by domestic manufacturers from any source, domestic or foreign. New orders are a good measure of demand for each industry and in aggregate. Shipments are the dollar volume of goods shipped by domestic manufacturers to any source, domestic or foreign.

ECRI FUTURE INFLATION GAUGE (FIG)
Source: Economic Cycle Research Institute (ECRI)
The FIG is a weighted average of eight key economic data series designed to predict cyclical swings in the inflation rate. The index generally turns up before an acceleration in inflation and vice versa. The components used to construct the index are industrial materials prices, real estate loans, insured unemployment rate, yield spread, civilian employment, federal and nonfederal debt, import prices, and the percentage of purchasing managers reporting slower deliveries.

ECRI WEEKLY LEADING INDEX
Source: Economic Cycle Research Institute
The composite index, designed to be clearly cyclical, is constructed as a weighted average of seven key economic data series designed to predict economic conditions in the near term. The index is designed to turn down before a recession and turn up before an expansion. The components are money supply, JOC-ECRI Industrial Markets Price Index, mortgage applications, bond quality spread, stock prices, bond yields, and initial jobless claims.

EMPLOYMENT COST INDEX
Source: Bureau of Labor Statistics
The Employment Cost Index (ECI) data are based on a survey of employer payrolls in the third month of the quarter for the pay period including the 12th day of the month. The survey is a probability sample of approximately 3600 private industry employers and 700 state and local governments, public schools, and public hospitals. The ECI measures changes in labor costs of money wages and salaries, and noncash fringe benefits in nonfarm private industry and state and local government for workers at all levels of responsibility.

EMPLOYMENT SITUATION
Source: Bureau of Labor Statistics
Payroll Employment is a measure of the number of jobs in more than 500 industries, except for farming, in all states and 255 metropolitan areas. The employment estimates are based on a survey of larger businesses. This release is the single most closely watched economic

statistic because of its timeliness, accuracy, and its importance as an indicator of economic activity. Payroll figures are reported each month by the Bureau of Labor Statistics in their Employment Situation Report. The report also provides information on average weekly hours worked and average hourly earnings, which are important indicators of the tightness of labor markets—something the Federal Reserve pays close attention to when setting interest rates. An index of aggregate weekly hours worked is also included in the release, which gives an important early indication of production before the quarterly GDP numbers come out. An estimate of the labor force, employment, and unemployment is provided in a parallel survey of U.S. households.

EXISTING HOME SALES
Source: National Association of Realtors
Each month the NAR Research Division receives data on existing single-family home sales from over 650 boards and associations of realtors and multiple listing systems across the country.

FACTORY ORDERS
Source: Bureau of the Census
The Factory Orders release includes the dollar volume of new orders, shipments, unfilled orders, and inventories reported by domestic manufacturers. It is more comprehensive and detailed than the advance release of durable goods activity 1 week earlier. Data are reported for numerous industry groupings, plus the total and specialized aggregates.

There are four separate concepts reported for each industry group. New orders are a good measure of demand for each industry and in aggregate. Shipments are the dollar volume of goods shipped by domestic manufacturers to any source, domestic or foreign. Shipments are a good measure of supply for each industry and in aggregate. Unfilled orders are the backlog of orders that have been received by domestic manufacturers, but not yet shipped. Unfilled orders are one indication of the balance between demand and supply, most often used to indicate an excess of demand relative to supply. Inventories are another key indicator of the relative trends of demand

and supply, most often used to indicate an excess of supply over demand.

FOMC MEETING
Source: Federal Reserve Board
The Federal Open Market Committee of the Federal Reserve Board (FOMC) meets approximately every 6 weeks to consider whether any changes need to be made to monetary policy. The FOMC is comprised of the seven Federal Reserve Board members, including current Chairman Alan Greenspan, and five Federal Reserve District Bank presidents. The five presidents on the FOMC rotate among the 12 bank presidents across the nation.

FOMC MINUTES
Source: Federal Reserve Board
The minutes of each FOMC meeting are released a few days after the FOMC meeting. The minutes generally include a discussion of the economic and financial factors the FOMC considers when making a decision regarding the direction of monetary policy. The minutes also indicate whether the Fed has a bias toward future monetary tightening or easing.

GROSS DOMESTIC PRODUCT
Source: Bureau of Economic Analysis
Gross Domestic Product (GDP) is a measure of the total production and consumption of goods and services in the United States. The Bureau of Economic Analysis (BEA) constructs two complementary measures of GDP, one based on income and one based on expenditures. GDP is measured on the product side by adding up the labor, capital, and tax costs of producing the output. On the consumption side, GDP is measured by adding up expenditures by households, businesses, government, and net foreign purchases. Theoretically, these two measures should be equal. However, due to problems collecting the data, there is often a discrepancy between the two measures. The GDP price deflator is used to convert output measured at current prices into constant-dollar GDP. This information is used to

define business cycle peaks and troughs. Total GDP growth of between 2.0 percent and 2.5 percent is generally considered to be optimal when the economy is at full employment (unemployment between 5.5 percent and 6.0 percent). Higher growth than this leads to accelerating inflation, while lower growth indicates a weak economy.

IMPORT AND EXPORT PRICES

Source: Bureau of Labor Statistics

The overall Import Price Index measures the price change of products purchased from other countries by U.S. residents. The overall Export Price Index measures the change in the prices of domestically produced U.S. goods shipped to other countries. These indices are calculated using a method similar to that used to calculate the Consumer Price Index (CPI). Every month, the Bureau of Labor Statistics collects net transaction prices for more than 20,000 products from over 6000 companies and secondary sources. These prices are then weighted according to the relative importance (i.e., the share of expenditures) of the product in 1995.

INDUSTRIAL PRODUCTION

Source: Federal Reserve Board

The Industrial Production (IP) Index measures the change in output in U.S. manufacturing, mining, and electric and gas utilities. Output refers to the physical quantity of items produced, unlike sales value, which combines quantity and price. The index covers the production of goods and power for domestic sales in the United States and for export. It excludes production in the agriculture, construction, transportation, communication, trade, finance, and service industries; government output, and imports. The IP Index is developed by weighting each component according to its relative importance in the base period. The information for weights is obtained from the value added measures of production in the economic censuses of manufacturer and minerals industries, and from value-added information for the utility industries in Internal Revenue Service statistics of income data. The weights are updated at 5-year intervals to coincide with the economic census. The current index base year is 1992.

INTERNATIONAL TRADE

Source: The Bureau of the Census and the Bureau of Economic Analysis of the Department of Commerce

The balance of trade represents the difference between exports and imports of foreign trade in goods and services. Merchandise data are provided for U.S. total foreign trade with all nations, detail for trade with particular nations and regions of the world, as well as for individual commodities. Trade data are available dating back to 1982. A great deal of detail is available on the destination of U.S. exports and the country of origination of U.S. imports. Thus, the importance of one country's economy may be analyzed in terms of U.S. trade. The report can further reveal to what extent overseas growth is contributing to the U.S. economic performance.

INTERNET SALES (E-COMMERCE SALES)

Source: Bureau of Census

These data cover sales of goods and services over the Internet, intranet, EDI, or other online systems that may or may not be paid online.

ISM INDEX (FORMERLY NAPM)

Source: Institute for Supply Management

The Institute for Supply Management releases a monthly composite index based on surveys of 300 purchasing managers nationwide representing 20 industries regarding manufacturing activity. Index values above 50 indicate an expanding economy, while values below 50 are indicative of contraction. This so-called diffusion index is calculated as the percent of positive responses plus one-half of same responses. The index is seasonally adjusted for the effects of variations within the year, differences due to holidays, and institutional changes. An index value above 43.9 over a period of time generally indicates an expansion of the overall economy. The index is a composite of nine similarly constructed indices including new orders, production, supplier delivery times, backlogs, inventories, prices, employment, export orders, and import orders. Information on activity in each of the 20 industries is provided separately. The ISM Survey also provides price changes for 14 key inputs.

ISM NON-MANUFACTURING INDEX (FORMERLY NAPM NON-MFG.)
Source: Institute for Supply Management
The Institute for Supply Management Non-Manufacturing Index is based on surveys of 370 purchasing and supply executives. Membership of the Business Survey Committee is weighted to correspond with each industry's contribution to GDP. Index values over 50 percent indicate an expansion, while values below 50 percent indicate contraction. There are 10 separate indices reported, but business activity is considered the most important. The other nine indices are new orders, supplier deliveries, employment, inventories, prices, backlog of orders, new export orders, imports, and inventory sentiment. The ISM Non-Manufacturing Index is similar in form to the ISM Manufacturing Index, which is older and more established. The Non-Manufacturing Index is also referred to as the ISM Services Index because the services industry is the largest component of the index. Other industries are covered, however, such as construction, mining, and transportation among others.

KANSAS CITY FED MANUFACTURING SURVEY
Source: Federal Reserve Bank of Kansas City
The Kansas City Fed surveys roughly 300 manufacturing plants that are representative of the district's industrial and geographic makeup. Surveys are sent to plant managers, purchasing managers, and financial controllers. The indices are calculated by subtracting the percentage of total respondents reporting decreases in a given indicator from the percentage of those reporting increases. The indices, which can range from 100 to -100, reveal the general direction of the indicators by showing how the number of plants with improving conditions offset those with worsening conditions. Index values greater than zero generally suggest expansion, while values less than zero indicate contraction.

MONTHLY MASS LAYOFFS
Source: Bureau of Labor Statistics
Mass layoff statistics are compiled from state initial unemployment insurance claims. Each month, states report on establishments that have at least 50 initial unemployment insurance claims filed against them during a consecutive 5-week period regardless of duration.

These establishments then are contacted by the state agency to determine whether these separations lasted 31 days or longer, and, if so, other information concerning the layoff is collected. Quarterly Mass Layoff Reports include the additional information. The reports list how many layoff events occurred and how many people who are eligible to receive unemployment compensation were affected. Layoff events are segmented by state and industry.

NEW HOME SALES
Source: Bureau of Census
Data for this report are compiled from telephone or personal interviews of about 10,000 builders or owners of about 15,000 selected building projects. To provide nationwide coverage of building activity, a multistage stratified random sample procedure is used to select some 820 building permit-issuing offices and a sample of more than 70 land areas not covered by buildings permits.

NEW RESIDENTIAL CONSTRUCTION
Source: Bureau of Census
The New Residential Construction press release provides statistics on the construction of new privately owned residential structures in the United States. Data included in the press release are (1) the number of new housing units authorized by building permits; (2) the number of housing units authorized to be built, but not yet started; (3) the number of housing units started; (4) the number of housing units under construction; and (5) the number of housing units completed. The data relate to new housing units intended for occupancy and maintained by the occupants. They exclude hotels, motels, and group residential structures, such as nursing homes and college dormitories. Also excluded are "HUD-code" manufactured (mobile) home units and units that are created in an existing residential or nonresidential structure. A housing unit, as defined by the Census Bureau, is a house, an apartment, a group of rooms, or a single room intended for occupancy as separate living quarters.

PERSONAL INCOME
Source: Bureau of Economic Analysis
Personal Income mainly measures the income received by households from employment, self-employment, investments, and transfer

payments. It also includes small amounts for expenses of nonprofit organizations and income of certain fiduciary activities. The largest component of Personal Income is wages and salaries from employment. Personal Income is released after the Employment Report and thus can be estimated by the payroll and earnings data for the Employment Report. Therefore, income releases generally do not shed much additional light on current conditions. Disposable income refers to personal income after the payment of income, estate, certain other taxes, and payments to governments.

PHILADELPHIA FED SURVEY
Source: Federal Reserve Bank of Philadelphia
Every month, the Philadelphia Fed sends out a survey asking respondents to assess general business conditions as well as company business conditions. Answers are given based in the current month versus the previous month, and the outlook for 6 months from the current month. An indicator is presented for a decrease, no change, an increase, and a diffusion index.

PRODUCER PRICE INDEX
Source: Bureau of Labor Statistics
The Producer Price Index (PPI) is a family of indices that measures average changes in selling prices received by domestic producers for their output. The PPI tracks changes in prices for nearly every goods producing industry in the domestic economy, including agriculture, electricity and natural gas, forestry, fisheries, manufacturing, and mining.

There are three primary publication structures for the PPI: industry; commodity; and stage-of-processing. The industry structure organizes products according to the Standard Industrial Classification (SIC) system. Thus, prices of products from the same industry are computed together. The commodity structure organizes products by material composition or similarity of end uses.

PRODUCTIVITY AND COSTS
Source: Bureau of Labor Statistics
The productivity and associated cost measures describe the relationship between real output and the labor and capital inputs involved in

its production. They show the changes over time in the amount of goods and services produced per unit of input.

RETAIL SALES (MARTS)
Source: Bureau of Census
Retail Sales include merchandise sold (for cash or credit at retail or wholesale) by establishments primarily engaged in retail trade. Services that are incidental to the sale of merchandise, and excise taxes that are paid by the manufacturer or wholesaler and passed along to the retailer, are also included. Sales are net after deductions for refunds and allowances for merchandise returned by customers. Sales exclude sales taxes collected directly from the customer and paid directly to local, state, or federal tax agency. The monthly retail trade estimates are developed from samples representing all sizes of firms and kinds of business in retail trade throughout the nation. This survey is composed of a sample selected from the retail employers who made FICA payments.

RICHMOND FED MANUFACTURING SURVEY
Source: Federal Reserve Bank of Richmond
The Richmond Fed surveys roughly 190 manufacturing plants that are representative of the district's industrial and geographic makeup. Surveys are sent to plant managers, purchasing managers, and financial controllers. The indices are calculated by subtracting the percentage of total respondents reporting decreases in a given indicator from the percentage of those reporting increases. The indices, which can range from 100 to -100, reveal the general direction of the indicators by showing how the number of plants with improving conditions offset those with worsening conditions. Index values greater than zero generally suggest expansion, while values less than zero indicate contraction. Unless indicated otherwise, data are seasonally adjusted.

RISK OF RECESSION
Source: Economy.com
The leading indicator is composed of four state and metro area indicators, two broad regional indicators, and two national indicators.

Because no single variable explains shifts in the business cycle, the variables are combined into a composite index. The advantage of aggregating the individual variables into a single index is that the volatility in the variables not attributable to changes in the business cycle is dampened. The components of the Economy.com regional leading index are as follows: housing permits (state or metro), manufacturing hours worked (state or metro), initial jobless claims (state only), trade-weighted index of the value of the dollar (state), Help-Wanted Index (metro where available, Census Division elsewhere), Consumer Confidence (Census Division), S&P 500 stock index (national), and Treasury yield curve, (national).

SEMI BOOK-TO-BILL RATIO
Source: Semiconductor Equipment and Materials International
Semiconductor Equipment and Materials International releases the results of a survey of U.S. manufacturers on a monthly basis. The 3-month moving average of shipments and new orders plus their ratio, named the book-to-bill ratio, are all included. A book-to-bill ratio indicates demand is outpacing supply in the equipment industry. Since chipmakers are the customers placing new orders, a ratio above 1 and rising is the usual signal of recovery in the semiconductor chip industry.

SEMICONDUCTOR BILLINGS
Source: Semiconductor Industry Association
This release reports the global dollar volume of integrated circuit sales on a 3-month moving average on a monthly basis. All types of semiconductor chips are included in the totals: microprocessors, memory, and others. The sales are reported individually for four regions: North America, Asia-Pacific, Japan, and Europe. The data are compiled from a survey of the largest global chip manufacturers.

SENIOR LOAN OFFICER OPINION SURVEY
Source: Federal Reserve
The report is drawn from a survey of approximately 60 large domestic banks and 24 branches and agencies of foreign banks. The Federal Reserve generally conducts the survey quarterly, timing it so that

results are available for the January, May, August, and November meetings of the Federal Open Market Committee. The Federal Reserve occasionally conducts one or two additional surveys during the year. Questions cover changes in the standards and terms of the banks' loans and the state of business and household demand for loans. The survey often includes questions on one or two other topics of current interest.

TREASURY BUDGET
Source: Department of Treasury
The Treasury Budget is a monthly account of the surplus or deficit of the U.S. government. Detailed information is provided on receipts and outlays of the federal government. The information is provided on a monthly and fiscal year-to-date basis. The major sources of data include monthly accounting reports by Federal entities and disbursing officers, and daily reports from the Federal Reserve Banks. These reports detail accounting transactions affecting receipts and outlays of the federal government and off-budget federal entities, and their related effect on the assets and liabilities of the U.S. government.

UNIVERSITY OF MICHIGAN CONSUMER SENTIMENT SURVEY
Source: University of Michigan
The University of Michigan Consumer Research Center conducts a telephone survey of 500 consumers. Consumers are asked questions about personal finances, business conditions, and buying conditions. The survey employs a rotating panel design. Each month, 60 percent of the consumers are added to the sample for the first time, while the remaining are interviewed a second time. Households are asked five questions that include (1) a rating of household financial conditions, (2) a rating of expected household financial conditions a year from now, (3) a rating of expected business conditions a year from now, (4) expectations for the economy for the next 5 years, and (5) buying plans. The responses are seasonally adjusted. An index is constructed for each response and then a composite index is fashioned based on the responses.

VEHICLE SALES
Source: Auto Companies' Press Releases
Light vehicle sales are divided between cars and light trucks (sport utility vehicles, pickup trucks, and vans). Light vehicles sales include both sales of vehicles assembled in North America that are sold in the United States and sales of imported vehicles sold in the United States.

WHOLESALE TRADE
Source: Bureau of the Census
Companies provide data on dollar values of merchant wholesale sales, end-of-month inventories, and methods of inventory valuation. Monthly wholesale trade, sales, and inventories reports are released 6 weeks after the close of the reference month. They contain preliminary current month figures and final figures for the previous month. Statistics include sales, inventories, and stock-to-sale ratios by 3-digit SIC code along with standard errors. Data are both seasonally adjusted and unadjusted. A mail survey of about 7100 selected wholesale firms is the method of data collection. Firms are first stratified by merchant wholesale sales, inventories, and major type of business (determined from the latest census of wholesale trade). All firms with wholesale sales or inventories above applicable size cutoffs for each major type of business are included in the survey. The sample is updated every quarter to reflect "births" and "deaths"; adding new employer businesses identified in the business and professional classification survey and dropping companies that are no longer active wholesalers.

B

Sample Economic Reports

The following material presents three sample reports covering gross domestic product (GDP), the employment situation, and national manufacturing data from the Institute of Supply Managers (ISM). These reports are included as appendix material to illustrate the reports that are issued by official sources and that are widely available to the public free of charge. In these sample reports, lengthy tables have been eliminated due to space and formatting issues. The text is presented in its entirety.

"Gross Domestic Product" (GDP) is a quarterly report that is released by the U.S. Department of Commerce, Bureau of Economic Analysis, in three time frames as data is made available. The first report for every quarter is the "advance," which is the first indication of how the economy performed for that particular quarter in comparison with the prior quarter. The next one for the quarter is the "preliminary" report. Of particular note in the preliminary report is the revision—if any—from the advance report. For example, if the preliminary report showed an upward revision in the GDP rate, that

*would indicate that the economy was growing more strongly than pre-
viously indicated. The third report is the "final" for that quarter.
Again, the most keenly watched aspect of the final report is if the GDP
rate is revised and by what degree and why. GDP reports may be
viewed at the BEA Web site at http://www.bea.gov. (My annotations on
the GDP report appear in italics.)*

SAMPLE GDP REPORT

GROSS DOMESTIC PRODUCT:
FOURTH QUARTER 2001

(PRELIMINARY)
8:30 A.M. EST, THURSDAY, FEBRUARY 28, 2002

Real gross domestic product—the output of goods and services produced by labor and property located in the United States—increased at
an annual rate of 1.4 percent in the fourth quarter of 2001, according
to preliminary estimates released by the Bureau of Economic Analysis.
In the third quarter, real GDP decreased 1.3 percent.

The GDP estimates released today are based on more complete
source data than were available for the advance estimates issued
last month. In the advance estimates, the increase in real GDP was
0.2 percent.

*(As stated above, the most significant feature of the preliminary
GDP report is the revision from the advance report issued the month
before. In this case, the revised GDP shows a stronger economy,
growing at an annual rate of 1.4 percent, up from the advance estimate
of 0.2 percent. Further, as stated in Chapter 5, the GDP reading that
is most closely watched is the "real" rate, reflecting constant 1996
dollars to factor out the impact of inflation.)*

The increase in real GDP in the fourth quarter reflected positive
contributions from personal consumption expenditures (PCE) and
from government spending that were partly offset by negative contributions from private inventory investment, from nonresidential
fixed investment, from exports, and from residential investment.
Imports, which are a subtraction in the calculation of GDP,
decreased in the fourth quarter.

The upturn in real GDP growth in the fourth quarter reflected accelerations in PCE and in government spending, and a smaller decrease in exports that were partly offset by larger decreases in inventory investment and in nonresidential fixed investment, and a downturn in residential investment. There was also a smaller decrease in imports in the fourth quarter.

Footnote:—Quarterly estimates are expressed at seasonally adjusted annual rates, unless otherwise specified. Quarter-to-quarter dollar changes are differences between these published estimates. Percent changes are calculated from unrounded data and annualized. "Real" estimates are in chained (1996) dollars. Price indexes are chain-type measures.

The price index for gross domestic purchases, which measures prices paid by U.S. residents, increased 0.4 percent in the fourth quarter, the same as in the advance estimate; this index decreased 0.1 percent in the third quarter. Excluding food and energy prices, the price index for gross domestic purchases increased 1.9 percent in the fourth quarter, compared with an increase of 0.6 percent in the third. The fourth-quarter upturn in the price index also reflected acceleration in PCE services prices associated with the treatment of insurance payments resulting from the September 11th terrorist attacks. The increase in benefit payments is treated as a reduction in the average net premiums paid for insurance services. Excluding the insurance-related price effects, the gross domestic purchases price index decreased 0.3 percent in the fourth quarter, following an increase of 0.6 percent in the third.

Real personal consumption expenditures increased 6.0 percent in the fourth quarter, compared with an increase of 1.0 percent in the third. Real nonresidential fixed investment decreased 13.1 percent, compared with a decrease of 8.5 percent. Nonresidential structures decreased 32.6 percent, compared with a decrease of 7.5 percent. Equipment and software decreased 4.8 percent, compared with a decrease of 8.8 percent. Real residential fixed investment decreased 5.0 percent, in contrast to an increase of 2.4 percent.

Real exports of goods and services decreased 12.2 percent in the fourth quarter, compared with a decrease of 18.8 percent in the third.

Real imports of goods and services decreased 6.9 percent, compared with a decrease of 13.0 percent.

Real federal government consumption expenditures and gross investment increased 11.6 percent in the fourth quarter, compared with an increase of 3.6 percent in the third. National defense increased 9.4 percent, compared with an increase of 3.2 percent. Nondefense increased 15.7 percent, compared with an increase of 4.2 percent. Real state and local government consumption expenditures and gross investment increased 9.4 percent, in contrast to a decrease of 1.3 percent.

The real change in private inventories subtracted 2.19 percentage points from the fourth-quarter change in real GDP, after subtracting 0.81 percentage point from the third-quarter change. Private businesses reduced inventories $120.0 billion in the fourth quarter, following decreases of $61.9 billion in the third quarter and $38.3 billion in the second.

Real final sales of domestic product—GDP less change in private inventories—increased 3.6 percent in the fourth quarter, in contrast to a decrease of 0.5 percent in the third.

Gross domestic purchases

Real gross domestic purchases—purchases by U.S. residents of goods and services wherever produced—increased 1.7 percent in the fourth quarter, in contrast to a decrease of 1.0 percent in the third.

Current-dollar GDP

Current-dollar GDP—the market value of the nation's output of goods and services—increased 1.1 percent, or $28.3 billion, in the fourth quarter to a level of $10,253.2 billion. In the third quarter, current-dollar GDP increased 0.9 percent, or $22.3 billion.

Revisions

The preliminary estimate of the fourth-quarter increase in real GDP is 1.2 percentage points, or $27.1 billion, higher than the advance estimate issued last month. The upward revision to the change in real GDP primarily reflected a downward revision to imports of goods and an upward revision to personal consumption expenditures for nondurable goods (see the Technical Note).

	Advance	Preliminary
	(Percent change from preceding quarter)	
Real GDP	0.2	1.4
Current-dollar GDP	−.1	1.1
Gross domestic purchases price index	.4	.4

2001 GDP (Revised)

Real GDP increased 1.2 percent in 2001 (that is, from the 2000 annual level to the 2001 annual level), compared with an increase of 4.1 percent in 2000.

The major contributors to the increase in real GDP in 2001 were personal consumption expenditures (PCE) and government spending. The contributions of these components were partly offset by negative contributions of private inventory investment, exports, and private fixed investment. Imports, which are a subtraction in the calculation of GDP, decreased in 2001.

The deceleration in real GDP in 2001 primarily reflected downturns in private fixed investment and in exports, a deceleration in PCE, and a larger decrease in private inventory investment. There was also a downturn in imports in 2001.

The price index for gross domestic purchases increased 1.7 percent in 2001, compared with an increase of 2.6 percent in 2000.

Current-dollar GDP increased 3.4 percent, or $332.7 billion, in 2001. Current-dollar GDP increased 6.5 percent, or $604.3 billion, in 2000.

During 2001 (that is, measured from the fourth quarter of 2000 to the fourth quarter of 2001), real GDP increased 0.4 percent. Real GDP increased 2.8 percent during 2000. The price index for gross domestic purchases increased 1.1 percent during 2001, compared with an increase of 2.5 percent during 2000.

*   *   *

The "Employment Situation Report" issued by the U.S. Bureau of Labor is closely watched for both the economic trends that it conveys, and the psychological impact that it wields on consumer and investor sentiment. The employment situation will show, for example, if the unemployment rate is rising because companies continue to cut back their work forces in the wake of declining demand, or if the unemployment rate is falling because companies are expanding production. As stated in Chapter 6, often the unemployment rate is greatest just as the economy is turning around since companies have trimmed their work forces to the needed level to improve profitability. Conversely, the unemployment rate is often at its lowest just as the economy reaches a peak before the inevitable contraction begins. The "Employment Situation Report" may be viewed on the Department of Labor Web site at http://www.dol.gov. (My annotations on this report are in italics.)

Friday, February 1, 2002.
THE EMPLOYMENT SITUATION: JANUARY 2002
Employment continued to decline in January, and the unemployment rate decreased to 5.6 percent, the Bureau of Labor Statistics of the U.S. Department of Labor reported today. Nonfarm payroll employment declined by 89,000 over the month, as job losses continued in manufacturing and construction employment also fell.

(In this report, the most notable statistic is the unemployment rate itself, in this case 5.6 percent. As the report states, the unemployment rate declined to 5.6 percent from 5.8 percent for the previous month, which on the surface would indicate that more workers were employed. However, employment continued to decline with fewer individuals in the available work force, which offsets the positive view of the decline in the unemployment rate.)

Unemployment (Household Survey Data)
The number of unemployed persons declined in January by 337,000, to 7.9 million (after seasonal adjustment). The unemployment rate decreased by 0.2 percentage point to 5.6 percent, reversing an increase of the same size in December. The rate was 1.7 percentage points above its most recent low of 3.9 percent reached in October 2000. (See table A-1.)

In January, the unemployment rate for adult women decreased by 0.4 percentage point to 4.8 percent after rising by 0.3 percentage point in December. Jobless rates for adult men (5.2 percent), teenagers (16.1 percent), whites 5.0 percent), blacks (9.8 percent), and Hispanics (8.1 percent) showed little or no change.

Total Employment and the Labor Force (Household Survey Data)
Total employment fell by 587,000 in January to 133.5 million, after seasonal adjustment. The employment-population ratio dropped by 0.4 percentage point to 62.6 percent. Over the past 12 months, the number of employed persons has declined by 2.4 million and the employment-population ratio has fallen by 1.8 percentage points.

Over the month, the number of persons working part time despite their preference for full-time work decreased by 294,000 to 4.0 million, after seasonal adjustment. Over the year, however, the number of these persons working part time for economic reasons has risen by 685,000.

The civilian labor force fell by 924,000 in January, to 141.4 million persons. The labor force participation rate—the proportion of the population that is either working or looking for work— fell to 66.4 percent.

About 7.0 million persons (not seasonally adjusted) held more than one job in January. These multiple jobholders represented 5.3 percent of the total employed, the same as a year earlier.

Persons Not in the Labor Force (Household Survey Data)
In January, the number of persons not in the labor force who reported that they currently want a job rose by 163,000 to 4.8 million, seasonally adjusted. These individuals are not counted as unemployed because they had not searched for work in the 4-week period preceding the survey. Most had not searched for over a year.

About 1.5 million persons (not seasonally adjusted) were marginally attached to the labor force in January, up from 1.3 million persons a year ago. These individuals reported they wanted and were available for work and had looked for a job sometime in the prior 12 months. They were not counted as unemployed, however, because they had not actively searched for work in the 4 weeks preceding the survey. The number of discouraged workers was 319,000 in January, essentially unchanged from a year earlier.

Industry Payroll Employment (Establishment Survey Data)
Total nonfarm payroll employment fell by 89,000 in January to 131.2 million, seasonally adjusted. Since the recession began in March 2001, payroll employment has declined by 1.4 million. In January, job losses continued in manufacturing, and construction experienced

its first large employment decline since last April. Services employment was about unchanged over the month.

Manufacturing employment fell by 89,000 in January, compared with average losses of 137,000 a month in the fourth quarter of 2001. Within manufacturing, motor vehicle employment decreased by 22,000, reflecting temporary shutdowns for inventory control. Large employment declines continued in industrial machinery (−19,000). Primary metals and electrical equipment each lost 11,000 jobs in January, and employment in fabricated metals fell by 10,000. In non-durable goods manufacturing, declines continued in printing and publishing (−8,000) and textile mill products (−4,000).

Elsewhere in the goods-producing sector in January, construction employment fell by 54,000, despite relatively mild weather across most of the country. The decline was spread throughout special trades (−33,000), heavy construction (−16,000), and general building contractors (−5,000). Mining lost jobs for the third consecutive month in January. This industry's employment had been on a growth trend since September 1999, reflecting expansion in oil and gas extraction. January's employment decline was primarily in metal mining (−2,000).

Employment in the services industry was about unchanged in January following a net decline of 192,000 in the fourth quarter of 2001. Help supply services employment was essentially unchanged in January; employment has fallen by 661,000 since its recent peak in September 2000. Computer services lost 18,000 jobs in January and has dropped by 34,000 since June 2001. Hotels lost 7,000 jobs in January; since peaking in March 2001, employment in this industry has declined by 124,000. In contrast, employment gains continued in health services in January, and social services had an above-average increase of 15,000.

Elsewhere in the service-producing sector, employment was unchanged over the month in transportation and public utilities, following seven consecutive monthly declines that totaled 211,000. In January, employment in air transportation rose after seasonal adjustment because extremely light holiday-season hiring by air courier services resulted in fewer layoffs than usual. Communications continued to lose jobs; since its peak last July, employment has declined by 26,000.

In finance, both depository institutions and mortgage brokerages continued to add workers, aided by low interest rates. Employment in security and commodity brokerages was little changed in January, following a large decline in December.

Wholesale trade employment continued its downward trend in January. The industry has lost 145,000 jobs since its peak in November 2000. Employment in government was essentially unchanged in January.

Following losses that totaled 241,000 in the last 5 months of 2001, retail trade posted a seasonally adjusted gain of 62,000 jobs in January. Seasonal hiring for the holidays in department, apparel, and miscellaneous retail stores (such as toy stores) had been very light. As a result, there were fewer seasonal layoffs than usual in January, resulting in large employment gains after seasonal adjustment. An employment decline of 22,000 in eating and drinking places more than offset the small gains of the prior 2 months and brought total job losses in the industry since July to 129,000. In January, car dealers added 4,000 jobs, following similar increases in November and December.

Weekly Hours (Establishment Survey Data)

The average workweek for production or nonsupervisory workers on private nonfarm payrolls edged down by 0.1 hour in January to 34.0 hours, seasonally adjusted. Following an increase of 0.3 hour in December, the manufacturing workweek edged down by 0.1 hour to 40.5 hours in January. Manufacturing overtime was up by 0.1 hour to 3.9 hours.

The index of aggregate weekly hours of production or nonsupervisory workers on private nonfarm payrolls decreased by 0.4 percent in January to 148.1 (1982=100), seasonally adjusted. The index has fallen by 2.7 percent from its recent peak in January 2001. The manufacturing index fell by 0.9 percent to 92.6 in January 2002 and has fallen by 9.7 percent since January 2001.

Hourly and Weekly Earnings (Establishment Survey Data)

Average hourly earnings of production or nonsupervisory workers on private nonfarm payrolls were unchanged in January at $14.59, seasonally adjusted. This followed a gain of 5 cents (as revised) in December. Average weekly earnings fell by 0.3 percent in January to $496.06. Over the year, average hourly earnings increased by 4.0 percent and average weekly earnings grew by 2.8 percent.

* * *

The Institute for Supply Management (ISM) (formerly the National Association of Purchasing Management) puts out a monthly national manufacturing report that gauges the activity in this sector. As a diffusion index, the ISM's monthly report is evaluated on the basis of whether the reading is above or below 50.

A reading above 50 percent indicates that the manufacturing economy is generally expanding. Below 50 percent, the sector is generally declining. According to ISM, a reading over 42.7 percent, over time, indicates that the overall economy, as measured by gross domestic product (GDP), is generally expanding. Below 42.7 percent, it is generally declining. The distance from 50 percent of 42.7 percent, ISM explains, is indicative of the strength of the expansion or decline. The reports may be viewed at the ISM Web site at http://www.ism.ws. (My annotations on the ISM sample report, below, appear in italics.)

SAMPLE REPORT

February Manufacturing ISM *Report On Business*®

PMI at 54.7 percent

(The headline number of 54.7 percent captures the market's attention first. Clearly, this number is well above the 50 percent mark for the diffusion index and indicates an economy that is growing. Market analysts and savvy investors would also compare this number with the previous month's reading—in this case 49.9 percent in January—to determine the relative rate of growth or decline in the economy.)

New Orders, Production Growing
Supplier Deliveries Slower
Employment, Inventories Decline
Exports, Imports Growing

(Tempe, Arizona)—Economic activity in the manufacturing sector indicated growth in February, ending 18 consecutive months of decline. The *overall economy* grew for the fourth consecutive month, say the nation's supply executives in the latest *Manufacturing ISM Report On Business®*.

The report was issued today by Norbert J. Ore, C.P.M., chair of the Institute for Supply Management™ Manufacturing Business Survey Committee and group director, strategic sourcing and procurement, Georgia-Pacific Corporation. "February signals the turnaround for manufacturing based on a strong PMI reading and an accelerating trend in new orders and production. Most of the indexes are heading in the right direction at this point. Employment is still soft, but it is a lagging indicator and will need a number of months of growth before it recovers. Pricing power is still lagging, but should begin to develop if the trends in new orders and production continue."

ISM's Backlog of Orders Index indicates that order backlogs grew for the first time after 21 months of decline. ISM's Supplier Deliveries Index reflects slower deliveries for the second consecutive month. Manufacturing employment continued to decline in February as the index fell below the breakeven point (an index of 50 percent) for the 17th consecutive month. ISM's Prices Index remained below 50 percent as manufacturers experienced lower prices for the 12th consecutive month. New Export Orders grew in February for the second consecutive month. February's Imports Index decelerated slightly, but registered growth for the third consecutive month. Comments from supply executives fell into two groups this month. One group continued to express concerns with regard to business conditions, while the other indicated that things are starting to improve.

ISM's PMI is 54.7 percent in February, an increase of 4.8 percentage points from the 49.9 percent reported in January. ISM's New Orders Index rose from 55.3 percent in January to 62.8 percent in

February. ISM's Production Index rose 9.2 percentage points from 52 percent in January to 61.2 percent in February. The ISM Employment Index is at 43.8 percent for February, an increase of 1.2 percentage points when compared to the 42.6 percent reported in January.

ISM's Supplier Deliveries Index rose to 52.3 percent from 51.7 percent in January. ISM's Inventories Index is 39.5 percent. ISM's Customer Inventories Index declined slightly to 41.5 percent from January's 43.5 percent indicating a faster rate of inventory liquidation when compared to January. ISM's Prices Index in February is 41.5 percent, a decrease of 2.4 percentage points from January's 43.9 percent. ISM's Backlog of Orders Index rose from 44.5 percent in January to 53 percent in February.

ISM's New Export Orders Index registered 51.1 percent, up 0.3 percentage point from January's 50.8 percent. Imports of materials by manufacturers grew, as ISM's Imports Index is 52 percent for the month, down from January's 52.1 percent.

"The overall picture shows growth in manufacturing activity during the month of February," added Ore. "The PMI hasn't been above the 50 mark since July 2000, so this is certainly welcome news. Manufacturing has struggled and hopefully this signals the beginning of a strong recovery. It is encouraging that 13 industries reported growth in new orders. It appears that the inventory liquidation is nearing completion as customers' inventories are quite low. Upward movement of prices for aluminum, copper, nickel, and steel give credibility to the development of pricing power in some industries as we head toward the second quarter."

Of the 20 industries in the manufacturing sector, 14 industries reported growth: Wood & Wood Products; Primary Metals; Fabricated Metals; Miscellaneous (a preponderance of jewelry, toys, sporting goods, musical instruments); Rubber & Plastic Products; Tobacco; Leather; Chemicals; Transportation & Equipment; Glass, Stone & Aggregate; Food; Industrial & Commercial Equipment & Computers; Electronic Components & Equipment; and Printing & Publishing.

"There were no reports of commodities in short supply. Commodities reported up in price are: Aluminum, Copper, Nickel, and Steel. The commodities reported down in price are: Caustic Soda,

Chemicals, Corrugated Containers, Natural Gas, High Density Polyethylene, Resins, and Steel," Ore stated.

FEBRUARY 2002 ISM BUSINESS SURVEY AT A GLANCE

	Series Index	Direction Feb vs Jan	Rate of Change Feb vs Jan
PMI	54.7	Growing	From Contracting
New Orders	62.8	Grng	Faster
Production	61.2	Growing	Faster
Employment	43.8	Contracting	Slower
Supplier Deliveries	52.3	Slower	Faster
Inventories	39.5	Contracting	Faster
Customer Inventories	41.5	Too Low	Lower
Prices	41.5	Decreasing	Faster
Backlog of Orders	53.0	Growing	From Contracting
New Export Orders	51.1	Growing	Faster
Imports	52.0	Growing	Slower

THE ECONOMY AT A GLANCE

Overall Economy	Growing	Faster
Manufacturing	Growing	From Contracting

PMI

The PMI indicates that the manufacturing economy grew during the
month of February with an index of 54.7 percent. This is the first
month of growth for the manufacturing sector following 18 consecutive months of decline and is significant when compared to January's
49.9 percent. A reading above 50 percent indicates that the manufacturing economy is generally expanding; below 50 percent indicates
that it is generally contracting.

A PMI in excess of 42.7 percent, over a period of time, generally
indicates an expansion of the overall economy. The February PMI

indicates that both the overall economy and the manufacturing sector are growing. Ore added, "The past relationship between the PMI and the overall economy indicates that the average PMI for the months of January and February (52.3 percent) corresponds to 3.5 percent growth in real gross domestic product (GDP). However, if the PMI for February (54.7 percent) turned out to be the annual average for 2002, this would correspond to a 4.4 percent increase in GDP."

Month	Feb'02	Jan'02	Dec'01	Nov'01	Oct'01
PMI%	54.7	49.9	48.1	44.7	39.5
Month	Sep'01	Aug'01	Jul'01	Jun'01	May'01
PMI%	46.2	47.9	43.9	44.3	42.3
Month	Apr'01	Mar'01	Feb'01	Jan'01	Dec'00
PMI%	43.2	43.2	42.0	41.7	44.2

New Orders

ISM's New Orders Index indicated growth in February for the third consecutive month. The index is 62.8 percent, 7.5 percentage points greater than the 55.3 percent registered in January. A New Orders Index above 50.8 percent, over time, is generally consistent with an increase in the Census Bureau's series on manufacturing orders (in constant 1987 dollars). Industries reporting increases for the month of February are: Wood & Wood Products; Fabricated Metals; Miscellaneous (a preponderance of jewelry, toys, sporting goods, musical instruments); Primary Metals; Electronic Components & Equipment; Rubber & Plastic Products; Chemicals; Food; Industrial & Commercial Equipment & Computers; Printing & Publishing; Furniture; Transportation & Equipment; and Instruments & Photographic Equipment.

New Orders	%Better	%Same	%Worse	Net	Index
February 2002	39	47	14	+25	62.8
January 2002	26	52	22	+4	55.3
December 2001	24	46	30	−6	55.5
November 2001	24	44	32	−8	48.4

Production

ISM's Production Index is 61.2 percent in February up from 52 percent in January, an increase of 9.2 percentage points. This is the third consecutive month that the Production Index has been above 50 percent, indicating growth in manufacturing production. An index above 49.5 percent, over time, is generally consistent with an increase in the Federal Reserve Board's Industrial Production figures. Of the 20 industries reporting, those registering growth in February are: Wood & Wood Products; Tobacco; Primary Metals; Fabricated Metals; Miscellaneous (a preponderance of jewelry, toys, sporting goods, musical instruments); Glass, Stone & Aggregate; Apparel; Rubber & Plastic Products; Transportation & Equipment; Chemicals; Industrial & Commercial Equipment & Computers; Food; and Printing & Publishing.

Production	%Better	%Same	%Worse	Net	Index
February 2002	33	54	13	+20	61.2
January 2002	22	54	24	−2	52.0
December 2001	21	52	27	−6	50.3
November 2001	20	52	28	−8	48.2

Employment

ISM's Manufacturing Employment Index remained below 50 percent in February for the 17th consecutive month. The Index registered 43.8 percent in February compared to 42.6 percent in January, an increase of 1.2 percentage points. An Employment Index above 47.6 percent, over time, is generally consistent with an increase in the Bureau of Labor Statistics (BLS) data on manufacturing employment. Wood & Wood Products is the only industry reporting growth in employment.

Employment	%Higher	%Same	%Lower	Net	Index
February 2002	9	68	23	−14	43.8
January 2002	7	65	28	−21	42.6
December 2001	3	70	27	−24	39.2
November 2001	5	61	34	−29	35.7

Supplier Deliveries

ISM's Supplier Deliveries Index indicates delivery performance is slower when compared to January (a reading above 50 percent indicates slower deliveries). At 52.3 percent, the index is 0.6 percentage point higher than January's 51.7 percent. The industries reporting slower supplier deliveries in February are: Primary Metals; Furniture; Instruments & Photographic Equipment; Miscellaneous (a preponderance of jewelry, toys, sporting goods, musical instruments); Fabricated Metals; Electronic Components & Equipment; Printing & Publishing; and Transportation & Equipment.

Supplier Deliveries	%Slower	%Same	%Faster	Net	Index
February 2002	9	85	6	+3	52.3
January 2002	6	88	6	0	51.7
December 2001	5	86	9	−4	48.0
November 2001	4	88	8	−4	47.8

NOTE: A list of commodities in short supply is available at the end of this report.

Inventories

The rate of liquidation of manufacturers' inventories accelerated slightly in February as the Inventories Index registered 39.5 percent, down from the 40.5 percent reported in January. The Inventories Index has been under 50 percent for 25 consecutive months. An Inventories Index greater than 41.3 percent, over time, is generally consistent with expansion in the Bureau of Economic Analysis' (BEA) figures on overall manufacturing inventories (in constant 1987 dollars). Three industries reported higher inventories in February: Leather; Glass, Stone & Aggregate; and Rubber & Plastic Products.

Inventories	%Higher	%Same	%Lower	Net	Index
February 2002	10	64	26	−16	39.5
January 2002	10	58	32	−22	40.5
December 2001	9	55	36	−27	38.2
November 2001	9	55	36	−27	37.9

Customers' Inventories

Customers' inventories in February were perceived as lower when compared to January. The Customers' Inventories Index is at 41.5 percent, 2 percentage points lower than the 43.5 percent reported in January. The only industry reporting excessive customers' inventories in February is Primary Metals.

Customer Inventories	%Reporting	%Too High	%About Right	%Too Low	Net	Index
February 2002	88	8	67	25	−17	41.5
January 2002	88	11	67	23	−13	43.5
December 2001	91	11	66	23	−12	44.0
November 2001	89	12	65	23	−11	44.5

Prices

ISM's Prices Index indicates manufacturers continued to pay lower prices in February. With the index at 41.5 percent, this marks the 12th consecutive month the index has been below 50 percent. The index is 2.4 percentage points lower than January's 43.9 percent. In February, 9 percent of supply executives reported paying higher prices and 26 percent reported paying lower prices, while 65 percent reported that prices were unchanged from the preceding month.

A Prices Index below 46.6 percent, over time, is generally consistent with a decrease in the Bureau of Labor Statistics (BLS) Index of Manufacturers Prices. Primary Metals; Fabricated Metals; Instruments & Photographic Equipment; Transportation & Equipment; and Electronic Components & Equipment are the industries reporting paying higher prices for the month.

Prices	%Higher	%Same	%Lower	Net	Index
February 2002	9	65	26	−17	41.5
January 2002	7	69	24	−17	43.9
December 2001	3	58	39	−36	33.2
November 2001	3	55	42	−39	32.0

NOTE: A list of commodities up in price and down in price is available at the end of this report.

Backlog of Orders

The Backlog of Orders Index grew in February after 21 consecutive months of contraction. ISM's Backlog of Orders Index (not seasonally adjusted) registered 53 percent, indicating growth in manufacturers' backlogs. Of the 88 percent of respondents who measure their backlog of orders, 23 percent reported greater backlogs, 17 percent reported smaller backlogs, and 60 percent reported no change from January. Fabricated Metals; Furniture; Rubber & Plastic Products; Wood & Wood Products; Miscellaneous (a preponderance of jewelry, toys, sporting goods, musical instruments); Primary Metals; Transportation & Equipment; and Industrial & Commercial Equipment & Computers are the industries reporting an increase in order backlog during the month.

Backlog of Orders	%Reporting	%Greater	%Same	%Less	Net	Index
February 2002	88	23	60	17	+6	53.0
January 2002	89	16	57	27	−11	44.5
December 2001	88	13	53	34	−21	39.5
November 2001	89	14	49	37	−23	38.5

New Export Orders

ISM's New Export Orders Index for February registered 51.1 percent, an increase of 0.3 percentage point when compared to January's index of 50.8 percent. The industries reporting growth in new export orders in February are: Instruments & Photographic Equipment; Electronic Components & Equipment; and Industrial & Commercial Equipment & Computers.

New Export Orders	%Exporting	%Better	%Same	%Worse	Net	Index
February 2002	74	11	78	11	0	51.1
January 2002	73	10	79	11	−1	50.8
December 2001	79	12	68	20	−8	47.6
November 2001	74	13	73	14	−1	48.6

Imports

Imports of materials by manufacturers grew in February as the Imports Index registered 52 percent, a 0.1 percentage point decrease when compared to January's report of 52.1 percent. The six industries reporting growth in import activity for February are: Tobacco; Fabricated Metals; Printing & Publishing; Electronic Components & Equipment; Transportation & Equipment; and Chemicals.

Imports	%Importing	%Higher	%Same	%Lower	Net	Index
February 2002	75	10	81	9	+1	52.0
January 2002	75	9	81	10	−1	52.1
December 2001	74	12	75	13	−1	50.3
November 2001	72	11	75	14	−3	49.9

Buying Policy

Average commitment leadtime for Capital Expenditures rose 6 days to 99 days. Average leadtime for Production Materials declined 2 days to 43 days. Average leadtime for Maintenance, Repair, and Operating (MRO) supplies rose 1 day to 21 days. [See table on next page.]

In Short Supply

No commodities reported in short supply.

Up in Price

Aluminum; Copper; Nickel; and Steel (also shown down in price).

Down in Price

Caustic Soda—10th month; Chemicals; Corrugated Containers— 13th month; Natural Gas—13th month; High Density Polyethylene; Resins; and Steel—10th month (also shown up in price).

Data and Method of Presentation

The *Manufacturing ISM Report On Business®* is based on data compiled from monthly replies to questions asked of purchasing and supply executives in over 400 industrial companies. Membership of the Business Survey Committee is diversified by Standard Industrial

Percent Reporting

	Hand to Mouth	30 Days	60 Days	90 Days	6 Mos.	1 Year+	Avg. Days
Capital Expenditures							
February 2002	25	8	16	21	23	7	99
January 2002	27	6	20	20	21	6	93
December 2001	28	8	18	21	21	4	86
November 2001	29	7	16	20	22	6	92
Production Materials							
February 2002	25	47	17	7	2	2	43
January 2002	21	48	16	10	4	1	45
December 2001	23	45	18	9	3	2	46
November 2001	20	48	19	8	3	2	47
MRO Supplies							
February 2002	53	35	10	2	0	0	21
January 2002	54	37	8	1	0	0	20
December 2001	57	32	9	2	0	0	20
November 2001	55	32	11	2	0	0	21

Classification (SIC) category, based on each industry's contribution to Gross Domestic Product (GDP). Twenty industries from various U.S. geographical areas are represented on the committee.

Survey responses reflect the change, if any, in the current month compared to the previous month. For each of the indicators measured (New Orders, Backlog of Orders, New Export Orders, Imports, Production, Supplier Deliveries, Inventories, Customers' Inventories, Employment, and Prices), this report shows the percentage reporting each response, the net difference between the number of responses in the positive economic direction (higher, better, and slower for Supplier Deliveries) and the negative economic direction (lower, worse, and faster for Supplier Deliveries), and the diffusion index. Responses are raw data and are never changed. The diffusion index includes the percent of positive responses plus one-half of those responding the same (considered positive).

The resulting single index number is then seasonally adjusted to allow for the effects of repetitive intrayear variations resulting primarily from normal differences in weather conditions, various institutional arrangements, and differences attributable to nonmoveable holidays. All seasonal adjustment factors are supplied by the U.S. Department of Commerce and are subject annually to relatively minor changes when conditions warrant them. The PMI is a composite index based on the seasonally adjusted diffusion indices for five of the indicators with varying weights: New Orders—30%; Production—25%; Employment—20%; Supplier Deliveries—15%; and Inventories—10%.

Diffusion indices have the properties of leading indicators and are convenient summary measures showing the prevailing direction of change and the scope of change. A PMI reading above 50 percent indicates that the manufacturing economy is generally expanding; below 50 percent that it is generally declining. A PMI over 42.7 percent, over a period of time, indicates that the overall economy, or Gross Domestic Product (GDP), is generally expanding, below 42.7 percent, it is generally declining. The distance from 50 percent or 42.7 percent is indicative of the strength of the expansion or decline. With some of the indicators within this report, ISM has indicated the departure point between expansion and decline of comparable government series, as determined by regression analysis.

Responses to Buying Policy reflect the percent reporting the current month's leadtime, the approximate weighted number of days ahead for which commitments are made for Production Materials, Capital Expenditures, and Maintenance, Repair, and Operating (MRO) Supplies, expressed as hand-to-mouth (five days), 30 days, 60 days, 90 days, six months (180 days), a year or more (360 days), and the weighted average number of days. These responses are raw data, never revised, and not seasonally adjusted since there is no significant seasonal pattern.

The *Manufacturing ISM Report On Business®* is published monthly by the Institute for Supply Management™. The Institute for Supply Management™, established in 1915, is the world's leading educator of supply management professionals and is a valuable resource for decision makers in major markets, companies, and government. In May 2001 the membership of NAPM voted to change the association's name from the National Association of Purchasing Management to the Institute for Supply Management™ to reflect the increasing strategic and global significance of supply management. For further information, see the ISM Web site at *www.ism.ws*. The report has been issued by the association since 1931, except for a four-year interruption during World War II.

The full text version of the *Manufacturing ISM Report On Business®* is posted on ISM's Web site at *www.ism.ws* on the first business day of every month after 10:10 a.m. (ET).

Index

About the Author

Rob Stein is an economist, portfolio manager, and senior partner of Astor Asset Management, LLC in Chicago, which uses a macroeconomic model to make investment decisions. (Visit the Astor Web site at www.astorllc.com.) Stein, who started his career as an analyst at the Federal Reserve, is also founder and senior economist of StockBrokers.com, a network of financial Web sites for the brokerage and investment industry. Stein writes frequently about the economy and the markets, and he has been featured in the *Wall Street Journal, BusinessWeek,* the *New York Times, USA Today,* and Reuters. He also appears on CNN, CNBC, Fox News, Bloomberg, and other national programs.

Stein is also the founder and president of the Dream of Jeanne Foundation and serves as vice chairman on the Board of Trustees for Glenkirk. Both organizations help the mentally challenged participate fully in all areas of community life.